SONIC HARVEST
TOWARDS MUSICAL DEMOCRACY

I am folklore

VILLA LOBOS

SAM RICHARDS

SONIC HARVEST

TOWARDS MUSICAL DEMOCRACY

AMBER LANE PRESS

Published in 1992 by
Amber Lane Press Ltd
Church Street
Charlbury
Oxford OX7 3PR

Printed and bound in Great Britain by
The Guernsey Press Co. Ltd
Guernsey, Channel Islands

ISBN: 1 872868 07 X

Programme

Thanks are due to many. In most cases their names are in the book. Special thanks to Frank Denyer for encouragement, information, and the interview which led to the chapter on his music. Likewise to Lou Gare for the interview about AMM and some aspects of Cornelius Cardew's work. Also to Peter Flux for reading the chapter on Sean O Riada and offering some useful comments; to Mark Joseph for talking and listening a lot, even though we rarely talked about my book; and to Judith Scott for guidance and editorial assistance — it was all useful. And of course to my parents Ron and Doris for being understanding beyond the call of duty.

Overture

The Music of Sean O Riada

PROGRAMME NOTE

This is a personal account. It might also raise some universals.

The particulars are stages on a journey: certain composers, an improvisation group, folk revivalists, village singers, bands, internationalism, politics, spirituality. I only discuss those I have participated in actively or as a fascinated onlooker.

There are two main themes: the way music assimilates or expresses democracy, the dominant political myth of our era, and one of its consequences — a tension between the mythology of 'the roots' and the necessity to innovate.

There is a conclusion, and there's no harm in stating it now. The twentieth century is remarkable in its invention, discovery, rediscovery, and assimilation of a vast orchestra of sounds from banging two sticks together to synthesizers. At some points on the journey I have assumed that choices had to be made. But this is not necessarily so. Every possibility can be viewed as a seed. Composers are beginning to take up the challenge to gather in the sonic harvest.

The September of 1987 found me in Cuil Aodha in the West Cork Gaeltacht, the home of the late Sean O Riada. O Riada's musical importance is mainly recognized in Ireland. It may be that his concerns were so germane to Irish culture that his voice appears nationalist elsewhere. If this is so it is a half truth.

O Riada was known to me principally through recordings of his traditional music ensemble Ceoltoiri Cualann, a band which included the piper Paddy Moloney who was later to lead The Chieftains.

Some years earlier, when touring Ireland as a musician, I had been whisked around Donegal in a car by some students. O Riada enthusiasts to a man, they played a tape of a live performance at the Dublin Gaiety Theatre three times without a break as we drove through that wild and beautiful county, peat stacks outside cottages, mountains, and plenty of bars in every village. Rarely have I had such an experience of music fitting a landscape, the Irish experience suddenly becoming comprehensible. O Riada's musical arrangements, combining form, texture, instrumentation and climax were an auditory mirror of what I saw. It came as no surprise to me to learn later that he was a trained classical musician who also composed, as I was unreliably informed, "a bit like Schoenberg". This description was wide of the mark, but the conjunction of folk arranger and twentieth-century classic composer was compelling.

It summed up the exact crisis of musical direction that I had sensed for years.

Now, in 1987, I couldn't avoid it any longer. With John Faulkner at the wheel (John is English, an old friend, and as good an Irish style fiddle player as you could wish for) we drove into Cuil Aodha and took out our bags. Within minutes I was standing in the porch of the house where Sean O Riada had lived until his death in 1971.

We stayed there for a few days. It could have been two, three, not more than that. Peadar O Riada, Sean's son, was now living there on his own, buzzing in and out of Cork City, busy on his own music, and continuing some of his father's work. You didn't meet or spend time with Peadar. You experienced him. He moved, talked and thought at speed with intensity. It was a relief when he smiled or tended his chickens.

One night the three of us stayed up talking till four in the morning. We sat in the kitchen, cutting off hunks of bread and some very tasty cheese. I had little to say. I was content, through my ignorance of such matters, to listen to John and Peadar ranging around Ireland and the Irish and, of course, music. Circling in my memory of that discussion are threads of politics, philosophy, religion, with hefty wedges of a more global awareness than Ireland alone could offer. We had some booze — enough to loosen up. And somewhere in the core of all those words I remember someone saying something to the effect that what was important was the connection between Self and the realities of life, time and place, realities which could be approached in many ways. Catholicism was merely the vehicle through which these had to pass for so many Irish people, but the main thing was that it happened at all.

It may sound like a vague straw in the wind to pick out of a four-hour conversation, but I felt, and still feel, that within this grand speculation lay the key to the riddle of Sean O Riada, his vacillating between traditional and folk forms and the equally strong pull of contemporary music of the concert hall. It also began to open up a whole series of musical and philosophical concerns which I had kept dormant for over twenty years for the simple reason that I had neither means nor courage to confront them. But when Peadar played us extracts from a new LP of his and his father's arrangements of psalms sung in the Irish language by the Cuil Aodha choir I knew exactly what we had been talking about. Clearly composers and singers had managed to fulfil some potential which went beyond the vehicle of the Christian psalms.

On my return to Dublin a few days later I found the best music shop in town and bought every recording of Sean O Riada that I could lay hands on, along with books, appreciations and critiques. It was, of course, as much my own concern as O Riada's. How did you even begin to reconcile the apparent opposition between folklore and the contemporary music scene? Was there any relationship at all? Was the split between grass roots local culture and high art merely a reflection of a simple Marxist view of history? Or did it say something further about music and culture that, as yet, had not been voiced?

As I listened to what I heard as commercial cocktails in which traditional music had been face-lifted by rock beats and synthesized paraphernalia, I wondered where O Riada would have placed popular music and jazz in his scheme of things. Or the strange meeting between his protégés The Chieftains and the rock singer Van Morrison in which traditional songs normally delivered cool and deadpan were given full expressionist treatment wildly outside even the remnants of traditional style. For that matter, where would I place this odd concoction? And did it matter?

O Riada's story is illustrative of many of the themes in this book. It also became, for me, a symbol of the creative dilemmas encountered on my own path.

He was born in 1931 in Cork. He was no man of the soil in the hackneyed sense, although the distinction between high and low culture is utterly different in Ireland from that in England. His family had an interest in classical matters. His great-grandfather, for example, had translated Homer's *Odyssey* into the Irish language. O Riada himself studied classics and music at the University in Cork. His musical ability and knowledge must have been accomplished, for he went straight from university to Radio Eireann as assistant director of music.

His time at Radio Eireann was short. He wanted to get into Europe and continue his musical studies. He came under the influence of Messiaen in Paris, found out about Schoenberg and serialism, and composed to such a standard that he was able to broadcast his own piano music on French radio.

It has often been said that O Riada found a point of contact between serial composition and the basic cyclic form of traditional Irish music. Classic serialism is based on the composer's arrangement of the twelve chromatic notes in a chosen order. This order is then repeated throughout the composition with the twelve possible transpositions. The series can be used backwards, or by inverting the intervals, or by using the inverted version backwards. The basic intention is to create certain relationships between notes, these relationships underpinning the composition. O Riada's point was that in the big songs and airs of Irish tradition a similar cyclic process of variation was at work. The shape of the basic melody stayed the same from verse to verse, period to period, but was infinitely susceptible to decoration and variation by the soloist. One feels that the connection with serialism is tenuous, but it provided O Riada with a framework from which he could reject classical form, something he felt compelled to do, one feels.

On his return to Ireland O Riada got into the swing of a musical career. In 1955 he accepted the post of musical director at the Abbey Theatre in Dublin, and had the experience of working closely with a specific group of players. At the theatre his duties involved him in all kinds of musical arrangement and direction. The annual Geamaireacht, or Christmas pantomime, required helpings of folk, popular, and other idioms, and apparently O Riada took to this with relish. Likewise writing incidental music for plays, especially Irish plays, was a skill he exercised to widespread approval. It was in 1960, when a folk influenced play *The Song of the Anvil* by Bryan MacMahon was being produced, that O Riada first experimented with the sound of traditional folk instruments. This may well have been the first time that arranged Irish folk music was played to a large audience, a phenomenon that has continued to the present with such groups as The Chieftains, Planxty, De Dannan, and many others. In direct lineage, O Riada is the original master of these disciples.

Important and accomplished though his work in the theatre was, it was O Riada's radio and film exposure that brought him to public attention, most notably in his score for George Morrison's film *Mise Eire (I Am Ireland)* in 1959. Morrison had heard O Riada's large-scale work for string orchestra, *Hercules Dux Ferrariae*, and felt that he was the man to compose the music for his film. O Riada turned in a score for a fifty-one piece orchestra and it was recorded by the Radio Eireann Symphony Orchestra.

The main musical material for *Mise Eire* is Irish folk melody. The glorious tune *Roisin Dubh* is prominent, and traditional tune-spotters can have fun singing along with the familiar melodies. Maybe today we can be pardoned for hearing slushiness in the music but this perhaps misses the point. It was film music for a popular audience and was innovative for its time.

It does not detract in any way from O Riada's musical score to point out that the subject matter of the film — a political, social and historical documentary about Ireland — made it good box office. In addition, Morrison's technique as a film-maker broke a certain amount of new ground. He writes of "drawing on all resources of film, still photographs, graphics, newspapers, documents, and music and using a number of commentators and voices..."
Mise Eire was followed up by another film, the second part of an intended trilogy, *Saoirse?*, for which O Riada also wrote the music. To quote Morrison again: "*Saoirse?* illustrates how the bourgeois revolution of 1916 ... could not sustain itself and deteriorated, ultimately, into civil war and neocolonialism". This is also why *Saoirse?* has never been as popular as a film, in Ireland, as its predecessor. *Saoirse?* makes no concessions to romantic nationalism.

The composition that had first drawn Morrison to O Riada, *Hercules Dux Ferrariae* (1957), is an example of his classical style. It is for string orchestra, uses elements of serialism, has a passage of effects slightly recalling Bartók's 'night music' style, and a strong sense of form. It is an austere work, although it has a lush Waltz, surprisingly described by one critic as "grimly fatalistic". O Riada's orchestration is inventive but there is no way in which this work courts the experimentation which characterized the contemporary European avant-garde. The sections are all in easily recognizable classical forms: a statement of themes, a modernistic twelve-note *Lento*, *passacaglia*, *rondo*, another *Lento*, and a final *Giocoso*.

The impression is of a competent composer, aware of the modernistic options available to him, but unwilling to really plunge into their depths. The hold on classicism is tight and, despite the note rows, the piece comes over as a theme and variations. Or, it could be said, classical form was not part of O Riada's conception (he never wrote in sonata form, having rejected it early on), yet the forms he did use in miniature for each section hang together as much by intuition as by any structural planning. The austerity comes from the audible struggle to make a moderately large-scale work hang together. It is classical in sound and feel and non-classical in conception.

This feeling permeates much of his composed work. It is eclectic, forever trying to establish its style. And, of course, this reflects on a wider level O Riada's varied involvement with popular, film, classical, traditional, and folk music.

There is a sense in which it could be said that he never quite knew which kind of composer he was. This raises an important question: is there any reason why one should know? Isn't this but a response to the labelling tendency of a culture which makes composers and their music into commodities which must have an identity? Or is this a superficial reading? Does 'knowing what kind of musician you are' indicate a deeper search for a place in society and thus in oneself? Do we thus define ourselves in terms of what we believe may be acceptable? This is one of the key issues of musical democracy. Despite our political democracies, are composers still subject to pressures far more subtle than outright force when it comes to knowing who and what they are?

Part of the appeal of folk music for O Riada may well have been that it sidesteps these issues, for it implies a certainty, if not a simplicity, of form. No longer does the composer have to wrestle with the grandiose, the metaphysical, the structural. These are implied and embedded by tradition. The music itself suggests a social order that is at least predictable, if not stable, and the audience response, in Ireland at least, is direct and uninhibited.

It was in 1961 at the Dublin Theatre Festival that Sean O Riada publicly aired his new direction with the band Ceoltoiri Cualann. Now with the new folk band another side of the composer emerged.

In fact, Ceoltoiri Cualann had been in the making ever since O Riada's introduction of folk instruments for the Bryan MacMahon play *The Song of the Anvil*. The idea of forming a band to play that kind of music had been in O Riada's head ever since. Eamon de Buitlear gives some of the background. He was working in a fishing-tackle shop in Dublin when O Riada came in and filled out a form for a gun licence. Eamon de Buitlear recognized the name, and that was the beginning of their association. O Riada asked which musicians would be useful in his new group. A number were suggested. He was introduced to traditional musicians John Kelly, Sonnie Brogan, Paddy Moloney and Sean Potts. Later came Michael Tubridy, Sean Keane, and Martin Fay. Eamon de Buitlear recalls:

"He was able to use Martin Fay to great advantage in the slow airs, because, having the classical training, he was able to get the kind of long, clear notes Sean wanted and which sometimes come very difficult to traditional musicians."

We can see from this statement that for whatever reasons O Riada may have been turning to traditional music he was bringing his own ideas as an arranger and composer to bear. The majority of musicians in Ceoltoiri Cualann were not, like Martin Fay, classically trained. They were folk musicians from the pubs, the country, the ceilidh bands, and had learned their techniques in the tried and tested way — by ear, mainly, and by osmosis. Eamon de Buitlear continues:

"But no, they didn't welcome at all some of the things Sean was doing. At the time they thought he was gone completely crazy, playing this kind of musical arrangement to some of the traditional tunes they had been playing for years and years. They were very much against it, but later they were very much in agreement with what Sean did."

As a composer and musical talent O Riada was compelled to put his stamp on his source material. He was carrying out a modern composer's experiment but he could not succeed without traditional musicians.

In comparison to some of the folk musicians he had gathered round him, O Riada was less experienced in Irish traditional music. As Paddy Moloney has described, the question of who was master and who disciple was never utterly clear.

"...when I played with him, he'd leave it free and open. He wouldn't stop you if you did just what you felt like doing. But afterwards he would ask me: 'Why do you do this?' He was trying to find out my approach to harmony, my ideas, what I had to offer. Although it may have been right or wrong he was quite fascinated. I would demonstrate how I would do a tune and he would demonstrate how he would do it. We had some very funny sessions."

The group was highly successful, and a number of recordings are still available, preserving the sound of a unique experiment in the marrying of folk music and musical arrangement. Particularly worth hearing is the live performance at Dublin's Gaiety Theatre from the spring of 1969, the one that I heard three times without a break in that car drive in Donegal. The skills of the musicians and the yelps of delight from the audience leave us in no doubt that this was a 'big' experience.

But for Sean O Riada it was an experiment which, once successful, lost its interest. Paddy Moloney again:

"Ceoltoiri Cualann was disbanded in 1969. I was there the evening of the launching of the publication of *Hercules Dux Ferrariae*. It was in the Hibernian Hotel and Sean just made a statement in an interview for radio: 'I am disbanding Ceoltoiri Cualann. My experiment is finished.' That's it. I was very disappointed because Eamon and myself were very anxious to keep it going. I actually phoned up at two o'clock in the morning and asked Ruth [Sean's wife] would she get him to reverse the situation, to take back the statement. But that was the end of it."

Part way through the life of Ceoltoiri Cualann, Sean O Riada and his family had moved to Cuil Aodha in the West Cork Gaeltacht following his appointment as music lecturer at University College, Cork. Here he applied his fertile mind to writing psalms and settings of the Mass in Irish and founded the Cuil Aodha Choir, a remarkable ensemble which continues under the guidance of Sean's son Peadar.

O Riada's move to Cuil Aodha allowed him to absorb himself in native Irish culture in a rural setting. Traditional singing had always been highly developed in the area. There is a school of native poetry, and, as my brief visit in 1987 suggested, Cuil Aodha has the right feel for someone interested in traditional culture. This is an idealized picture, of course, and O Riada himself was not fool enough to think he could retire to the country in seclusion. He still visited Dublin, toured with Ceoltoiri Cualann, lectured in Cork City and so on. Yet the disparity between Dublin and Cuil Aodha *is* symbolic, and fits with the polarities which characterize O Riada's life and work: rural / cosmopolitan; folk and traditional music / modern European styles; Ceoltoiri Cualann / the symphony orchestra; the Irish language / English; the old / the new; and ultimately we might say, borrowing Lévi-Strauss's classic structural distinction, the 'raw' and the 'cooked'. It is these polarities which run through the lives of a huge number of twentieth-century artists. It would seem that some can ride above or over them: others never reach integration, and it is these figures perhaps who provide us with the greatest insights into this crucial question of twentieth-century culture, and in particular how creative minds have turned to, flirted with, plundered, or otherwise orientated themselves to folk culture. To begin to see how this relates to Sean O Riada we need to explore the man and his music a little more.

One day, when Peadar had gone into Cork to work (I'm not sure where John was), I was left in the house alone for an hour or so. I knew that Sean O Riada was the brains behind the development that led directly to The Chieftains. I knew I liked the two records of Ceoltoiri Cualann that I had at home. I knew that he was a trained musician and composer, although I had not yet heard recordings of his music. I knew that those moments on the Ceoltoiri Cualann records which most revealed the classical composer, the harpsichord solos for instance, sounded slightly incongruous to me. I knew that O Riada was a force to be reckoned with in the recent development of Irish culture. That was about all I knew. The house told me much more.

Above all, it was the house of a musician. Of course, Peadar, also a musician, was now living there, so there was every reason to feel music everywhere. But I had the distinct impression that little had changed since Sean's death sixteen years before. The piano didn't seem to have been moved, pictures on the wall, carpets, furniture — all seemed ingrained, almost unused. As synchronicity would have it, it was also sixteen years since I had left the world of the musical avant-garde to become absorbed in folklore.

An inviting coincidence.

I played his piano. I believe there was an old harmonium there too. If so, I probably played that. The house was dark, unconscious, waiting. Behind the kitchen was a large work room. I dared to look in. It contained literally hundreds of old records, tapes, books, documents, files of musicological material, notebooks, manuscript paper. The tapes were labelled mainly in handwriting. They told of great Irish pipers, *sean nos* singers, comparative studies of musical styles, a lifetime of study and absorption.

I didn't touch anything. It wasn't that I hadn't asked permission. I just didn't want to touch. I felt that I was not the one to disturb the way things were, to blow off the dust, or to feel entitled to any comment or reaction other than the feelings I allowed the room, the house, the unfinished work to arouse in me. I really didn't have to allow them. They overwhelmed me.

The enigma that faced me was the riddle of the musical experimenter, able to grapple with complex forms, serialism, orchestration, rooted in the history of European concert music, who decides consciously to devote at least a portion of his life to a music which he knows is unorganizable, simple in form (although not detail) and, once revived, arguably phoney. I wasn't only looking into Sean O Riada. Nor was I merely seeing myself, although that was clear enough. I was aware that I was finally asking the question that had been gnawing away for nearly two decades and was now placing me near despair: is there any integration possible between these two musical traditions, the folk and the contemporary, the raw and the cooked? And if so, is it necessary? And if not necessary then why is it found in virtually every composer from the classical era to the present?

A few years have passed. It has now become clear to me that this is a recurring problem of the modern creative psyche, not, incidentally, only in the art of music. The fact that I felt it so acutely didn't argue for me being particularly modern or creative, but it did suggest that I felt the almost unbearable pressure of this duality which surely couldn't be mine alone. And so it proved. The more I learnt about Sean O Riada the more I became convinced that something like this had been going on for him too.

Sean O Riada was a musician in search of a language. He was pulled hither and thither in this search. European classical composition on the one hand, Irish traditional on the other — both demanded his attention, and indeed he remained committed to both. One writer recognized how deeply this apparent pull of opposites went: "It was an agonizing dilemma absorbing all his attention because first and foremost he wished to be a real communicator... All his life one will find him engaging in this dualism or dialectic — as if seeking the truth like the Ancient Greeks he admired so much in some Golden Mean between violent extremes".

The matter could not be put better. More than in search of a language, O Riada sought an identity. It is no accident that he made a determined attempt to Gaelicize his life. He was born John Reidy. Becoming Sean O Riada is a gesture in the direction of an identity he preferred. I can't help feeling that it was John Reidy who wrote the classical style music and Sean O Riada who got into the traditional idioms.

Then, in another determined gesture, he announced to his wife and family one day: "We're all going to speak Irish in this family from now on". Apparently his Irish wasn't even all that good, but he worked on it and became fluent.

It seemed that for most of his musical output, film music apart, he was never to reconcile the opposites that were within him. (The major exception to this was his work with the Cuil Aodha Choir.) For the most part his excursions into traditional music, brilliant though they were on a musical (that is to say a *musician*'s) level, stir up a hornet's nest of questions.

If traditional music is so powerful, what need has it of an O Riada? We have seen from the interviews with two of his musical associates that he altered their styles and conceptions of musical performance. The traditional players didn't understand or even like his ideas at first. To the fiddle player who learnt his music aurally, style, decorations and all, and normally played in the pub or the kitchen, the idea of pizzicato string accompaniments, O Riada himself on the harpsichord, dropping in and out of tunes according to an arrangement, not even always playing the full tune on some occasions, playing other tunes in counterpoint — all these were baffling innovations which, it

must be said, Irish music could have survived without. O Riada's choice of
singer was also significant. Sean O Se was no traditional singer. If anything
you'd describe him as an amiable, light Irish tenor, quite unsuited to *sean nos*
style singing, or anything vaguely traditional.

Would Irish music have survived without an O Riada or a group like The
Chieftains? This is unprovable either way. I just happen to have a very strong
hunch. But let us speculate for a while what the possible outcomes might have
been without the intervention of well-meaning arrangers, popularizers and
folklorists.

What would we say if traditional music *had* survived without them? Could
we ever prove the matter? Perhaps all we need say would be that the cultural
impulse to continue these forms was such that they were obviously important.
We could leave it to the folklorists and sociologists to say why. But if the
music *hadn't* survived, what then? Clearly the opposite would be the case: the
culture itself didn't have the impetus and that would be that. We could mourn
or rejoice over the death of the old but we couldn't do much about it.

I do not wish to minimize O Riada's work but there does seem to be a case
for saying, given the possibility of the survival of the fittest (a better way of
putting it would be 'most fit'), his involvement was a matter of personal
ideology. And we have already seen this ideology slugging it out between
O Riada the traditionalist and John Reidy the modernist composer. The field
of this battle is, in this case, peculiarly Irish. In Ireland there is a spoken and
musical language to turn to, and a history that can never be viewed
apolitically. We should remember that it was only in 1946 that a full
symphony orchestra emerged from within Radio Eireann. Then in 1953 came
the Radio Eireann Singers, and in 1958 the Radio Eireann String Quartet. The
lack of such facilities before these dates is enough to prove that Ireland's
official culture did not function at the same level as virtually everywhere else
in Western Europe. (Significantly, however, its folk culture had always been
lively.)

But one can get sidetracked into a purely local, Irish framework, important
though it was — and is. The fact is that Sean O Riada's response to a search
for personal and national identity followed a very familiar course. We might
call it 'back to the roots', with all that that implies. Other classical composers
have also been prone to it. Many are still. In Ravel we hear Spanish and
French folk influences; the Spanish and Latin American nationalists are full of
them; Milhaud gleefully plundered Latin and jazz idioms; Bartók's courtship
and marriage to Hungarian and Rumanian folk music is well known as is
Vaughan Williams' similar relationship with the English folk tradition. Grieg
in Norway, Grainger in England, the Stravinsky of *The Rite of Spring* and *Les
Noces*, Britten, Holst, Janácek and, indeed, some of the Americans with their
somewhat fey usage of early jazz idioms — all have gone 'back to the roots'
in search of an identity. O Riada, then, for all his Irishness, followed a path
that had been made available by the very invention and ideology of folklore as
the soul of the people. This dates back to the German philosopher Herder and
the Romantic era, and served progressive nationalist purposes in the late
eighteenth and early nineteenth centuries.

I shall return later to the nuts and bolts of the ideology of folklore and 'the people' . But it should be noted, in passing, that it is not only the classical twentieth-century composers who have self-consciously buried themselves in, or at least tested, the soil. The musical significance of the folk (the people, call them what you will) has also been acknowledged outside the formal concert hall. Most notably there have been many folk revivals in the second half of this century. It would seem that America led the way, and there the movement was consciously ideological if not political. The early days of the folk revival in America had definite radical sympathies. Britain followed, and subsequently the rest of Europe and ultimately, it seems, the world.

In many cases, particularly in England and parts of Western Europe, grass roots traditional music seemed to have little impulse to survive. By the 1950s the kind of singing and music-making on a local level that the folklorists looked for was definitely on the wane. By the 1970s, when I began researching in the Westcountry, it was a rare breed. Self-conscious folk revivalism, therefore, always had to fight for survival. It just wasn't germane to mass culture, despite protestations otherwise.

For the musician who, like Sean O Riada, wishes "to be a real communicator" (and which composer doesn't?), and especially for the composer aware of twentieth-century developments, the availability of a plethora of musical options is a challenging and difficult business. O Riada himself, one instinctively feels, found it more than challenging, and there is evidence that, in times of despair, he simply didn't feel up to it. As was perceptively written of him: "Unlike an artist in a stable framework which he can both rely on and refine, O Riada found a world in which there was chaos between the incongruous poles of serialism and Gaelic *sean nos.*"

And this is crucial. Composers in previous centuries had a stable framework, so the question of style, idiom, options, identity was partly dealt with. The same was true of the *sean nos* singer in Connemara, of the village musician on Dartmoor, as of folk musicians everywhere. Society was more narrowly drawn. Your musical idiom tended to fit the stratum you were born in. This does not imply static traditions. There was plenty of crossing of boundaries. Paradoxically it usually meant quite the opposite. Dare I say that in those eras when nobody was too concerned with labels, everybody just made music. And the music they made was whatever was appropriate to the circumstances. But as circumstances were likewise more sharply drawn, perhaps we could say restricted, there was no need for an identity crisis over idiom, purpose, or relationship to listeners.

One of the greatest benefits of the Romantic era was that it liberated the individual. No longer was an artist prepared to be a craftsman artisan, albeit a brilliant one like J.S. Bach. Art acquired another function. The mundane world did not satisfy the Romantic curiosity. Artists were hooked on the peak experiences of life — those moments of transcendence which took you beyond yourself. Vast numbers of them smoked opium, or tortured themselves and their partners in deliciously tragic love affairs, got into the sexual fringe. Many still do. The Romantic legacy is not extinct.

Once the artist *expected* to express himself first and foremost, however, the identity crisis was on. The Romantic era also conceptualized folklore and so offered those inclined a convenient escape route. O Riada tried to take it but was, when it came to it, unfulfilled. This undoubtedly contributed to his depression towards the end of 1961. Of that period in his life Louis Marcus wrote: "While he maintained something of his public ebullience, in private he was sometimes close to tears and, I feared, to losing his reason". Those who have known this dark region understand that the problem is not restricted to any one factor. One may pin it on the artistic struggle which, for a committed artist, is writ large when he or she realizes that all previous efforts are just *not it*. But the source of the despair is deeper.

For artists, their creative output and ideas are a metaphor for who they are. Their identity, sense of personal worth, and quite possibly their income are all dependent on this metaphor. When their work goes well everything else seems to follow, and even if it doesn't the artistic temperament can cope because that at least is fulfilled. Unpaid bills, colds and sore throats, ups and downs in personal relationships are minor nuisances, but not devastating. But let the identity of the work collapse and the entire universe looks bleak.

The artist who vacillates between possible paths, as O Riada did, has as many possible identities as he has paths. Where a pull in two directions is equally strong the identity is in danger of splitting. The classical / folk polarity is a particularly insidious one because it is so shot through with ideological extremes. Consciously or unconsciously one knows that the concert tradition bears the weight of historical class ideology and, particularly in the Irish setting, is identified with Anglo-Irish and European culture. It is a cosmopolitan, urban tradition, exclusive, and yet from its workings comes music that changes consciousness, sometimes on a wide scale. It is the arena of the individual. The folk tradition is pretty well the opposite extreme, yet is likely to be associated with unforgettable characters, friendships and relationships of real human warmth. The psyche naively asks: "Which?", not realizing that you can have both or even that both are necessary.

These are big questions once you get caught up in them. One way out is to affect arrogance, which at least masks the fear, although it comes from the same root. Another, more productive solution, is to make the determined effort to *rise above your art* so that its problems are no longer dominant. Yet another is to plunge into the abyss with the intention of finding the elusive identity no matter what. Or you can give up.

O Riada never gave up. He was too committed. He *did* affect arrogance. He *did* know something of the abyss. Although he had never quite risen above his art there is strong evidence in his music for Cuil Aodha that his search was fruitful.

The recording of the Cuil Aodha Choir that Peadar gave me remains one of the most treasured in my large collection. It consists of settings of psalms by Peadar and his father, sung either solo or in choral unison, accompanied on the harmonium with occasional touches from folk instruments such as the tin whistle.

Part of the compelling quality of the psalm settings comes from the quality of the voices. The classical singer learns to breathe and control a large reservoir of air. This produces tone, volume and projection. Articulation is carefully considered, and all vowel and consonant sounds are, to a degree, standardized. The folk singer works in an entirely different way, especially the Irish singer with any instinct for *sean nos* style. Large reservoirs of air in the lungs are not called for in small, informal settings, and as variation in volume is not part of the style the classical techniques of control are not necessary. The most prized skills are decoration of the vocal line, and shades of tone colour. These are more easily achieved by using a lot of head tone. This gives the effect of open-throatedness, nasality and occasional humming tones. Classical singers find it almost impossible even to approximate this style which, incidentally, is not regarded as folk singing in Ireland. *Sean nos* is Irish language classical tradition.

To hear a choir of men singing in something like this style over slow-moving harmonium drones is to hear a unique and stirring form of music. The melodies have an Irish traditional shape to them, and use appropriate scales. We'd call them modal, I suppose.

One of O Riada's late works was the *Cuil Aodha Mass* and was presented in this style. One wonders, had he lived beyond the tragically early age of forty, would he have pursued this? Or would he have tired of it as he did Ceoltoiri Cualann? It is of no consequence, as the choir seems safe in Peadar's hands.

While O Riada was producing religious works for the Cuil Aodha Choir, I was still banging my head against a brick wall known as Community Arts. During the late 1960s the only way possible to get Arts Council or Southwest Arts funding for my folklore work and local projects in the Westcountry was under this fairly contentious banner. For that reason I had to think about it a lot. A great deal of hot air was wasted on dogma in those days. The home base that had to be defended against our chosen Philistine opponents was the slogan 'process not product'. The doing and participation were deemed to be more important than what you produced, a position I could never accept, having always believed that if the work was genuine there was no essential split between process and product. This had applied to Beethoven and Bach as equally as it did to Cage or, indeed, the farmer who strolled down to the pub, had a pint and sang a couple of songs.

However, it wasn't all claptrap. Those of us who thought this way had a point, but it wasn't worth all the lobbying, hate campaigns and lost sleep. I was left thinking that the ideal situation would be for an artist to work in the community, taking the highest artistic skills of that community as a starting point, yet producing original and satisfactory 'products' into the bargain. On hearing the Cuil Aodha Choir I realized that this was not merely an inspiring possibility. Someone had already done it. It had come from the creative struggles of Sean O Riada and, to put it no finer, may have cost him his life. Although I was unaware of it at the time, this was my first perception of musical democracy in action. The composer was fulfilled and expressing himself, pulling no punches, the performers likewise and, in the process, learning a lot about themselves. The community, too, was involved.

As a footnote, there is a story that O Riada used to relish telling. As an excursion into the macabre it takes some beating, but I fear it may also tell us something startling about the state of his psyche. It was an idea he invented for a musical horror film entitled *The Killer Chord.*

The main character in the story is a composer — no prizes here. He has spent considerable time working on the hypothesis that if sound can smash a glass it can also be made to have far more lethal consequences. After much experiment he manages to compose a chord which will kill anyone who hears it. The rest of the story is taken up by Louis Marcus:

"His next work is announced with the startling news that the final chord will not be played in rehearsal and that the orchestral parts for it will be distributed only as the concert begins. Tension mounts as we see the work performed and observe not only the musicians and audience in the concert hall, but also the millions listening at home or on car radios. As the final moment approaches, the composer, who conducts the piece himself, stuffs his ears with impenetrable plugs. Then the fatal chord is played. The orchestra and audience collapse dead, people slump by their firesides all over the country and cars with radios slaughter hundreds as they career out of control. The composer, calmly removing his ear plugs, has survived."

Perhaps it is better not to comment too closely on the implications of this tale. Suffice it to say that there is an unconcealed anger projected on to those who listen to, and presumably don't understand, the composer. But the contempt, of course, is the composer's.

I began to see in what I understood of O Riada a symbol of my own journey. Although hardly acknowledging it, I too had felt angry, perhaps for more years than I cared to admit. What about? Maybe it was just that I hadn't found my spot.

In the 1960s I took my lead from the American John Cage, the Englishman Cornelius Cardew and, perhaps inevitably, the European avant-garde, figureheaded by Boulez and Stockhausen. Alfred Nieman, my teacher, was also a considerable influence in the field of improvised music. Of the many scores I composed at that time I have allowed none to survive. They were for their immediate time and context — self-consciously so.

At the Drury Lane Arts Lab I saw and heard the Americans Morton Feldman, Earle Brown and Christian Wolff, all radicals at the time, experimenting with free forms, no form, indeterminacy and chance, all influenced by John Cage. I heard Satie's *Vexations*, a single page of quiet music which is repeated eight hundred and forty times to give a performance lasting roughly a day. Later, at college in Devon, I organized a performance of this work with a rota of four pianists.

Also at the Arts Lab I set up a day-long improvisation in which over twenty musicians were invited, none of whom knew what they were going to play before they got there. When they arrived their only instruction referred to which part of the building they should play in. The success of this depended entirely on the quality and sense of responsibility of the musicians, most of whom did their best, and many of whom eventually moved to other parts of the building and even into the street.

It was exciting, chaotic, utterly unpredictable, and took up the whole of a Sunday.

Just before leaving London in 1968 I encountered folk music. Initially it was the popular guitar-bashing, 'Fine Gal You Are!' stuff which jostled for position with protest material derived from Bob Dylan, or as it was then called, contemporary song. This was good for a laugh and an occasional gig in a youth hostel or whatever. It filled the tiny coffee houses like Bunjies near Leicester Square tube station, and was ever on the go in pubs just about everywhere. You heard folk songs on CND marches all mixed in with beat poetry, blues and anarchism. It was part of the style of the 1960s. But eventually it was the magnetic pull of the field recordings which had me firmly in their grip.

In the 1950s and '60s Peter Kennedy and his colleagues had worked for the BBC on a massive project to record the folk music of Britain. Much of this remains in the BBC Sound Archive and in Kennedy's private collection. Ostensibly they were gathering material for a radio series called *As I Roved Out*, broadcast on Sunday mornings to a large and enthusiastic audience. Kennedy describes recording the songs of Sarah Makem from Keady, County Armagh, "...on a portable magnetic tape machine in Sarah's kitchen, and since she could best remember the old songs when she was working, it meant following her around with the microphone, verse by verse, from the kitchen sink to the kitchen range and then back to the sink again."

Details such as this were as important as the actual songs and, for me, possibly more important than their content. They suggested an entirely different attitude to music-making from that favoured by the European classical tradition, including its extension into the avant-garde. In Devon in the 1880s the Reverend Sabine Baring-Gould had a similar experience trying to hand-notate the songs of an old woman on Dartmoor.

"Mr. Bussell and I, on another occasion, again visited Huccaby, this time to interview old Sally Satterly, who knew a number of songs. But she was busy, she had to do her washing. Mr. Bussell seated himself, inconsiderately, on the copper for the boiling, till she lighted the fire under and drove him off. I had to run after her as she went about her work, jotting down her words, while Bussell followed, pencil and music book in hand, transcribing her notes."

The humour of the situation was ripe. The two academics were earnestly doing their bit to rescue a heritage, and here was their source, totally unconcerned about the nature of the fine gentlemen's quest, unaware that they regarded her bits and bobs of traditional lore as the Holy Grail. It would be wrong to assume that the songs were more important to them than they were to her. She simply understood them in a different way.

Unforgettable to me was a series of recordings made by Peter Kennedy in a Suffolk pub, The Ship in Blaxhall. Some of these were available on a ten-volume compilation of commercially available LPs, *The Folk Songs of Britain* (originally issued by Caedmon Records in the United States, but available in Britain on Topic Records). At the Saturday night sing-songs an MC banged a cribbage board on a table, announcing with mock formality: "Order please, Ladies and Gentlemen, I have great pleasure to call on me dear old friend Mr. C.P. (Cyril Poacher) to oblige with *Nuttin'*." At which an out-of-tune squeezebox gave the singer a note (you could take your pick which one) and a gruff loud voice lolloped through a ballad which told of how the ploughboy's song so entranced a pretty maid that she threw away all the nuts she had been gathering and ended with a young 'un "to nurse up in the spring". The voice got progressively less in tune with the squeezebox, the choruses were full of massed "rite fal lals" reminiscent of Elizabethan madrigals, and everyone sounded — well — pissed.

This was light years away from the cosmopolitan, complex and demanding world of experimental music, and it was hard to believe that the two were probably taking place on the very same Saturday nights in any week of the year. Whatever the reasons, I was seduced into the warm womb of folklore and stayed there, resolutely refusing to emerge for over fifteen years. In that time, having moved to Devon, I amassed a considerable archive of recordings made in country pubs, farm kitchens and Gypsy caravans and at parties, booze-ups and local annual fairs. For much of the time this work received varying amounts of funding from Southwest Arts, ranging from barely tolerable to generous, depending on how well I could argue my case that this was community arts, the buzzwords of arts funding in the 1970s. In truth it didn't matter to me what you called it. Art it undoubtedly was. And it came from communities.

The richness of those years of research could not be denied, but as time went on a nagging voice became louder until I had to listen to it. "Is this it? What about new music? What about composing, exploration, improvisation? Can we really expect to build a new musical language out of folklore?" In fact, attempts to do so (my own included) tended to err on the leftish side of gauche.

The supremely powerful role model of Ewan MacColl was just about all I had to go on for many years, unless, of course, the Dylanesque appealed, which by this time it didn't. MacColl had hammered out an idiom of vernacular-inspired song which, at his best, produced some superbly singable material. He had also insisted on making it into a theory for others, a blueprint for writing songs according to socially relevant folk 'disciplines' (though I'm sure the old lady with the copper boiler knew little of these). There was a whole subculture of these effusions. By way of illustration, I quote a neat bit of pseudo-Marxist claptrap of my own which, I'm embarrassed to say, I sang in folk clubs over the length and breadth of the British Isles. With the alacrity of the would-be revolutionary, I managed to get the materialist view of historical development into two verses:

Two strong hands began the journey
Held a stone and started learning
Reached for the stars and made a home
Time to be moving on
Turned the soil and built the bridges
Crossed the ocean, worked the factories
With hand and heart a world we won
Time to be moving on

The inevitable outcome of this rhetoric (as if you couldn't guess) was that seeing as we made the world we bloody well ought to have it and it was the massed conspiracy of capitalist greed and power that damn well stopped us. Bastards! My usual recourse was to kick the telly or, occasionally, to write a song. This was a form of crass class consciousness which was not, I should add for the record, shared by the traditional singers of Devon, most of whom had something I lacked — experience of manual work.

But, naive words apart (and this is a critique rather than a confession), the musical idiom associated with many such songs could only be called deadly. It actually had nothing to do with what my rural friends were singing in their pubs. It was a kind of modal mish-mash that nodded nervously in the direction of popular idioms (you could put blues guitar to the above song, but not too mean) but didn't dare *enjoy* itself lest the meaning was lost, a problem Brecht had when he realized that Weill's music was just too popular.

When MacColl wrote in this style, which one of his greatest admirers affectionately called 'Ewan's Soviet style', he got away with it — if you agreed with him, that is. But then, he had dramatic flair and a powerful singing voice. His *The Ballad of Accounting* is a good piece of fighting, shocking poetry:

> In the morning we built the city
> In the afternoon walked through its streets
> Evening saw us leaving
> We wandered through our days as if they would never end
> All of us imagined we had endless time to spend
> We seldom saw the crossroads and small attention gave
> To landmarks on the journey from the cradle to the grave

So it wasn't just a matter of words and politics. Ultimately it was a musical question. As fifteen or so years passed I became aware of an old familiar desire to listen to and engage in new music from Cage onwards. By the mid-1980s there had been some interesting developments. Music had got cooler, less wild. The postmodernists Steve Reich and Philip Glass had emerged as a force to be at least noticed. The work of the Estonian composer Arvo Pärt was just becoming known. Morton Feldman had gone on to large-scale works; Cage seemed as prolific as ever, and as challenging. The confined folk 'disciplines' were beginning to feel more like self-flagellation. The potential world of sound was wider, far wider, than folklore seemed to permit. Rocked-up 'John Barleycorns' tended to fall short of both the folk and the rock experience, and it was to the likes of Sean O Riada that I gravitated, more to see if there were any clues for me personally than to get into the dynamics of folk in twentieth-century music, let alone musical democracy.

Sonatina in Four Movements

My Grandfather / Little Richard / Bartók / Webern

PROGRAMME NOTE

The polarities which characterized the musical career of O Riada, I suggest, are archetypal. The folk traditions, their implied sense of community, of continuity with the past, their apparent reliance on spontaneity and intuition are safe and warm and speak powerfully of home, family and the known locality. They also suggest undercurrents of undiscovered subconscious regions of experience, the psychic ragbag of centuries of human life, much of which is generally assumed to be unavailable to us in our complex modern culture. Folk proselytizers often speak of "getting back to" whatever it is we are supposed to be out of touch with — continuity, community, authenticity, social and psychological order. This relationship to folk culture tells us as much about ourselves as it does about the traditions which are its subject.

The inevitable question is why, in a historical era which has left such traditions behind with astonishing rapidity, there has been a widespread urge to return to them, investigate them, and use them for the basis of music-making. This urge would seem to be independent of explicit ideology as it runs through the work of composers, performers and folk revivalists from conservative to revolutionary.

The search for meaning is most usefully carried out in action. When action (in this case musical action) leads the way it is possible to reflect from time to time on how it makes us feel. Without this feeling there can be no evaluation. In this sense there can be no theory of action. There can only be action, the nature of which changes constantly. We may search for meaning later. This echoes the way Jung explained the unconscious. We can say practically nothing about it until it becomes manifest, in which case it has moved into consciousness. At that point we may surmise from the evidence available what has been going on. This seems to be the case in musical action.

In musical democracy such self-knowledge is a necessity. My method, for present purposes, is to describe my musical actions, leading eventually to an evaluation.

Casting about for a point of entry, where better to begin than with the investigator's formative experiences as a child in Brixton, London, in the 1950s?

- 1 -

My mother got her songs from four sources: her father, youth hostelling, political movements, and the radio. Her father, Jack Edmondson, known to his mates as Eddie, lived in working-class, industrial, frequently unemployed Preston, Lancashire, and sang most of the time. His singing was an embarrassment to his seven children, who thought it a trifle common.

The folklorists hadn't got to him so he made no distinction between the patriotic songs of Peter Dawson, old ballads such as *The Golden Vanity*, music-hall comedy items, and the semi-operatic light classics typical of the up-and-coming Josef Locke — *The White Horse Inn*, that sort of thing. He sang at home when he was making the beds, one domestic chore he performed regularly. Most evenings he warmed his cap, lit a Woodbine, and buzzed off to the pub and an enthusiastic audience. Years later I managed to learn one of his songs, having recorded it from the singing of a retired lorry driver called Archie in Newton Abbot, Devon. He preceded his rendition with: "Now here's one I bet you've never heard before." It was called *The Muffin Man*.

> Ding dong ding dong
> There were more ping pongs than there were ding dongs
> Just then a smart young lady came along
> And the curate said ding dong
> What's this? said the vicar, with your ding dong there
> That's my wife I do declare
> Said the curate: Bugger it I've been there
> With me ring a ring a ring ding dong.

I must have disappointed Archie's sense of the exclusive when I told him that this was my grandfather's song. His self-esteem was more than restored when I explained that I had been searching for years for someone who knew all the words. This was true. Of the hundreds of songs I recorded over more than fifteen years of fieldwork this one, daft and knockabout as it is, gave me a greater sense of discovery than many a more literary effort. It was a song which 'belonged' to me because I had heard my mother talk about it, cursing the fact that she couldn't remember more than snatches.

O Riada the modernist, the innovator, is perhaps paralleled by my father's taste in modern jazz. True, the fit isn't exact. But there was no denying the exploratory, urban, modern sound of my father's record collection. As soon as we got a gramophone he piled up 78 records of Charlie Parker, Dizzy Gillespie, Erroll Garner, Gerry Mulligan, the Modern Jazz Quartet, Thelonious Monk. In post-war Britain these were still to some extent a specialist taste. Dizzy Gillespie's frantic, noisy, and wonderfully brash number *The Champ* was a bone of contention in our house. It was just too much for my mother's quieter tastes and only found its way onto the turntable by special dispensation. Charlie Parker, with his endless chromatic improvisations, was another source of difference. My parents found a point of compromise in the more refined forms of traditional jazz. They took me to hear the Mick Mulligan Band with George Melly singing. I wrote George a fan letter because he made me laugh when he sang *Organ Grinder Blues* strutting about like a monkey. I missed the sexual symbolism. He sent a letter back and said I wrote very nicely for a chap of nine.

The family gramophone was my first experience of musical democracy. It was one of those old-fashioned contraptions that could stack up eight records at a time and play them automatically in order. As our tastes differed my mother, father and I took turns, alternating our choices. It used to bother me that as there were three of us and as the gramophone took eight records someone was going to be one short. It never occurred to me to have two less. I experimented with stacks of nine but it seriously interfered with the machine's precomputerized brain.

While I was having lessons in egalitarianism via this new-fangled piece of technology I could hardly be expected to have been aware that live voices, like my grandfather's, were daily slipping into silence.

Jack Edmondson died in the 1950s. Thirty years later, trying to recover his songs was like searching for Christ's grave in Kashmir. Even when found there were question marks about its authenticity. I had blown the inheritance of a family tradition by a few decades.

Cajoling my mother was tantalizing. A few lines, a remembered gesture of the hand, anecdotes, a few more lines — then "Your Uncle Freddie would be the only one who might know". I visited Fred in Yorkshire a couple of times. My visits were a chance for a few pints and an update on the family. For the songs: "Your Mother would know..."

"She said you might..."

What with one thing and another it was "Oh bugger it, have another pint. It's my turn. You sing us a song." So I ended up doing the singing. This convinced me that any direct contact I might have with folk tradition was pure romance.

- 2 -

In the mid-1950s popular music went through its now legendary revolution. Rock and roll and skiffle introduced, in clumsy fashion perhaps, a form of egalitarianism into music. Skiffle, in particular, was music that anyone could make. Get a guitar (it didn't have to be a good one), learn a few chords, stick a broom in a tea chest, and wrap some bog paper round a comb, and there you were — musicians. Rock and roll was more subject to commercial hype and the star system, but it was, as one began to hear like a stuck record, music that the young could genuinely identify with. Its history has been written many times, and is currently rather fashionable. The essential points were that it was extrovert, rebellious, it made sex permissible, and it wasn't difficult to play. It was immediate.

The beginnings of modern pop music in the mid-1950s signalled some democratic principles forcibly. One type of music is not intrinsically 'better' or 'worse' than another, although within each framework there is an aesthetic. The standards this refers to are only valid *within*.

On the positive side, everyone could participate in rock and roll to some degree. If you didn't want to play it you could dance to it. And the type of dance associated with the music didn't involve going to classes to learn set steps. As an *educative* experience this music and dance taught that in musical matters and, by extension in most other areas of life, no one had to accept what another said no matter how authoritative the other might appear to be. Parents said it was rubbish. The reply was infuriatingly simple: "I like it". What right had one's elders to assume they were betters? "Anyone could make that racket" wasn't a criticism. It was a statement of the appeal of the music in question.

It was part of the ethos and hype of the new popular music that effort and study were old-fashioned and boring. It had an autoerotic message. If you want it, you can have it now. Pop music was only one important expression of this cultural trend. It induced the *having* mode into life on a mass level. Maybe this was a natural reaction to a century which, until then, had been austere, the escapism of Hollywood notwithstanding.

This liberation is one explanation of the style and assumptions of the new popular music. Morals could get stuffed. Authoritarian systems were instantly suspect and a sham. I'm just old enough to remember Edwardian-clad blokes twirling their pony-tailed birds around in the aisles of the cinema as Bill Haley rocked around the clock, or Little Richard screamed "The Girl Can't Help It" as on screen Jayne Mansfield swayed her magnificent arse. I was seven at the time.

At that age I was a damned nuisance with my rock and roll and skiffle. My father once took me to a theatre to see Lonnie Donegan and his Skiffle Group. Good progressives, my parents obviously believed in giving the child what he wanted, though I can hardly feel that my father with his sophisticated jazz tastes derived much in the way of musical stimulation from the experience.

Strangely enough, I am left with hardly any *musical* impression. I suppose Donegan and his group sounded a bit like their records, many of which I had worn out within weeks of getting them and could sing along to with utter precision. But I do not recall which songs I heard, or how they compared to the recorded versions. My only memory of any substance is of the double bass player. On a number of occasions he twirled his bass around on its spike. In the frantic numbers he lay the instrument sideways on the floor, jumping all over it without stopping playing. I presume he kept in time.

Many rock and rollers did the same. Little Richard, by far my favourite, stood at the piano, baggy suit shining and, from time to time, balanced on one foot and attacked the piano with the other. Jerry Lee Lewis, in between pounding away on the keys, got both elbows and forearms on the job, then left his seat, turned around, and gave the keys a bash with his bum. Elvis Presley's wiggles were legendary and scandalous. British performers tended to be pale imitations, but they all did their bit in the quest for the outrageous. Screaming Lord Sutch predated many more theatrical presentations of the next few decades.

From time to time this wild style got too much for Little Richard and he devoted himself to God, getting his hair cut neat, wearing respectable clothes, and only singing gospel songs. Perhaps his struggle with his own ambiguous sexuality had something to do with it, but he seems to be a classic case of "enjoying yourself is wicked, God is good". I found his evangelism a profound disappointment, feeling then, as I do now, that his early rock and roll recordings hit a nerve of energy unsurpassed by any other singer of the time.

It is worth reflecting on what this music taught by example. Its primary appeal was to *sensation*. It hit you in the gut and got you moving. It did not engage thought. It annihilated the *thinking* function. There was only one moment worth considering — now. Therefore it eschewed the past. Although popular music had always had this tendency, in rock and roll it became a creed.

It was continuous in texture. A simple formula was repeated throughout, often the twelve bar blues taken at speed, without much variation of instrumentation. This contrasts with much classical music in which changes of orchestration are part of the composer's art and add considerably to the interest of the symphony, concerto, or whatever. Continuity is something rock and roll shared with folk music and many forms of jazz.

It was outrageous and theatrical. It was more than a musical performance. From the start rock was music theatre. It had its own sense of ritual. All music has this, but rock and roll's rituals were novel and stunning, exuberant, confrontational.

The music was raunchy, something that wasn't lost even on a seven-year-old. Fundamentally this was a product of how it made you want to move. Popular dancing to date had been a rather polite affair with its waltzes, foxtrots and quicksteps. Suddenly music made an appeal from the hips on down, was low-centered and sexual.

Finally we might say that the music was so simple that it gave the appearance of ease and accessibility. Everyone was equal in the face of the music — with the one important exception of the old and therefore 'square' who could be relied on to hate it. This equality did not extend to the performers. They were elevated as stars. Their musical skills did not need to be anything more than rudimentary, but their personalities had to be exceptional and marketable. They had to feed and fulfil the fantasy.

- 3 -

All things contain the seeds of their opposite, especially when stated to extremes. The lake dried up quickly and totally, despite the fact that the music of pure sensation had been an influential teacher. The feeling that pop music had become tiresome, especially in Britain in the early 1960s (Cliff Richard, Adam Faith, bubble gum and plonking bass lines), was one of my routes into classical music. Another was that I was now learning to play the piano. As soon as someone becomes a *participant* in music a quantum leap into a different level of awareness is ready to emerge. How this manifests itself is unpredictable except that it generally implies a broadening, a tolerance.

Having moved from Brixton to Ealing, in West London, a move which I can only say struck me as 'up', it may have been that classical music suddenly became more available. Certainly Ealing Grammar School (which I did not attend) had a big reputation for music under its brilliant teacher John Railton. Its musical presence was definitely felt in the borough. Railton organized a Brahms concert locally. I went along.

What struck me most about Brahms' Fourth Symphony, the first orchestral work I heard live, was that it took nearly half an hour of my life to listen to it. I heard it in a dark and unspeakably dismal church in West London. I hated churches, but loved the music. It provided aural sensations I had not previously experienced. A few years of courtship with classical music (favourites, for the record, were Bach, Debussy, Sibelius) inevitably led to an encounter with twentieth-century music.

Unconsciously at the time (I was hardly to know where this would lead) my chosen preferences stated the themes which Sean O Riada was later to exemplify. Bartók and Webern, when contrasted, contain a twentieth-century musical polarity which suggests both directions.

Bartók represents the direction which takes folk music as a major source of inspiration and language. The later Webern is the serialist *par excellence* and leads directly to the post-war avant-garde. Bartók's example led me to folk revivalism, finding me, some years later, in Westcountry pubs, farm kitchens and. Gypsy camps, struggling to convince arts funding bodies that this was musical activity meriting equal consideration to that of the classical tradition — a point of view which was eventually to become self-evident to the extent that local arts associations began to create posts for folk *amimateurs*. Webern led me, more immediately, to post-war serialism, and its apparent opposites — indeterminacy, improvisation. Bartók seemed raw, Webern refined.

Bartók's *Music for Strings, Percussion, and Celeste*, the first of his compositions I heard, made a huge impact. Yet it was his relationship with folk music which provided the greatest grounds for thought. In all but the modernistic third movement (Bartók's 'night music' style) it was possible to hear, actively hear, Hungarian and Rumanian folk music. At the time I knew little about Bartók and nothing about him as a folklorist. Certainly Hungarian folk music had been no part of my experience, other than the rhapsodies of Liszt and Brahms that were regularly churned out in school assemblies as our daily dose of what was good for us. (An interesting combination, our assemblies: prayers, hymns, school notices, and classical music!) Bartók and his colleague Kodály made it clear that so-called Hungarian Gypsy music as used by Liszt had little to do with the real thing they claimed to have found.

So whatever my forgotten source, somehow I knew that folk influences were indisputably present in Bartók. My response to Bartók was every bit as immediate as it had been to Little Richard less than a decade earlier. In the realm of feeling and evaluation, though, something else was happening which, at this stage, didn't spill over into conscious thought.

The clearly audible folk influences meant that it was possible to hear in the music traces of a people, a culture, very different from my own. Of these people I knew little, so the only resource was to conjure up stereotypes. Depending on mood this could be an invigorating or a frustrating project. The wildly stamping Magyar dance which forms the basis of much of the final movement of *Music for Strings, Percussion, and Celeste* could suggest an imagery of vast plains, horse-riders, bandits. Then the mental camera zooms in to a settlement where a small community celebrates a wedding or a feast day with bagpipes, drums and swirling dancers. Imaginative suppositions. The folk influences could therefore be heard as cultural fossil imprints, no less clear in outline for not being there. The rock in which they are embedded is, of course, Bartók himself.

Yet in another mood it was possible to feel that all that really counted was the rock — Bartók. The third movement seemed to offer this possibility. So did the first, a huge structure of chromatically interweaving counterpoint reaching a dramatic climax of a type not heard in most folk music.

In those moments in which Bartók had assimilated folk styles to the extent that he no longer needed to state them, even the faintest and most noble traces of pastiche were eliminated. His musical world was then populated by his own authenticity as a composer. This offered no problems of perspective. It was when I could 'hear the joins' that the difficulties occurred.

This dualism is a version of the O Riada syndrome. When Bartók arranged folk melodies, or wrote directly in their manner, he was less perplexing than when a Hungarian dance suddenly leapt out of a string quartet. As a young pianist one of my favourites was the *Six Rumanian Dances* — mainly because I could play them on the piano. They bore a similar relation to Hungarian traditional music as Sean O Se's light tenor, O Riada at the harpsichord, did to Irish balladry. Neither are unpleasant.

But Bartók the composer is heard at full stretch in works such as the Third String Quartet, which comes over to unsympathetic ears as perhaps strident. In such moments, no matter how national his musical personality, like the O Riada who flirted with serialism and European concert styles, Bartók is apparently furthest from his chosen roots. The folk influences are no longer an adornment, a creed, or an ideological presence. The composer no longer consciously speaks their language. It has become part of his creative psyche, taking its place alongside the assimilated influences of Stravinsky and Schoenberg. Rather than striving for authenticity he speaks authentically: an important difference.

- 4 -

Much as Bartók captivated, it was a first hearing of Webern that took me all the way. One evening I turned the radio on to the music programme and heard the most inexplicably strange sounds: a few notes on violin or cello, one loud one soft, a pizzicato or two, perhaps a brass phrase here, woodwinds there. None of them seemed to add up to a melody which my ear could 'follow'. It was music of scattered patternings, splinters, no apparent tonal centre, unpredictable conjunctions of instrumental timbres constituting an aural tapestry which seemed to proceed to a plan that was not offered up for conscious inspection.

The feeling was that this music could only be approached in the moment because it contained no reference to anything that had gone before. This was an illusion, but a powerful one. I had to use my intuition.

The radio announcer gave out that we had been listening to Webern's *Symphony Opus 21*, stressing the *n*, presumably in case anyone should confuse it with Weber. Who was Webern?

Next day in Ealing Public Library I was mortified to find that he had been shot by accident after the end of the War in 1945. Yet his techniques of composition had been developed by European composers who were very much alive, Boulez and Stockhausen being pre-eminent. For the next few years until I left London most of my time was spent in attending concerts of new music, reading about it, analyzing it, composing, improvising, and spending my student grant in record shops.

Webern had actualized an *internal musical democracy*. That is, as far as the actual music itself was concerned, each note has equal value. There is no leader or hierarchy of degrees of the scale. Each note has an exact place in the scheme of things and willingly occupies that position as part of a harmonious plan. One note is *impelled* to the next, not due to the dictates of functional harmony, but because a patterning of intervals has been set up by the composer. Each sound *chooses* to do what it inexorably *has* to do. The plan was based on the composer's order created in the twelve-note series which occurred in predetermined patterns throughout each piece.

I began to fill out the history which had led to Webern's use of serialism.

Schoenberg's invention of serialism earlier in the century had been in response to the problems presented by the breakdown of traditional harmony, melody and form. In pre-twentieth-century classical music there had been a musical reason for one sound to proceed to the next. Much of this was found in functional harmony. In Mozart or Bach, no less than in folk music, one note followed the next because of the expectations of musical hearing within the culture. Frequently the composer's art consisted of balancing the expected with the unexpected. The ear would assume a phrase to go in one direction. The composer could gently, wryly, dramatically, or violently push it in another. Whatever, it was a framework, but it inevitably contained the seeds of its own destruction as inspired minds stretched it to its limit. Much music composed at the turn of the century was already treading a tightrope on the edge of tonality. Schoenberg had the courage to fall off and see whether the fall was really all that dangerous, a matter which he never resolved. His excursions into atonal music suggested to him a need for some kind of new formal principle.

If all the twelve notes had equal weight, which is a rough and ready definition of atonality, they could be arranged into a fixed order which would serve as a basis for composition. Webern, Schoenberg's pupil, took this idea further than his master. Some composers used serialism almost as a convenience within a traditional context. They used traditional forms such as sonata form, variations, rondo, or whatever, but filled them out with twelve-note serial technique. Sean O Riada's use of serialism is typical. One senses that it is nineteenth-century music with note rows, which is not to say that it is thus condemned, but simply to observe that it represents music in transition. Webern, however, created a serial universe in which the form and detail of each piece had a precise logic of its own. Yet, contrary to falling into the possibility of merely manipulating a mechanical system, Webern used it to compose real music.

In the post-war school of integral serialism the sounds got wilder, more unusual and more demanding. Early Boulez, Stockhausen, Nono, Berio accentuated these responses. Not only the twelve notes of the chromatic scale were ordered into a series. The same went for durations, attack, register, dynamics.

Most importantly the *internal musical democracy* of a style of composition in which all constituent parts were equal had, in Webern, produced a music which, although sometimes difficult to play, was at least approachable. My piano technique at the time at least allowed me to bash through the *Variations* for piano with some sense of satisfaction. When I got piano music by Stockhausen or Boulez out of the library I pored over it for days on end to perfect a few bars with no certain knowledge that I was playing it correctly. The sense of immediate satisfaction I had got from Little Richard, Brahms, Bartók and Webern was missing. Even learning to play this music became, for me, an intellectual exercise.

This is not to decry the mainstream avant-garde of the immediate post-war era, but much as I enjoyed listening to it I had to admit that I was not cut out to play it, even less compose it. This became doubly true when I realized that what I lacked in ability to read the dots was compensated for by a flair for improvisation. The *internal musical democracy* didn't extend outwards to the performer. To play this music, with its egalitarian world of sound, required specialists of an order not previously known. It was in this frame of mind that I gravitated to the work of John Cage and Cornelius Cardew.

At a time when popular culture was caught up in hippiedom, Hendrix, and hashish, the challenges issued by the musical avant-garde struck me as more interesting by a mile, obviously less commercial, and uncompromising. As a student I staged a concert of new music at the Questors Theatre in Ealing. In the final item a friend of mine, wearing frogman's flippers, tied up the audience with a ball of string, while I put a hammer through a row of glasses on stage. On that occasion I also performed John Cage's *Water Music*, which calls for a pianist to also play a transistor radio, a siren, a nightingale warbler, and a duck call which is immersed in water to sound like a fart in the bath. My understandably anxious mother sat in the audience with a friend from work. Apparently her friend's comment was: "Well, Mick Jagger thinks he's hip!" Jagger, of course, had recently emerged as a prime symbol of rebelliousness. Our friend's comment was astute.

One of the characteristics of such performances was the deadpan way in which they were carried out, as if the performer saw nothing in the least unusual about what was going on. In this way the concert platform was constantly parodied, indicating that we thought it stuffy.

Cage had demonstrated how to reflect questions and criticism back to one's questioners. "What's it all about?" — "Why does it have to be about something?". Or: "My dog makes better noises!" would draw forth "I compliment you on having a musical dog". Having been accused of this I once wrote a random piece for dog and orchestra. According to what the dog did the orchestra responded in given ways. It wasn't getting the orchestra that was the problem. It was getting anyone to lend me a dog for the purpose.

Cage's influence was, and remains, profound. But being American he was not a figure I could observe at close quarters. Cornelius Cardew, however, was operating in and around London, constantly issuing challenges even to Cage's anti-orthodoxy.

Revolutionary Study No. 1

Cornelius Cardew

PROGRAMME NOTE

Demos — rule. Kratos — people. Democracy = rule by the people. But how?
Which people? All of them? All classes equally? Immediately or some time in
the future? According to which values, which traditions? What if rule by
prevailing values implies the will of a conservative majority? Oppression by
consent?

How is it organized? Directly in gatherings of "freemen orderly
assembled" in manageable-sized groups to make just laws as in the Rhode
Island constitution of 1641? How is that different from anarchism? Or via
representatives — in which case do 'the people' really own power or do they
devolve it to the elected? What steps are taken to encourage personal power
and freedom? Do traditional systems of thought, morals, music get in the way?
How can they be questioned? Is the questioning inevitably the role of
minorities? How do minorities fit into representative democracy? Is democracy
the same as freedom?

Is a new view of the Universe necessary to make demos kratos more than a
slogan?

Post-war avant-gardism signalled dissatisfactions and possibilities. It was
first necessary to turn the world upside down. In British music Cornelius
Cardew was a seminal figure. He introduced ideas of responsibility and
democracy — into the notating of music, the relationship of performers to
notation, to each other, to the composer, to themselves, sometimes inviting
them to play in ways he could not predict even in outline. It is not surprising
that in an important phase of his development he rejected European models
and admired John Cage. America, after all, is where the modern concept of
democracy comes from. It is an essential element in the American Dream.

In the London of the 1960s the musical avant-garde found its most challenging
figure in the person of Cornelius Cardew. Even when the music left me
irritated, mystified, or just plain bored (which did happen) I gave it the benefit
of the doubt because the quality of ideas was so apparent, the challenge to the
established musical order so profound.

Cardew had produced a number of works under the influence of the
European avant-garde tradition. Although I eventually familiarized r.ıyself with

many of these they failed to excite my curiosity as much as the work he produced as he moved progressively away from their assumptions.

There was a series of three concerts at the Commonwealth Institute. The year would have been 1967. Cardew was prominent in all of them. They all lasted about two hours non-stop. One was the first complete performance of his *Treatise*, a 193-page graphic score of huge proportions with circles, lines, triangles, dots, squares, sweeping and curving effects and relatively few notes of music specified. The performers brought their own musical experience to bear on this graphic stimulus which was, nevertheless, 'composed'.

Another of these concerts was an improvised one given by AMM — Lou Gare, Eddie Prévost, Lawrence Sheaff, Keith Rowe, and Cardew.

And one concert was a performance given by Cardew, John Tilbury and others of four avant-garde works mainly from America. They were played simultaneously, again for two hours. In La Monte Young's *Piano Piece #1 for David Tudor* John Tilbury treated the piano as a horse. He first cleaned its 'teeth' (the keyboard) with a huge toothbrush, then placed a bucket of water under it, then stuffed strands of hay into it. Meanwhile, the other players produced amplified screeches, bangs, long sustained and occasionally delicate moments. Pieces of fruit dangled on long lengths of string over one area of the stage. From time to time Cardew cut a string. I can't recall whether he ate the fruit.

These quasi-Dadaist gestures were fun and had a point to them (if a pointless point) and for a while Cardew seemed very close to them, but it is wrong to judge his work in the 1960s by them alone. Underpinning the entirety of Cardew's career was a penetrating intellect, deep conviction, talent, courage, and an almost prophetic sensitivity to the issues of contemporary direction.

In terms of musical democracy Cornelius Cardew raised a huge number of issues, as relevant now as they were then, but as little understood. The pity is that since his death in 1981, aged 45, musical experimentation, with few exceptions, has lain dormant, perhaps in rhythm with the more materialistic phase in society that was gathering momentum at that time. Playing music under Cardew's direction, something I did only infrequently, was an extraordinarily exciting process in which I came as close as I ever had to feeling in touch with a personal and musical sense of potential, self and value.

His background was musically conventional. From the ages of seven to fourteen he was a chorister at Canterbury Cathedral. From 1953-57 he studied composition and piano at the Royal Academy of Music. He and Richard Rodney Bennett gave the British premiere of Pierre Boulez's *Structures for Two Pianos*, a virtuoso work of post-Webern integral serialism. The musical establishment of the 1950s may not have liked Boulez, and certainly didn't understand his music, but no one could deny the challenges it gave the performers.

From 1957-58 Cardew studied electronic music in Cologne where he met Karlheinz Stockhausen. Boulez and Stockhausen were the twin luminaries of the European avant-garde, deeply involved in extending serialism as a principle of composition. Stockhausen, in the manner of a Renaissance master, required the collaboration of assistants in some of his works, especially the large-scale pieces, and Cardew served in that role from 1958-60, working on *Carré* for four orchestras.

It was in Cologne that Cardew encountered American avant-garde music. John Cage, the composer, and David Tudor, the pianist, were playing in Germany, and made a deep impression. Cage's most remarkable claim, and the one that established him in musical consciousness, was that he was disregarding tradition. This was what new music in Europe badly needed, caught up as it was in what had become a serial religion.

Almost from his earliest works Cage enjoyed creating new sounds. He had used percussion instruments, metal sheets, frequency recordings associated with the gramophones of the time, gongs immersed in water to produce wonderful sliding tones, and had invented the prepared piano whereby bits of wood, rubber, screws, plastic and so on were inserted between the piano strings. This changed the piano into a one-man percussion orchestra. Schoenberg's now legendary remark was that Cage was "not a composer, but an inventor — of genius".

Cage's early works are delightful. They reflect his interest in Oriental philosophy and his determination — perhaps we should say his natural inclination — to proceed independently of European tradition. The percussion pieces are forceful and exciting, and the music for prepared piano with or without voice is extraordinarily sensitive and does induce a state of listening which has a meditative effect.

At a crisis point in his life he felt he had to choose between a Jungian psychologist and Zen Buddhism. As he had no faith in psychoanalysis he got deeper into Oriental philosophy, particularly Zen. He took to heart the notion of composing music without the ego. He invented systems based on chance in which pitch, attack, duration, register, and so on were determined by throwing dice, tossing coins, using imperfections on manuscript paper, and reference to the classic Confucianist book of changes, the *I Ching*. His *Music of Changes* for piano is a terrific work, every bit as complex and difficult to play as its European serial counterparts, and as remote from conventionally bred listening habits.

Although some of Cage's gestures were calculatedly surreal, there was a serious challenge in his way of thinking and composing. His mentors, the Zen Buddhist Daisetz Suzuki, the medieval German mystic Meister Eckhart, hip philosopher Buckminster Fuller, and the greatest publicist for media study, Marshall McLuhan, all contributed in significant ways to his work. As Cage had a decisive effect on Cardew it is worth summarizing his ideas as they were in the 1960s.

One of Zen's assumptions, common to much Buddhist thought, is that the individual's attachment to things, objects, the Self, and ultimately even to one's own enlightenment are hindrances to its realization. The story of the monk Bodhidharma no doubt pleased Cage. The monk was speaking with a Chinese emperor who had built temples, monasteries, copied sacred books of teachings, and so on. He asked Bodhidharma what merit he had gained. The monk's reply was "None whatsoever". The emperor then asked Bodhidharma to explain the first principle of Buddhism. The reply was "Vast emptiness".

The emperor pursued the matter further: "If everything is emptiness, who is standing in front of me?" Bodhidharma's reply was: "I have absolutely no idea".

This extreme denial of the *having* mode of existence is echoed in Eckhart's writings in a Christian context. He maintained that the highest state of being was to *have* nothing. Man need not be bound or tied to what he apparently owns, not even God. One of Eckhart's famous prayers was: "Therefore I pray God that he may quit me of God". A Zen Buddhist would instinctively understand.

Fuller and McLuhan provided a twentieth-century framework for Cage to put these ideas into action. Fuller was an advocate of the power of intuition, and maintained that all new realizations in science, invention, and art had been produced by a phenomenon "transcendental to humanity's self-disciplined objective concentrations of thought and deliberate acts".

McLuhan's acceptance of modern media with their implied challenge to culturally conditioned ways of thought gave Cage the material philosophy to back up his spiritual beliefs.

Cage's mission was to compose music with no interference from his conscious choice. To many this was an abrogation of the responsibility of the composer. A careful examination of Cage's work reveals that he has never actually succeeded for the simple reason that he was attempting the impossible. The composer makes a conscious choice to compose in the first place. To choose to compose by chance is a personal decision. The actual systems of chance Cage invented are a result of his own conscious choice and taste. He happened to have a remarkably well-ordered mind, and his compositional procedures reflect this. Within a Buddhist framework one could argue that composing by chance lays the composer's *karma* bare. This enhances uniqueness rather than obliterating it. Other composers who tried to work by chance operations, and I include my own early efforts, produced remarkably different work. Chance was a discipline, not an invitation to randomness.

For example, it was obviously important to make sure that the chance system you had invented actually worked. On a composition summer school a group of students was set the task of producing a very short composition ready for the next class. I decided to use the positions of stars in the night sky. I would estimate as accurately as possible their relative positions and dot these in ink on clear transparent paper. This would then be placed over manuscript paper at any angle, giving each performer a unique reading. I sat on a roof one night and assiduously made the transparency, not aware of the fact that the glossy surface of the paper would not take the ink. Next morning every single mark was gone, resulting in utter silence. Composing by chance indeed lays the composer's *karma* bare.

If any sound could become part of a piece of music, sounds being allowed to happen by chance, it wasn't a big step to Cage's most extreme piece *4'33''* in which the performer does not intentionally make any sounds at all. For Cage it was a compositional necessity to discover that chance methods could result in silence. Cage was attempting to let sound happen. The Europeans bossed it about.

After the mid-1950s Cage's music became more anarchic. He incorporated theatrical elements into performance, frequently with hilarious effect. *Water Music* is one example we have already seen. When I played it, blowing the duck call into a bowl of water splashed my glasses and I had difficulty in reading the score. This meant I got out of time. In other pieces all sorts of inventive effects prevail. A clockwork fish whose tail flips is placed on the strings of a grand piano, sustain pedal down. A contact microphone is placed on a performer's throat, amplifying water as he drinks it, or carrots as they are crunched. Transistor radios become musical instruments, the performers carrying out instructions from the score to move wavebands and manipulate the volume. A notorious performance of one such piece took place late at night when all the available radio stations had gone off the air. The result was hardly any sound with the occasional blip from far distant stations. One assumes that Cage didn't mind. That was chance.

Cage's lectures could rarely be followed as words. Many of them were 'written' by chance, and spoken into electronic gadgetry which distorted his voice, played it back at different speeds, and often came out at a deafening volume. It was not unusual for four or more lectures to be delivered simultaneously in this fashion. I heard one in the late 1960s at the Shaftesbury Theatre when Cage and his associates were over touring with the Merce Cunningham Dance Company. The lecture lasted an hour, after which Cage asked for questions. In the upstairs balcony few were left at the end. I was one. As I recall, Yoko Ono was another.

So this is the picture in which we can place Cardew in the early 1960s: repelled by European serialism, attracted to the much broader approach of Cage and the Americans and, like Cage, prepared to go wherever his own experiments suggested. But in order to interpret Cardew's work from this point onwards, especially in terms of its contribution to musical democracy (which is great), we must probe a little deeper into the whys and wherefores of his preference.

A good place to start is with a summing up made by one of Cardew's closest associates, the pianist John Tilbury. In a sleeve note accompanying a memorial double album of Cardew's music, Tilbury writes:

"What he admired was Cage's rejection of the commodity fetishism that had invaded musical composition, for which the super-objectivity of serialism and its corollary, the preoccupation with the perfection of the ideal object, was largely to blame. What also impressed him was Cage's liberation of the performer from the constraints of oppressive notational complexities, and perhaps most of all the 'democracy' inherent (at least in theory) in Cage's scores. And here is the crux, because this concern for freedom and democracy, displayed in a number of highly sophisticated indeterminate compositions from the early sixties, tough in an abstract and intellectualised fashion, informs Cardew's entire musical career."

It is worth examining this statement in detail beginning with the notion of 'commodity fetishism', the absence of which Cardew apparently admired in Cage's work. It is possible, given Tilbury's involvement with Cardew's later Marxist-Leninist rejection of avant-gardism, that he wrote these words wise after the event. Was this classical Marxist critique really foremost in Cardew's thought in the 1960s? I doubt it, but in a sense it doesn't matter. Consciously or not, opposition to the notion of composed pieces of music in their status as commodities underpinned much of Cardew's work, especially as it became more innovative.

To look at the matter from basics: a fetish is an object without which activities which are socially or individually considered normal cannot take place. A fetish is a magic object which is given life force, or supernatural powers. Marxism begins with an appraisal of the role and nature of commodities in capitalism. These commodities (objects, things, products of labour) have use value and exchange value and are fetishized. In other words, the economic system *depends* on the production and exchange of commodities — at its crudest, things to sell. Thus a form of 'supernatural' power is invested in material things. As the system itself is assumed to be eternal, life in any shape or form cannot continue without commodities.

In materialist society, the way we relate to *things* embodies, or is symbiotically related to, social and personal relationships. Thus, commodities have the status of objects of worship because they are used as a yardstick of value. To *have* something, a commodity, is to make a statement about oneself. Modern society tends to emphasize the *having* mode rather than what the psychologist Erich Fromm called the *being* mode. Fromm suggests that the *having* mode is now embodied in our language. Over the last couple of hundred years, roughly the period of industrialization and capitalism, language has placed everything as potentially in the *having* mode. Fromm says: "Some decades ago, instead of 'I *have* a problem', the patient probably would have said, 'I *am* troubled'; instead of 'I *have* insomnia', 'I *cannot* sleep'; instead of 'I *have* a happy marriage', 'I *am* happily married'."

This act of *having* — a car, a washing machine, a Ph.D., a company, a business empire, sex — is an agreement with the inescapable fact that commodities have exchange value which is a result of the division between the means of production and human labour. The forms of social organization in relation to how things are made (owners and labourers, producers and consumers, divisions of labour) are the substance of social relations.

The argument goes that because these relationships are endemic to materialist society, the way we think and feel, they can also be seen in the arts. If artists strive to produce ever more perfect fixed masterpieces, the things they produce echo and reinforce the social relationships we assimilate as if they were 'natural'. The composer produces the fixed and final form and detail of a piece of music. The performers take on the role of operatives, devoting much time and energy to realizing that piece. People who do not have the technical resources to play music (and this is particularly true of the fiendishly difficult post-war European avant-garde) may sense that they *have* 'no technique', rather than looking at what they *are* in relation to music. The musical composition is seen as a thing in itself and is, if not literally at least metaphorically, an object of exchange for sale. The business side of music then comes into play: agents, promoters, recording companies, concert halls, ticket prices, publicity, grants and awards, colleges to train the next generation of producers, and so on. In order for this network to function, the objects of worship, the pieces of music, must be recognizable and repeatable. Otherwise there is no commodity. This is the typical state of music in the Western art tradition for the last four hundred years, but is far more apparent in the music of mainstream popular culture, which is based on discs which can bought and owned, and all the associated commercial paraphernalia from concert tours to T-shirts.

John Cage, as we have seen, didn't play this game according to the rules. He began to compose systems in which virtually anything might happen, one performance of a piece being potentially very different from the last. His series of *Variations* did not specify sounds. *Variations IV*, for example, deals only with sound in space. It consists of a set of instructions as to how to use intersecting lines to show at which points in a room or building sounds should be made. As a predictable, repeatable commodity, therefore, the piece is useless — unless it is recorded (which it was, making nonsense of the placement of sound in space).

On a basic psychological level this was much of the appeal of Cage to people such as myself in those turbulent barrier-breaking years of the 1960s. By any generally applicable yardstick what he did was utterly useless, yet it was intriguing. It had no aesthetic, no culturally conditioned ideas of beauty and form, no purpose. If anyone asked "What's the point?" you knew they'd missed the point. No one ever asked "What's the point?" when it came to selling shirts, fridges, or armaments. A post-war society in which the Bomb was a constant threat couldn't get away with silly simple questions when it had so much to answer for.

Cage's approach has never been politically motivated *per se*. He would not have been over-interested in Marxist interpretations of his work, although he later espoused Maoism for a time, thankfully ignoring all Mao said about art. He was putting into practice his idiosyncratic interpretation of Zen Buddhism in which the highest purpose is to have no purpose at all. That is, not to judge or discriminate, but to open our ears, minds, and lives to whatever happens to be. If Cage had a political critique at all it was that Man's egotistical interference with life's processes was at the root of his mismanagement of the universe. Tinkering around with one's thought processes alone, no matter how apparently well-motivated, was liable to be counterproductive in the end. The title of one of his lectures, the one I heard at the Shaftesbury Theatre, gave it away: *How to Improve the World, You'll Only Make Matters Worse*.

It was Cage, also, who clarified that there need no longer be any distinction between musical sounds and what had hitherto been thought of as noise.

I played the cello (which I can't play) in a performance of Cage's *Concert for Piano and Orchestra* at Highgate Church. As the score could be taken at any speed I could go slowly enough to work out roughly where the notes were, which I did with great devotion. There were plenty of effects — slides, pizzicati, and so on, and what Cage called "auxiliary sounds" — any sounds not made on your instrument, an illustration of the assimilation of noise into his musical world. At Highgate Church I was placed up in a gallery. This meant I could lean across and, with the end of the bow, hit one of the huge hanging lights. It had a wonderful bell-like tone.

In a performance at the Drury Lane Arts Lab I decided that my auxiliary sounds would be exploding cigarettes. I bought a box of pellets in a joke shop and placed them in all the cigarettes in a pack. When the sign for auxiliary sounds occurred I lit a cigarette and waited. Some of the explosions were spectacular and had great theatrical effect.

The following day I went into a sandwich bar in Tottenham Court Road. I ordered a sandwich and a cup of coffee. I ate the sandwich and then lit a cigarette: this one had a far louder bang than any I had used in the Cage piece. Strands of tobacco landed up not only in my coffee but all over a woman's sandwich, and in various other cups of tea and coffee. Every head in the place turned towards me. Having recovered from the shock I descended into uncontrollable laughter and had to leave. I regarded this incident as a perfect illustration of many aspects of Cage's philosophy. But back to Cardew.

Cornelius Cardew assimilated Cage's work, but as a musician with ideas of his own he was not a disciple. Time and again in Cardew's work and writings we come across the idea of *responsibility*. He devised events, broadly musical in nature because they involved making sounds, in which the performers were invited to bring a commitment of responsibility to realizing his scores. To do this he had to trust. Cage and serialism had liberated musical sound from the functional harmonic constraints of the last few hundred years. So there was no longer any preconceived pattern in which one sound had to lead on to a limited choice of others.

This meant that, ideally, anyone could participate, provided they came with a responsible attitude. Cardew experimented with ways of creating performing situations in which players were invited to *take responsibility*, a form of direct democracy. At this time Cardew was doing more than being a democrat: he was acting it out and sharing it.

One of the bases on which he was able to do this was that his performers trusted him. For much of the 1960s Cardew worked with performers who knew what he was about: John Tilbury, AMM, David Bedford, Christopher Hobbs (his first student at the Royal Academy) and a number of others whose names were often associated with Cardew.

How did this work in practice? I have already referred to the monumental 193-page graphic score *Treatise*. By any standards it is visually sensational (John Tilbury's word for it), the work of a refined graphic artist, reflecting the way Cardew was earning his living at the time. At the bottom of each page are two blank musical staves. Above these, occupying most of the page, are graphic symbols. Running through the middle of each page is a continuous straight line, only occasionally broken. Some of the graphic symbols are visual games played with musical notation. Lines sweep out of treble and bass clefs, musical notes are drawn connected by series of curving or parallel lines, all in different sizes and shapes. The majority of the signs have no apparent connection with conventional notation: circles, triangles, intersecting or parallel lines, enigmatic-looking drawings, and so on. Cardew once said that the sound "should be a picture of the score, not vice versa". It is the performer's job to fill in the details.

The score's visual beauty and accomplishment was important in gaining the trust of performers. Cardew worked with people who knew and trusted him anyway. But anyone else looking at *Treatise*, even if they were baffled by it, would recognize that there was a powerful mind behind it and, at least, a highly competent graphic artist.

I played solo piano versions of another, less ambitious, graphic piece of Cardew's, *Octet '61*, on many occasions. Although the graphic references are more directly musical, what one plays is suggested rather than prescribed. As a performer I had to bring my own invention to bear. My method was to improvise from the score frequently at home, trying out different approaches — a quiet, slow piece, a loud, active one, a mixture of the two, deliberate references to styles that interested me, sometimes no conscious references at all. None of these would necessarily figure in public performance, but my familiarity with the score meant that I was able to produce a satisfactory piece of music each time.

As no method of working was specified, other performers approached the piece in their own ways. Many wrote out in full what they were going to play. If played in groups there might be a group agreement as to the general character of the interpretation. All this had the effect of getting musicians thinking closely, often discussing, and *participating* fully in the composer's idea. On occasions I found that I wasn't happy with a performance. This forced me to consider why. Perhaps I hadn't given everything to the piece, or perhaps I was consciously trying to make 'good' music rather than letting the musical impulse flow. Although I never played in *Treatise* I imagine that it offered a grand scale version of these challenges.

Treatise could in theory be played by anyone, whatever their level of musical expertise, on any instruments. The performance I heard at the Commonwealth Institute included amplified and acoustic sounds, conventional musical instruments — rarely played conventionally — balloons squeaking, bottles, tin cans, transistor radios, all fairly standard fare for the time.

The crucial factor, for me as an audience member, was not what the score looked like, how it was organized, what the relationship of the performers to score/composer consisted of, nor Cardew's personal philosophy of life as expressed in music. It was far more simple than that: was it stimulating to listen to? And it was not possible to give a precise answer.

As with the work of Cage and his American followers, what one heard passed through passages of delicacy, fearsome volume, protracted periods in which little changed, silence, surprising and unusual sounds and combinations of sounds, excruciating sounds, cacophony, repose, and so on. My response after about an hour was that I wanted to join in and could see no reason why I shouldn't. There was no apparent form to speak of, as in conventional (ie European avant-garde) music. Level of technique was no qualification. All sounds could be assimilated. Why, then, should be there be any distinction between performers and audience? It was not that I didn't *like* the music. Like didn't come into it. One experienced this music for what it was, but an hour was enough to convince me that my contribution would be as valid as anyone else's, providing I could see a score. After all, I could make a balloon squeak as well as anyone.

The same issue had come up in a group that I organized as a student. I had written what was, I suppose, a Cardewesque graphic piece for free interpretation, and was rehearsing it one evening at college with a group of players. One player was late. We had already gone through the instructions and started playing when he turned up. He was a Japanese jazz sax player of no particular technique but great enthusiasm. He unpacked and assembled his instrument and joined in immediately. I, as composer and rehearsal director felt that this wouldn't do and whispered to him disapprovingly: "You can't see the score". His cheerful reply was: "No, but the others can" — which could only have come from a country which developed Zen Buddhism. Now, with *Treatise*, I was feeling that same response. On reflection I feel it was a very young response, but no less real for that.

My desire to participate in Cardew's music was soon satisfied. In 1967 he produced a piece called *The Tiger's Mind* and called for volunteer performers. It was the first time I had ever seen a score which consisted entirely of written words. There was a Daypiece and a Nightpiece. Each was a kind of prose poem in which characters, such as tiger, wind etc., were given roles. Cardew arranged two performances at the Middle Earth in Covent Garden, home of a great deal of acid rock in those days. The first performance was without an audience, although I do not recall him ever calling it a rehearsal. It was played one afternoon for two hours, a standard time length it seems, with Cardew himself sitting at a table listening. Afterwards he gave a few comments. I was the only performer he singled out for negative criticism. I had chosen to play the part of Wind and had taken literally the idea that when Wind blew it pushed everything in front of it. Therefore I pushed a chair around for about a quarter of an hour, enjoying the sound it made scraping loudly across the floor. Cardew didn't like it. After his criticism I even felt a bit victimized. After all, I had interpreted his score.

The second performance was public and televized. I can't recall all the participants, but there were a good dozen of us. We started before the audience entered and, again, did the usual two-hour stint. I have a memory of beginning by bowing the rim of a full glass of water. Every so often I drank some water and went back to bowing. The diminishing quantity of water produced sounds of increasingly lower pitch. I believe this comprised my first half-hour's worth.

How did it feel in this large ensemble of improvisers? The strange thing was that this was never discussed, yet I am left with an impression of feelings to this day. Excited to be involved, yes. Trying hard, perhaps too hard, to produce sounds as interesting as those I had heard in concerts. And here was an important point: is there such a thing as entirely 'free' improvisation? Although we may land up in passages that feel new to us, our responses and gestures are largely a matter of what we already know. There *was* an avant-garde aural tradition in London in the late 1960s. Every performer had heard it, and all, consciously or not, played within it. Some of us were playing Cardew-like because we were in a piece by Cardew, not at all what he would have necessarily wanted. It is interesting that he had once written that *Treatise* should ideally be played by musical innocents. None of the performers in *The Tiger's Mind* would have qualified for that label. So, for all the freedom involved, I was aware for much of the time that I was playing in a piece by

Cornelius Cardew. Yet there was something supremely satisfying about it. Those odd, unplanned moments in which you find yourself totally empathizing with another performer, or even the whole group, take you outside your narrow self, and induce a feeling of oneness with others, with sound, with life.

The most positive aspect of the experience was one of total equality. Many of the other players were more experienced than I, yet there was no element of competition in our playing. Perhaps this was what Cardew had picked up on in our private performance when I pushed the chair around. It was a gesture that was calculated to dominate the proceedings. In my mind that was what the Wind did when it blew strongly.

The most remarkable feature of this performance of *The Tiger's Mind* was that Cardew had appealed for players and accepted everyone who came along. There were no auditions, yet he couldn't have known some of the performers. It is possible to imagine a situation in which irresponsibility could have ruined the entire project. Cardew's gesture of trust was, therefore, absolute. And one felt that, even though he had an aloof persona.

In 1968 he produced *Schooltime Compositions*, his most oblique score. It was presented in a small mock exercise book, emphasizing its educational nature. There are some pages of musical notations, imprecise, schematic, but the rest is diagrams, a quasi-scientific experiment, words, drawings, observations, hints, none of which have any instructions whatsoever.

I heard this played at the International Student Centre, Euston, and enjoyed it immensely. It was based on Cardew's literal understanding of the word 'opera' as many people working together. That was the atmosphere of the piece. A large space was filled with people intently busy at their chosen activities. The music was much more delicate than I had expected.

Revolutionary Study No. 2

Cornelius Cardew continued

Cornelius Cardew's large-scale work *The Great Learning* and the formation of The Scratch Orchestra were achievements which it is impossible to over-estimate. They also led eventually to his wholesale renunciation of all his previous work and avant-gardism in general. By the early 1970s Cardew had identified himself with Maoism, then Marxism-Leninism, producing agitprop music, and conventionally notated songs and instrumental works. He was still in this phase of his development when he was killed by a hit-and-run driver in 1981.

When I went to college in Devon in 1969 it was not long before whatever was going on in London began to assume a certain remoteness. I quickly took on the provincial point of view that not everything of importance happened in London, nor was everything that happened in London necessarily important. So it was some years later that I caught up with what Cardew had been doing. By that time I was absorbed in folklore, and had entered a leftish political phase myself. There seemed to be an uncanny logic at work when I was first told that Cardew had forsaken the avant-garde, 'gone all political', and was arranging folk songs and setting revolutionary Maoist texts. I wouldn't say I had followed exactly the same path but there was enough similarity to give ground for thought.

The Great Learning consists of seven long pieces, some of which can last over an hour, and each based on a paragraph of text by Confucius in Ezra Pound's translations. In essence its theme is human conduct, or the moral authority which all human beings are capable of which Confucius locates *inside*. This echoes a statement of Cardew's about improvisation and self-discipline. The latter is an "essential prerequisite for improvisation. Discipline is not to be seen as the ability to conform to a rigid rule structure, but the ability to work collectively with other people in a harmonious and fruitful way".

Although it is concerned with Confucianist doctrine, it is, musically speaking, Cardew's most undoctrinaire work. Each of Cardew's previous works, for example, used or explored a type of notation — more or less conventional, graphic, textual. Now, in *The Great Learning*, any and every type of notation is pressed into service as needed. There are graphics; Paragraph 1 has a fully notated organ prelude; there are sets of instructions to performers, ways of playing, ways of responding to what others are playing. Cardew specifies instrumentation, something he hadn't done for a while: voices, pebbles, organ, an assortment of whistles and drums, cushions struck with wands, gueros, blown pipes, and a number of wood or metal percussion effects.

On another level, too, *The Great Learning* succeeds in combining differing levels of skill. Professionals and non-professionals can cooperate in its performance with little sense of hierarchy. Neither is there any hierarchy of musical preferences. The organ prelude to Paragraph 1 is non-tonal, yet elsewhere in the work there are tonal and modal references. It is a thoroughly composed piece, yet it offers scope for a degree of improvisation in places, and is totally concerned with how performers relate to one another.

Each Paragraph has a distinct character of its own. The pieces are compelling aural landscapes — dare I call them *mindscapes*? — in which the processes, effort and decisions of performers can be heard, almost as if the instructions are being thought aloud in musical sound. In some cases, Paragraph 7 being the most notable, the musical score is so brief that it could be written on a postcard, and yet there is enough material to last an hour without ever losing the sense of supreme discipline and concentration.

All the individual pieces have a strangely ceremonial feel to them, but Cardew was no parodist of ritualistic ideas from the annals of anthropology. *The Great Learning* is an abstract ceremony; it is not celebrating anything in particular other than the fact that a large group of performers can meet together and play this music. The ceremony is one of dedication, humanity, participation, ethics.

The Great Learning appeared to answer many of the questions Cardew had been asking. There are many features of the work which preclude its usefulness as a conventional commodity, a matter, we have seen, he instinctively responded to in Cage. Its entire ethos concerns the way performers relate to one another. Its parts do not necessarily go together in fixed and predictable ways (although some do). We could say, then, that it relies on being *live*. Recorded versions present the listener with only the aural aspect and, stimulating and (to my ears) beautiful though this can be, it is only a fragment of *The Great Learning*. The pieces require context, contact between performers, space, theatre, and a great deal of time.

The Scratch Orchestra was an outgrowth of *The Great Learning* and was originally connected with Cardew's composition class at Morley College, London. It was formed by Cardew, Michael Parsons and Howard Skempton. It was a large group, committed to performing in any context from grand concert halls to village squares. Every member could contribute compositions; they took it in turn to devise programmes; there was the by now familiar mixture of trained and non-trained musicians; and the orchestra as a whole was prepared to travel.

It was intended as a democratic organization without a specific leader. Cardew, however, was seen as the main force behind it, its father figure.

The Scratch Orchestra embarked on various projects and discussions. All kept a Scratchbook with notes, ideas, scores. Many of these scores were in an avant-garde code which would have baffled most trained musicians. They consisted of written instructions (often oblique or open-ended), drawings, experiments. It was a large ensemble of around fifty people at any one time.

Weekly meetings kept the members in touch, kept them playing. The Scratch Orchestra also gave a series of concerts. Each member of the Orchestra, starting with the youngest, had the chance to prepare a programme.

The Scratch Orchestra became a social unit. It embarked on a summer holiday tour in Cornwall where the whole group camped on a field at St. Tudy. Later they did the same thing on Anglesey. They played on village greens, in local halls, and occasionally gave the locals concerts. One assumes that their avant-gardism baffled a good few Cornish farmers. In one concert performers played their instruments with their hands tied behind their backs.

For a couple of years it seems to have been idyllic but, perhaps predictably, it contained the seeds of its own dissolution. The Scratch Orchestra, as an organization centrally concerned with democracy and egalitarianism, was unable to resist self-analysis as to its nature, function and political role. In the opinion of Lou Gare, one of its members:

"What happens when you work with a group is that you get a lot of energy which builds up, and people are always looking for ideas to explain what's happening. At the time political ideology was the thing — Mao's little red book and all that sort of thing — Marxist ideas. A lot of people took on a more religious thing — Buddhism or Chinese *I Ching* philosophy. Somehow the political ideas seemed to explain the way things could work in a group, rather than accepting that it *did* work and that you needed to keep feeding it with your energy to keep it going. The ideas became too strong for what was actually there to support them. So the whole thing crumbled and all you were left with was a sort of doctrine or ideology."

The nub of the argument put forward by The Scratch Orchestra's ideological group seems to have centred on contradictions between theory and practice. Two of its members offered an analysis based on an essay on D.H. Lawrence by Christopher Caudwell. Caudwell claimed that bourgeois society offered the artist a Hobson's choice: either accept the commercialized position of art, or rebel. If artists accepted the commercialization of art their work was no longer an unimpeded invitation to relationships between people in which "the art work is only like a machine which they must both grasp as part of the process". It also becomes a commercial, commodity-based relationship and, as such, automatically supports the whole social structure which validates it.

To rebel is an option but within bourgeois society rebellion can only be conducted on the terms of the status quo. In attempting to forget the market the artist concentrates increasingly on the art work itself rather than the human, communicative potential of art. Caudwell says: "The art work more and more exists for the individual alone".

This provocative analysis caused Cardew to review his entire career to date. He felt it necessary not only to attack other composers, but to repudiate all his earlier works. Avant-gardism seemed no longer viable or possible. It *was* individualistic, not accessible to many, concerned with itself. What if it was rebellious? Who cared? Caudwell's analysis had a point worth discussing and acting on.

Cardew had been one of the creators of The Scratch Orchestra as an outgrowth of his own work to date. Now The Scratch Orchestra introduced him to Marxism and utterly changed his career. From being the most exciting, challenging and highly talented luminary of experimental music in Britain he turned to writing tonal songs with revolutionary words, arrangements of industrial and Irish militant folk songs, and some instrumental works. The idiom was a curious mixture of the conventionally academic and the folkloric with few concessions to Romanticism. In his rejection of modernism, the avant-garde in particular, he became the first British postmodernist composer, I have heard it said.

It is too easy to suggest that the later Cardew simply turned to writing conventional music which bordered, sometimes, on the trite, an accusation which has been frequently made. Many of his political efforts are also imbued with a sense of irony, even parody. If they are uncomfortably simple they are *deliberately* so as a means of exposing the mythologies and values within bourgeois idioms.

So the last years of Cardew's life were spent in devotion to leftist politics. He felt it necessary not only to abandon but to repudiate all his earlier works, including his masterpiece *The Great Learning*. The title of one of his published collections of writings says it all: *Stockhausen Serves Imperialism*. He saw his years of commitment to *Treatise* as a misguided waste of time and energy.

The first years of his conversion were spent as a Maoist, something he later regarded as a mistake. The thoughts of the venerable Chinese chairman were fashionably unfashionable in the early 1970s. In most alternative arts festivals at the time you would encounter them. The *Little Red Book* was in the air. It explained in simple terms the true class nature of society, the necessity for revolution and how to bring it about.

At the Bath Other Festival the Ross and Cromarty Orchestra (an offshoot of the Portsmouth Sinfonia, itself an offshoot of The Scratch Orchestra) performed simplistic repetitive songs in praise of Mao. They neither sang nor played well but such criticism revealed, no doubt, the listener's hopeless enslavement to bourgeois ideology. They invited everyone to join in. Some did.

The folk group I was part of performed last on this occasion so we sat through the lot. We agreed that it was curious that the proletariat should be offered these hosannas via a self-consciously offbeat ensemble in a scruffy disused organ factory miles from the merest whiff of industrial smoke.

Cardew's Maoism was much more intelligent and musicianly, although at first inevitably gawky. His first political song, *Soon*, to a text by Mao, taken literally, turned out to be a *faux pas*. "Soon there will be a high tide of revolution in our country..." 'Soon' after, eight years to be exact, Mrs. Thatcher became Prime Minister — a revolution, true, but perhaps not of the type predicted. I do not intend this as a cheap criticism. Revolutionary idealism, based, as it often is, on an inadequate grasp of the practicalities of the political situation, has a nasty habit of ending up in disillusionment. I think of my many friends who were in leftist groups who now mutter into their beer that the "whole situation is hopeless", failing to see that the only hope is in the real situation. *Soon*, and songs like it, consciously foster a dreamlike idealism which courts this danger.

The uncomfortable question is: how else can we speak of this song and others like it? Are its outline and melodic ideas memorable? Cardew, slightly later, claimed to be enquiring into bourgeois ideology. Was he doing so here? Is the most astonishing thing about these pieces that they are by Cornelius Cardew?

This is a serious point. All his creative life Cardew had been ahead of the game. He accomplished this deftly by questioning the boundaries of musical composition and performance. His humanist instincts had led him into areas of musical democracy which found expression in The Scratch Orchestra. In demystifying the skill of the musician/composer he came close to annihilating his own deserved position. It is as if Cardew experienced some dys-functionality due to his position as an artist. What was he an artist for? Why? Who for? What was the point? The range of workable solutions is not as narrow as he began to assume.

Baffled critics of Cardew's conversion were hopelessly at sea with what he was trying to do. Yet he was doing what he had always done. He was, chameleon-like, challenging assumptions, with no obligation to what he had done before, nor to what his followers thought he was about. Was he still avant-garde, no matter how much he denounced its previous form?

Having taken a militant revolutionary stance he was no armchair socialist. He was a member of the Revolutionary Communist Party of Great Britain (Marxist-Leninist) and took part in many activities. He composed music for demonstrations against fascism, was arrested by the RUC for activities in Ireland, took part in international socialist festivals. *Bethanien Song* was written in 1973 as part of a campaign to save a children's hospital in a poor part of West Berlin. There was ideological piquancy here. The authorities wanted to build an arts centre in place of the hospital. His *Vietnam Sonata* celebrated the American defeat in 1975. He wrote *Resistance Blues* for a concert in Brixton prison in 1976. In 1980 he was imprisoned after opposing a National Front march in Camberwell, London.

His militant songs and settings of folk songs almost parody tonality in their total acceptance of its parameters. Cardew may have argued that any requirement to do otherwise is an example of bourgeois ideology at work. He predicted that if the revolutionary content does not touch the audience "you get the negative reaction either on the grounds that it's bad music, or on the grounds that it is an attack on the audience [on their bourgeois ideology]".

So we have to accept his challenge as he offered it on both fronts — musical and political — accepting that the one is the other in all but utterance. When a composer offers his politics first and foremost it is only fair that we allow him to do so.

Cardew found his cause in the proletariat, copiously quoting Marx and Lenin. It is notable, then, that his major sources were between fifty and a hundred years old, if one excludes Mao Tse-tung, whom he soon outgrew.

The leftist politics of Marxism-Leninism begin by *accepting* one of the fundamental premises of capitalism — that life can be reduced to, or explained by, material things. Although religion and the spiritual dimension in life played an ideological role in capitalism, as the twentieth century progresses these unmeasurables weaken to the point where the central object of worship is no longer Christ or God but capital itself. We are now a *having* society in which value is estimated according to our ability to accumulate wealth. The old Marxist-Leninist position accepted this as so but added that if only the proletariat could be woken up to its true *material* position it could fulfil its historic mission.

Did subsequent developments in Marxist thinking, notably Gramsci's introduction of hegemony, the role of education, culture and history, figure in Cardew's thinking? Gramsci had argued convincingly that in terms of classic Marxist theory the conditions for the proletariat to claim its freedom already existed. The major problem was its *consent* not to do so.

In various currents of thought the Marxist tradition developed. An important debate raging at the time of Cardew's political activities was that between the British historian E.P. Thompson, whose approach was broadly empirical, and Louis Althusser, whose theoretical formulations were broadly structuralist (although Althusser often denied this).

The work of Wilhelm Reich on the role of sexuality and the irrational was highly influential in the failed insurrection of Paris 1968. Before the Second World War Reich had suggested that failure to respond to freedom could be found in character structure and he reserved his greatest invective for what he called 'red fascists' — communists and leftists who changed the words but not the tune. The authoritarian temperament was as rife in the communist opposition as it was in the bastions of capitalism.

Reich himself was expelled from the Communist Party in 1933 over his attempt to link sexual and political revolution. Yet in his insistence on personal and mass psychology, character structure and orgastic potency Reich was forging the way for later, more refined probing of the essential question of why freedom is not generally claimed when it is available.

One of the implications of balancing the materialism of left and right with the spiritual or psychological dimension surely implicates the arts in their ability either to reinforce or loosen authoritarian character structure. Reworking established or popular idioms is no basic challenge. The work has to be done via words, thereby denying music's ability to signify anything on its own.

An alchemical mix of Reich plus structuralism had led into linguistics and semiotics. Roland Barthes attempted to uncover the implicit ideology in such areas as visual design in advertising, popular imagery and personalities, and sexuality. These constitute the mythologies of modern living. Although there is a questioning of the mythologies associated with traditional forms in some of Cardew's instrumental pieces, some of the revolutionary songs function as simple 'message' pieces with little *apparent* consideration of their manner of setting.

As I found in my own work at the same time, it was no longer clear who or what the proletariat was. The 1970s was the time in Britain when the microchip revolution fundamentally questioned all those classic Marxist modes — alienation, relation to means of production, the function and even the possibility of work and, significantly, the rise of white-collar trade unionism.

Is the proletariat a historical abstraction, a myth? Few people think of themselves as members of it. Politically, it could be argued, this very majority is the point at issue. The small minority who do accept the term may be regarded by revolutionaries as the vanguard, but this makes remarkably little impact. The real issue, as I was to find as a folk singer attempting to scrape a living, consists of confronting the majority who do not subscribe to 'correct ideology' (whatever that is), may find the label 'proletarian' offensive, outmoded and meaningless, and do not welcome instruction from blameless leftists who haven't had the grace to confront their own psychology. National and international revolutionary networks are regarded with a degree of healthy suspicion and disinterest. Experience shows where they lead.

Having left London I did not keep in touch with Cardew's activities for some time and found it provocativly synchronistic when I was told of his new direction. I too was involved in demonstrations, benefit concerts, campaigns and song-writing. These took me round picket lines, massed rallies, union branches, social clubs, and occasionally into theatres. After some years of observing where all this activity was getting, what if anything it was achieving, I began to ask whether it was a *substitute* for political activity, replete with intellectual hooliganism, patronage, and a great deal of knee-jerking. The musical avant-garde had been more honest.

The agitprop music Cardew produced in the last ten years of his life was good stirring stuff in the contexts it was intended for. There were many political songs written for specific occasions. Agitprop songs have an immediate function, and it is unfair to judge them in any other way. If they contribute to a campaign of justice one cannot deny them their usefulness.

It is remarkable that all ideological platforms that wish to express themselves in song or choral settings gravitate towards pretty similar *musical* idioms. Revolutionary socialism, Hitler's Nazis, trade union militants, patriotic clubs, world peace organizations — the worthiness or otherwise of the cause is of little account — all seem to embrace a musical idiom of astonishing consistency and conservatism. Cardew claimed that a group of people singing the *Internationale* was a "more complex, more subtle, a stronger and more musical experience than the whole of the avant-garde put together". Whether this sweeping statement could be proved is doubtful, but the same critique could be applied to people singing *Jerusalem* at a Women's Institute meeting or the audience belting out *Land of Hope and Glory* at the last night of the Proms. The difference in musical idiom is negligible. Only the words communicate different sentiments, but given all we now know about deep structures and their effect on psychology and thought patterns, semiotics, symbolism, linguistics, and McLuhan's earlier work on the way a medium *is* its message, we are justified in asking whether merely changing the sentiments is any real change at all. Naturally, each cause claims that its platform is the 'right' one, the correctness of the sentiments overriding all other considerations. This is patently ludicrous but it is painfully difficult for the converted to accept. Musical structures are thinking patterns which operate on a less literal, therefore more subconscious, level than words.

Does Cardew's later music, his use of folk or folk-like melody as vehicles, present an unsatisfactory picture following his years of genuine experimentation? His setting of socialist polemics such as *There Is Only One Lie, There Is Only One Truth*, the mere title of which annihilates one's right to an opinion, takes one's breath away in its wilful, naive gaucheness. Cardew may have argued that the very lack of expected technique emphasized the revolutionary content. You do, after all, hear the words.

In his instrumental music Cardew has much more to offer. One of the most interesting instrumental pieces is the *Thälmann Variations* for piano. It is a piece of real substance, a straight set of variations which leaves us in no doubt about the muscianly mind behind it. The theme can be heard in its development and restatement at various points and Cardew's use of chordal harmony, in the statement of the theme for example, is surprisingly lush. It is thoroughly tonal but not without experimentation. There are passages in it which recall sounds that the earlier Cardew might have used — not in idiom, but in texture. Rumbling passages at the lowest extremity of the keyboard are contrasted with delicate runs at the highest.

One of his last works, the *Boolavogue* for two pianos, is glorious. It rhapsodizes on the Irish folk tune of the same name — something Sean O Riada had also done. The tune itself gives any composer a head start. Although it is a tonal work, conventional in many respects, it is hard to imagine that a composer without some knowledge of the piano styles of the .avant-garde could have written it. Textures and uses of the piano that could be taboo in the conservatoire freely mingle with the tune, support it, contradict it.

Should we wish to locate these pieces in any tradition we would gravitate towards the social realism once approved in socialist countries. Cardew's efforts are more than worthy by comparison, although one has to say that a major reason why they merit discussion is, again, that they are by Cornelius Cardew, the man who led the British avant-garde. Can the composer. be decontextualized from his own life? Cardew couldn't escape the fact that due to the importance and influence his earlier music had anything he did was a *statement*.

Two of his statements were seminal. The first is paradoxical. In a most original way he questioned the whole idea of originality. One of the foundations of avant-gardism was that it sought out things which hadn't been done before. Although there is merit in this approach its less useful side is that it induces *originality fetishism*, whereby a crucial point of interest is newness. Taken to extremes this is as obviously dysfunctional as the insistence on the *new* in the mainstream marketing of clothes, movies or popular music. Cardew's challenge to originality fetishism was constructive and appropriate.

His other important statement was to reinstate tonality. He was not the only avant-gardist to do so. The minimalist school in America was gathering momentum at the time, as Cardew was aware. He had organized a performance of Terry Riley's *In C*, for example, one of the last things I saw him do before I left London. In the same programme was La Monte Young's vocal *Death Chant* which I took part in. The Young piece is literally a chant on certain syllables with melody all written out. It could hardly be called tonal in the conventional sense (there is no functional harmony) but it is melodic and has a tonal centre.

From the point of view of musical democracy Cardew's later career raises some fundamental questions. Firstly, organizations and ideologies ideally exist for people, rather than the other way round. They are created by people, but the moment they have power over people, including individual artists, they surrender their ethical position. Cardew's middle period works, *Treatise*, *The Tiger's Mind*, *Schooltime Compositions* and, notably, *The Great Learning*, existed for people, that is the performers and participants. They were also rewarding if challenging listening experiences. Although it would be too one-dimensional to say that his later works existed for ideologies, there is an uncomfortable *antidemocratic* problem, especially with the songs. If one disagrees with the ideology, wishes to refine it, regards it as unsubtle, unsophisticated, or even plain wrong (even from a sympathetic Marxist viewpoint) there is virtually nothing left of the piece.

Secondly, there was no reason to begrudge Cardew his position as a leader in experimental music because he increasingly adopted an advanced style of leadership. He rarely gave orders from above. He created situations designed to *enable* or draw out ideas and experience rather than prescribe what those experiences should consist of. And he called these situations compositions. There was always an element of risk, but he shared that risk. It made things exciting. He gathered a loose network of people who were in tune with his ideas, many of whom also became composers and improvisers.

Thirdly, the final phase of Cardew's output illustrates, in my view, what musical democracy is *not*. Proclaiming truths for the masses to follow, assuming a lack of ability on their part to relate to anything other than versions of conventional idioms and slogans, apart from being a political *cul de sac*, doesn't really show any awareness of contemporary developments in popular culture from the top twenty upwards. Ultimately we have to face it: if the music is flawed the ideology is flawed. What you do is not an expression of what you believe. It is the same thing. And this is so of music.

This is what makes *The Great Learning* such a masterpiece. It is brilliantly musical and its musicality is embedded in the ideas which motivated it. My recordings, which include Paragraph 7, which is purely vocal, are sumptuous in their ever-moving, ever-changing texture. It is utterly unimportant in Paragraph 7 that little seems to be happening or, to put it more accurately, the texture is continuous, because the minutiae of sound alteration and the eventual tonal resolution of a huge quiet discord are compelling to the point of meditation.

When in 1972 part of *The Great Learning* was performed at the Proms (establishment recognition) Cardew altered the Confucian texts to give them explicit socialist revolutionary content, and stipulated that banners announcing "A revolution is not a dinner party, it is an insurrection, an act of violence by which one class overthrows another" and suchlike should be held aloft during the performance. The BBC wouldn't have it, which is hardly surprising, and Cardew must have been able to predict that this would have been the case. Even if he had got away with it, did he seriously believe that the slogans would have changed anyone's mind, been a serious force in political education? Perhaps not. Perhaps he regarded the banners as creating a context for the music and therefore part of it.

Clearly Cardew came to believe that no matter how radical his experimental music had been, the system could eventually recuperate and be strengthened by it. Indeed, it needed its avant-garde in order to have a fund of new ideas to draw on commercially when the time was right. There are some grounds for this idea. Every system needs its *enfants terribles* in order to strengthen it, to test its boundaries and still come out on top as demonstrably fair.

But there's more to Cardew than this. *The Great Learning* gives us the clue in that it is a Confucianist piece. Despite Confucius' notion that genuine moral ability is located *inside* the individual, his basic concern is one of government by the wise. Cardew created the musical systems with his wisdom, systems flexible enough for the performers to discover their own inner responsibility within them.

Cornelius Cardew was a nonconformist in the best sense. He was not satisfied with timeworn, conventional situations in music, performance, notation, composition, context. He pushed them to the limit. *The Great Learning* is such an intriguing project because it marries Cardew's questioning spirit with conformity and order. Therefore it balanced his personality and drew two important opposites together.

Yet it was not only a personal matter that Cardew faced. He illustrates a version of the O Riada syndrome. In pushing the bounds of experimentation probably further than most of his contemporaries he necessarily found himself in a limited circle — not limited in numbers, although that may have been true too, but limited in *issues*. To continue with avant-gardism after the 1960s would have been pure introspection. Instead, one can turn to the unrefined, the raw, the people. To do so one has to construct a different set of myths.

Having got about as far out as it may have been possible for him to get, and as far away from the majority of the population, he made the gesture of favouring the majority — the masses, the proletariat — in his final phase of work. In doing so he took on romantic leftist myths, namely that there *is* such a thing as 'the people', ready to fulfil their historic mission.

Cardew considered that his initial political direction was mistaken and he was evidently modifying his line as actual experience inevitably taught him more. He understood well many of the contradictions brought about by his new line of development. As John Tilbury has written: "It is part of the tragedy of his death that, in the opinion of many, he was on the brink of achieving valid and meaningful solutions". We will never know what they might have been. We would dearly love to know what might have followed *Boolavogue*.

Occasionally in his writings Cardew produced some astonishingly apt comments from the point of view of musical democracy. In *Stockhausen Serves Imperialism* he asked the composer to take a "sober look at his own activity in the context of his local involvement in a musical community, and come to a point of readiness to work together to produce a positive atmosphere and real development". If we respect the man at all we need to take on *all* his output from first to last and understand the humanistic urge which lay behind it, no matter what form it took from time to time.

In 1980 I was deep in a folkloric trance. The group I sang with wanted to cut an album of industrial songs. I spoke to the folklorist A.L. Lloyd in his capacity of father-figure and artistic adviser to Topic Records. Lloyd was not all that interested. Albums of industrial songs had been done before, by his company. It was time to move on. "I'm more interested in what this fellow Cardew is doing," said Lloyd. I respected Lloyd. I was also astonished. Cornelius Cardew?

Improvisations

Alfred Nieman / Free Jazz / AMM

PROGRAMME NOTE

Does democracy include the right to specialize? If so how does such specialization survive under the will of the majority? Is a philosophy of exchange of socially desired products a subtext of democracy for artists? If so do they have real freedom? Freedom to starve or teach? Is there a way round these issues which avoids the commoditization of music?

One way of telling the history of Western classical music would be the story of tightening notation to the point of impossibility. From its origins as shorthand mnemonic through to the avant-garde music of the early 1950s it makes a logical and remarkably linear tale. By the mid-twentieth century it seemed that in modernist concert works the degree of specialization required had reached a high point. Alarmingly, the trend continues.

This was an inevitable consequence of the postwar generation pushing new techniques of composition to the limit — especially serialism. Performance of new music had become highly undemocratic despite the internal musical democracy of the serial aesthetic. It often bordered on the impossible. Not only did you have to be virtuosic. You needed a lot of time to rehearse, and an unusually specialist ear. Improvisation, in which there is no predictable result, emerges partly as an alternative to this nexus.

The rise of free and improvised music in the 1960s was no coincidence. The timely development of electronic music meant that the serialist's most complex concoctions could be interpreted with a precision that was probably beyond the human performer. If composers wanted ideally fixed renditions they could now have them. Improvisation was free to happen.

However, the matter is not quite that simple. Improvisation did not only occur in opposition to something, it also had its own positive lines of enquiry. Improviser Eddie Prévost has written of the group AMM: "Obviously, what we all had in common was a rejection of the predominating modes. However, I would repudiate the superficial assumption that we shared a camaraderie based upon a destructive dislike of an unsatisfactory form. *No intense long-term creative relationship is likely to be sustained upon a negative basis*" (my italics).

For composers, as opposed to pure improvisers, one attraction of writing pieces which demanded compositional input from performers was that they could experiment with mobile forms. Most of the Europeans tried this. Stockhausen and Boulez, for example, kept a tight control on the actual material played, but others composed looser structures. Performers were often asked to make decisions about the order in which sections or musical fragments were played. It became almost a cliché for a composer to announce that the music could be played as written, upside down or backwards.

American composers produced more radical situations. Earle Brown was inspired by the mobile sculptures of Alexander Calder. Brown explained: "As you walk into a museum and you look at a mobile you see a configuration that's moving very subtly. You walk in the same building the next day and it's a different configuration, yet it's the same piece, the same work by Calder. It took me a couple of years to figure out how to go about it musically."

Brown's offerings of musical freedom went much further than the Europeans. To his credit goes one of the first, if not *the* first, fully graphic score, *December '52*. It consists of a page of score with small rectangles and lines delicately placed: not a whiff of conventional notation in sight. As an abstract drawing it is beautiful. Most musicians at the time wouldn't have known what to do with it, despite some helpful rules from the composer.

So various forms of free, open or graphic notation arrived as options for composers. Some of Cardew's exercises in this genre have already been mentioned. His skill as a graphic artist served him in good stead, providing stimuli for what could in some cases be described as guided improvisations. The Italian Sylvano Bussotti presented a more expressionist use of graphic scoring in some of his pieces. Whereas Cardew's efforts tend to convey a sense of discipline and precision, Bussotti's explode off the page with passionate intensity. One of his graphic pieces was intended for three pianists at one piano producing some erotically suggestive theatre.

A librarian once told me that he had qualms about buying in Cardew's *Octet '61*; why should all the royalties go to the composer when the performers were just as responsible for the music produced? It was an interesting point which I considered for months. Discussing the matter with other musicians didn't help. Conventional musicians with no sympathy for such experimentation contemptuously dismissed the whole idea with aggression or mockery. This convinced me that something important was at stake. Yet the avant-gardists could be smug and equally negative in their determined stand to be different. Not for the last time I found myself in a position of trusting nobody's vested interest. In my late teens this was problematical for me: if there was a truth surely someone should know it. I was forced to the conclusion that the truth was that nobody knew the truth of anything.

I decided to carry out experiments. I interpreted free and graphic scores on the piano trying as hard as possible to derive all musical ideas from what I saw before me. Lines and squiggles might become analogous musical patterns; blobs or circles could become clusters of notes, and so on. Or I might take a less literal approach, simply staring at a page for minutes on end waiting for a moment when I would automatically play appropriate sounds merely by soaking in the atmosphere of, say, a Bussotti drawing.

These efforts would be tape-recorded.

Then I would try to clear my mind of what I had just played. I would turn to Mozart or Haydn, perhaps, or stop for a cigarette, or maybe start counting how many steps it took to walk round the block. (I had a notebook in which I kept such statistics.) When I was satisfied that I could play the piano without undue influence from what I had previously played I would attempt a free improvisation in any style I fancied. These would also be tape-recorded.

Comparing recordings of the 'scored' improvisations with the free ones revealed some interesting differences. The free playing implied decisions. What style? What form? Any form at all? What musical material? How long? Such matters were accounted for when a musical score, no matter how sketchy, was the point of departure. Now it was true that having pointers from the composer in certain directions still left decisions to be made in others, but there was undoubtedly a sense in which a score, no matter how unlike music it might look, shared responsibility, whereas the free improviser took it all on himself.

How far was it possible to go in experimental notation? I needed to know. As a young composer on Dartington Summer School in around 1968 I handed in a score for assessment by the visiting composer Hugh Wood. On one page were two stimuli: a postage stamp and the word FORCING.

Hugh Wood was charming about most of the scores he was offered. He commented in detail about the handling of the series, formal matters, instrumentation, and so on. When he came to my score he quickly passed it over with ''I take it this was a joke''. I was furious. It wasn't a joke and I had been too naive to see that it would be taken as such. This experience convinced me that my path was somewhere other than in the musical establishment.

I had hit the borderline between composition and improvisation and so I began to welcome encounters with any improvising musician.

Alfred Nieman's appearance in 1967 as improvisation tutor at Chiswick Polytechnic's evening classes was timely. He looked rather gentle. Tall, with crinkly fair hair and a slightly high-pitched speaking voice, he gave off an air of delicacy. But once he got down to work the superficialities disappeared. He explained little. Just that we were going to improvise music. He invited the class to bear in mind two rules: no tonal triads, 7th and 9th chords rather than octaves. For the untrained this probably didn't mean much. For me, who regarded classical harmony and counterpoint as an unnecessary war which could have been avoided by negotiation, it was manna from Heaven. (Nieman, for the record, didn't share my view of harmony and counterpoint.)

We were all going to begin by playing short piano solos. If you couldn't play the piano you could use the flats of your hands, fists, the whole forearm; you could pluck the strings inside. (One member of the class began a piece by slamming both forearms across as many keys as possible.) I could play well enough, but the idea of not always using my fingers appealed.

Nieman wrote some words on a blackboard: clowns, stormy sea, rush hour, clouds, midnight. Each member of the class would choose one of these impressionistic titles. Their improvisations would be recorded and played back with time for group discussion and guidance from Nieman.

Disingenuously he asked: "Shall I start?" He meant that he would.

It struck me years later that by giving the titles *and* giving an example of how they could be played he was determining so many important elements that it could almost be called composition. I now see what he did as *notation*. It may not be *composing* in the classical European sense, but someone who does such things is being a *composer* — assembling and predetermining certain elements which lead to music-making. Notation is any form of communication which causes music to be made. Some composers, myself included, have been happy to leave it at less.

My first effort was *Oxford Circus*. It owed something to Gershwin's *An American in Paris*, the bit where he imitates car horns with percussive major and minor seconds. Nieman liked it.

As the weeks passed we got on to duets, trios, songs, and then whole ensemble improvisations based on classical forms — sonata, variations, serial techniques. Skills developed. Listening developed. Eventually more mobile formal ideas were incorporated.

I got close to Alfie. I looked up to him. When the improvisation class did a public concert he asked me to play a piano solo. As I recall it sounded like early Stockhausen, pointillistic, based on rhythmic cells.

I was carefully monitoring my feelings. It was flattering to receive applause and overflowing encouragement from Nieman. It was also good for my self-esteem to hear the tapes back and realize that I had produced music of some quality. It was easy for these feelings to predominate. Yet it was impossible to silence the need to explore further, even if it meant leaving the arena in which I had established competence.

My main reservation was that this improvised music had a tendency to sound like composed concert music. It had an uncharacteristic fluidity, true, but its yardstick seemed to be connected with its closeness to identifiable models.

Nieman's approach to improvisation had a democratic flavour within the confines he set. Certainly no one was excluded. What was a challenge was the possibility — and it was no more — that a musical situation could be set up in which all players could function at their own level. Complete beginners with little technique could be trained to listen and respond, yet their contribution need not hold back those who had achieved a degree of virtuosity. In theory the old hierarchies of specialization and technique could be blurred, used constructively or dissolved. It is not surprising that Nieman's ideas have been highly influential in the world of music therapy.

For me, capable of improvising highly complex passages but less certain about writing them down or reading them, this was a liberation. I could *participate* in making the sounds I identified with. It was clear that I had to follow this line of thinking much further. Composing could be a matter of arranging for such situations to happen. A composition needed enough material given or suggested to form an identity, but not enough to predetermine all the details. This *social* aspect of music-making began to exert persistent fascination.

Some free jazz specialists presented Nieman with a problem which he dealt with by asking them to play another way. He was entitled to do that. I found, however, that if I wanted to form an improvisation group to play occasionally in public or private it was unlibertarian of me to try to alter someone else's experience of style. As a significant number of those who were willing to play came from a free jazz background it did present a problem which I was unable to solve.

The recordings the jazz people introduced me to — Ornette Coleman, John Coltrane, Albert Ayler, Archie Shepp — showed how far the jazz tradition had moved since my father had played his records of Parker, Gillespie, the Modern Jazz Quartet, Gerry Mulligan or Erroll Garner. The 'new thing' had reinvestigated some essential features of Afro-American music. Ensemble improvisation had been a feature of New Orleans street music before it was called trad jazz. Harmony was not a rigid twelve bar affair in early blues. But to these freedoms had been added the possibilities of loosening tonality, rhythmic playing which came in waves rather than beats, stretching instruments to breaking point resulting in shrieks, honks and howls, and an emotional intensity which resonated in your bones and blood. Behind it all lay the blues — not as a form or set of scales. Blues was a metaphor for black American social experience.

The young European whites who immersed themselves in this music rightly regarded improvisation as its *sine qua non* and looked for chances to play it. Whatever its political significance in America, its appearance in Europe was, again, not coincidental. At the same time as the European avant-garde had pushed serialism and notation as far as they would go until they exploded off the page in graphic protest, so jazz was also in danger of becoming a formalized concert art. In the 1950s the Modern Jazz Quartet represented an extreme form of this possibility. They appeared soberly dressed in dark suits, played delicate, safe, calculated and very composed music, refined, unchalleng-ing to white ears, even occasionally using classical forms such as suites, variations, fugue. This degree of refinement happened at the same time as its opposite was being born.

The experience of black Americans has fuelled the history of what whites have called jazz. Even the use of the word 'jazz', which, legend has it, meant 'fuck' in black slang, betrays a certain racism. The music is equated with animal functions, not necessarily only fucking, but dancing, funerals, parades, night clubs. Whatever, it wasn't regarded as an art form on a par with what whites did in concert halls. The Modern Jazz Quartet's stance was partly an attempt to go for this dignity, but it was done on white terms. What characterized the 'new thing' was that it finally disregarded what the hell whites thought of it. It came from the heart, the heart of black experience. And it built up a few myths of its own.

Ironically it began to get good white audiences. This was for a reason which is ignored by the standard *political* account of jazz that I have just summarized. Much of it was good music.

The problem when the white disciples of Coleman and Coltrane entered the European improvisation nexus was that idioms clashed horribly, rendering both powerless in the face of each other. The blues apparently had nothing to do with the European experience. So what happened in the midst of the post-serialist plinks and plonks was that fragments of another experience flashed across the texture, usually louder than everything else, making the experience unsatisfactory *musically*.

This was illustrated perfectly by a booking four of us did in a scruffy pub in Ladbroke Grove. Three of us turned up with boxes of tricks: bells, cymbals, things to prepare the piano, electronic gadgets, a cello, various drums. We began quietly, responding as much to what was going on in the pub as to each other. Suddenly the sax player swept into a solo and from there on it was a jazz gig plus funny noises. In our discussion afterwards the rest of us were told we had given little support, rhythm. We told him that it took him ninety minutes before he listened to what we were doing. We weren't doing anything, he said. That's because you weren't listening, we replied. We crossed that pub off our list. The landlord rightly regarded our music as terrible.

Were the free jazzers, in playing like their black heroes, paying homage rather than being themselves? Blacks, it seemed, played music. Their white followers played jazz. Black music stood as a symbol for alienation, or perhaps it was just plain dissatisfaction with existing musical options. But then, our unsupported sax player might have thrown the same accusation at us.

When I first came across the band AMM I was a student at the Guildhall School of Music and having a tough time orientating to an academic musical training in which Schoenberg and Webern were still regarded as modern composers.

There were other improvisers around but AMM, to this day, strike me as the most radical. Most importantly they were the only group I had encountered which had dealt with the usually disastrous meeting between free jazz and European avant-garde music. In order to do so they had to give up both, not as a rejection, but to establish their own tradition.

AMM began in the bosom of the Mike Westbrook jazz band. Through Westbrook's highly influential band passed many players who went on to become important members of the British new jazz scene — John Surman, Harry Beckett, Paul Rutherford and many others.

According to the sax player, Lou Gare, Keith Rowe "ripped the band apart with his guitar playing". He was playing very free, and some members of the band were not enthusiastic. But Gare and Rowe were kindred spirits and they left Westbrook's band and decided to go entirely for improvisation. They were following, to a degree, the path of the 'new jazz' as pioneered by Coleman. They were joined by drummer Eddie Prévost and Lawrence Sheaff and became AMM. Gare says: "We got more interested in improvisation and forgot about the jazz. It became an art expression of its own." Still, however, there were definite traces of Coleman or Albert Ayler.

Cornelius Cardew was at that time working on *Treatise*, which required adventurous improvisers, and had met Keith Rowe and invited him to play. Perhaps through this connection he heard of AMM and turned up to hear them at one of their regular sessions at the Royal College of Art in South Kensington. Soon after he joined.

In the summer of 1990 I interviewed Lou Gare in his home in Exeter. He had left London some years back. It was a warm September afternoon, so we sat in the garden drinking tea, talking, batting off the occasional insect. It was over twenty years since I had seen him in AMM — a time-warping experience for me. He made no bones about Cardew's influence on the group: "After Cornelius joined it became AMM music. Before that it was quite jazzy, Coleman, Ayler stuff, although the rhythm wouldn't be."

Cardew had better fortune, perhaps because he had more experience and determination than I as a student had, in working with free jazz musicians. He admired them, and for very similar reasons. Gare told me:

"He admired jazz musicians because they had this ability to improvise, and he was a composer, and improvisation was, I suppose, instant composition. You could present something which had a good musical shape, was interesting, and full of other musical qualities. They could do it without sitting down for several weeks or months labouring over it. It would just sort of happen. I think one of the stories was that he wanted to be a jazz musician. So he joined us. And maybe we wanted to be serious musicians."

When I saw them at the Commonwealth Institute, AMM was on stage well before the scheduled time of start. The members of the group appeared to be fiddling about with their instruments, adjusting microphones, and so on. I had enough experience of such things to realize that the distinction between what was considered to be the performance and what wasn't was being deliberately blurred. Lou Gare told me:

"I never used to do any warming up or tuning up or anything. You'd consider that as part of the playing. I attached a little bell on to my saxophone sling so when I got it out of the case the bell would tinkle. It would remind me that the music was already starting."

From then on the group improvisation lasted around two hours. As many of the performers had contact microphones fixed to instruments and sound sources there was an overall impression of amplified music. Typically there would be long passages of sustained sounds, or little happening, that would swell into hyperactive, deafening periods. All the time the players were looking for new ways of exploring their instruments.

There were times when the playing reached huge proportions of volume and relentlessness. A fair number of the audience walked out. It was unmusical by any previous definition. Melody, even as redefined by the most trenchant modernism, was almost absent throughout. Rhythm, in terms of a regular or even irregular pulse, was rarely heard, although there were showers of drumming from Prévost which obliquely punctuated the texture.

The fascination of much of the performance was in hearing how one group of sounds being played together gradually transformed into another. This was not done in obvious ways, as Lou Gare explained:

"One of the problems when people come and join in AMM [is that] someone will play something, then immediately they will echo it or play something complementary to it. But it doesn't seem to work like that. It works in an odd, oblique sort of way. You hear something going on, but all the time there's something else going on as well. But the two things do go together and obviously make something. But it's very difficult to explain how."

This is why the occasional visitors to the group usually had "...a disaster. You have to surrender yourself completely to what the group's doing, but also maintain a strong individuality — both together. I don't know how you can explain that to someone".

It was more than that. Surrender to the group while maintaining individuality is a prerequisite for any worthwhile improvisation. AMM consistently, and as a matter of *style* (which, it cannot be denied, they had), pursued a much more complex line. They went for a kind of anarchism in which the individual was free to play whatever he was driven to, knowing that the others were doing likewise. The permission given to each other to do this is what, paradoxically, produces a 'group mind'. This, at times, seems to function autonomously. Thus the space becomes safe despite its ability to sound abrasive or even violent. Prévost and Rowe have written in a sleeve note:

"Far from being a negation of individuality, the recording illustrates an ethic which allows each to express himself without fear of being subordinated or exploited. The players could share a timeless immersion in a world of sound, while simultaneously being free to pursue their individual paths. It was not uncommon for the musician to wonder who or what was producing a particular sound, stop playing, and discover that it was he himself who had been responsible."

This needs to be followed through on three counts. Firstly, the manner of playing and its implicit social relations are as radical a manifesto of direct musical democracy as we are likely to find. In composed music the composer takes responsibility for as many musical and behavioural matters as required. It may be little. It may be almost everything. In music that relies on a tradition as its major reference point (folk, jazz, whatever) decisions are made by default. In such cases there is an assumed reference point outside the immediate control of the performers. AMM's vital core is that it assumes equality of status as a formal quality of producing music. AMM, therefore, is a new form of social organization articulated in music.

Secondly, as a precondition of its activities AMM demands human qualities of trust and cooperation. These are not only necessary towards the other members of the group; they are also directed towards sounds and the instruments and objects that make those sounds. Although technique is introduced into the process, the fact that others are working simultaneously invariably means that each player has to be prepared for the unexpected and act responsibly. What is demanded here is a *spiritual* quality which, even amongst improvisers, is hard to find.

This willingness for dedication and surrender is easy to talk about, less easy to do. AMM's musical democracy, therefore, includes a degree of spiritual awareness. Lou Gare was quite explicit: "You felt the sound physically in your body. Or if you listened you could hear changes going on in your metabolic state. It's like meditating or something. You feel yourself change."

Real freedom comes about when individuals voluntarily choose what they inexorably must do. AMM enacts this. Lou Gare put it in a statement which should be enshrined in the annals of musical democracy for all time: "I suppose you're free by being totally committed to something. It's that kind of freedom. It's not the freedom to do anything you like. It's the freedom to do what the music likes. And what the music likes happens to be what you like as well. That way you're totally free.''

The third matter concerns AMM's relation to history. Although all sounds are permissible there is no doubt that AMM shows preferences for certain types. These tend to be those which were furthest away from traditional reference points. There was no quoting of harmonic or melodic structures unless they happened at random by turning on a transistor radio.

The only tradition which could be meaningfully referred to was that of AMM itself. It certainly had a style. Cardew used to argue that each instrument was a "traditional musical structure such as saxophone, piano, violin, guitar etc., in each of which reposes a portion of the history of music''. True though this may be it was the marked tendency of AMM to disregard musical history. The reason for this would presumably be that direct references or quotations would imply conditioned responses. As these are what many listeners survive on it is not surprising that AMM was specialist music.

The progress of AMM became inextricably tied up with that of Cornelius Cardew and The Scratch Orchestra. With Cardew's acceptance of political ideology came a change in his own personal perspective of AMM. Cardew's reinvestigation of history (tonality, conventional forms, etc.) was incompatible with AMM.

When the group toured Holland, Gare and Prévost did a duo performance, referring more to free jazz than they had done for years as AMM; Cardew and Rowe put on tapes of Chinese political songs and improvised with them as a backing.

Cardew did play with AMM towards the end of his life. Apparently they got together for a session, but Cardew's musical ideas were by now so different that the whole thing was a struggle.

Although the group did not play for some time it was eventually kept alive after Cardew's death by Keith Rowe and Eddie Prévost, and gradually played more. The pianist John Tilbury and the cellist Rohan de Saram joined the group, and it was this quartet which recorded a number of albums, including *The Inexhaustible Document*, issued on Matchless Records in 1987.

In *The Inexhaustible Document* some significant changes have occurred. It is unmistakably the old AMM with its predilection for noise, incidental sounds, long sustained passages, wavelike swells which take place over extended periods of time. So the democratic and spiritual aspects of AMM seem to remain the same, if not maturing. But there are passages of delicacy and sensuousness which were virtually unheard in the AMM of the 1960s. Tilbury plays successions of soft almost Debussy-like piano chords at one point. De Saram's cello whines melodies in harmonics. There are tonal references, for a short while a real tonal centre. Clashing gongs and cymbals at one point remind one of Tibetan sacred ritual music.

It would be impossible to account for these changes (they are probably unintentional) and foolhardy to try. It is sufficient to acknowledge that, at least on one recording, they can be heard and therefore, in the subtlest of ways, introduce history (even AMM's own history) into the style — from time to time. Gare, who does not play on *The Inexhaustible Document*, agrees that AMM is "much more polished now. It was much cruder. Now the sound is very accomplished", and admires Tilbury's pianism in particular.

AMM was by no means alone in experimental improvisation. It happened to be the group that I was closest to, most identified with. Many of the others seemed like a compromise in comparison, given to mere aural doodles. And many stayed too close to jazz.

What are the strengths of improvisation? Eddie Prévost has written:

"Western 'classical' music demands a solution to most of the technical problems of making music *before* the music can be performed. Where — although most improvised musics demand a high level of technical competence — the elaboration of a theme, on a chord sequence or the direct response of musical dialogue, demands the application of 'problem-solving' techniques *within* the actual performance."

Another strength is a precondition of *group* improvisation. The music has to be made through open relationship with the other players. In a fully written work anything outside the composer's instructions is not valid. In improvisation the opposite is true. Any composed or preconceived ideas inserted into the music are intrusive and possibly even anti-social. Within a free improvisation you have to remain open to whatever occurs. Even ideas which worked in a previous session may not necessarily be relevant to the current one.

The joy of improvising with players who are prepared to accept this approach can be found in those occasional moments (which become more numerous with sustained experience) where the 'group mind' takes over and an open space of absolute freedom emerges. Within this space you hear sounds — those made by yourself, others, and any in the environment — as a universe in themselves. As this universe is not outside (you are having a hand in creating it) and not inside you (you have to relate) the inescapable conclusion is that *it is you*. Or, less metaphysically, as you are participating in its progress there is no logical way of assuming what it would be like without you. From the listener this music requires great attentiveness.

Prévost says of the AMM experience that it "reveals the complexity of human beings who whilst innocently making music together perceived that they had found a more cogent basis for both music and life".

Bridge Passage

Who are 'the people' anyway? Are they the whole population, including those who don't subscribe to democracy, one country, one continent, one world — or maybe one small community? Are they those who conform to a point of view you happen to hold, no matter how nonconformist that view may be? Are all the others therefore disposable as deluded by false consciousness? Let he who is without this sin cast the first stone, I say.

Are 'the people' the majority? How do we assess their relation to music? By fraudulent pop charts? By what sells?

Is the gospel of 'the people' simply another way of saying we're all equal? So why aren't we musically equal? How is it that I can't play a Boulez piano sonata? Is it that I don't want to, or am so unsophisticated that I can't hear what is written? Improvisation — ah, that's easy. So how do I account for a friend who was a highly trained classical pianist who froze in Nieman's improvisation classes saying she couldn't, just couldn't. Is it the academic training that annihilates spontaneity?

Could there be a musical level outside the bourgeois concert tradition, not reliant on notation, specialization or donkey's years of practice in little rooms?

The search for folk music is typical of the age of democracy. It's part of the myth. It's not surprising that the Americans take it very seriously. Nor that it emerges as a study in Europe in the industrial period, when all was felt to be disappearing and there was uncertainty about what was coming. Precisely.

I had a friend who lived in Teddington (Lawrence Crawley, where are you now?) who had gathered a huge record collection. Determinedly eccentric, he lived in a shed at the bottom of the garden with only a bed and his records all round the wall. His tastes were wide-ranging, although he had a particular fondness for early music and Indian music. His entire collection was indexed in spidery biro. He should have been a librarian. The system worked brilliantly. He willingly participated in many of my Cage-inspired events.

To Lawrence goes the credit for the composition of *Music for Artificial Puddle and Gum Boot* which he and I performed at the Drury Lane Arts Lab. It was a punning piece of theatre. He stood behind a music stand and tuned his violin. Parodying the stuffy and incomprehensible spiel that generally preceded the performance of a new serial work on the radio, he announced in a Third Programme voice that the composer had provided the following notes. He then played a series of unconnected notes on the violin, slowly and very seriously.

My instruction was to create an artificial puddle and place a gum boot in it. I did this by taking a full watering can to the top of a large step ladder and pouring water onto a groundsheet. I placed my foot in a gum boot and brought it forcefully down in the puddle, splashing most of the front row, many of whom were used to such things. Seconds later a succession of fireworks went off on a balcony outside. Lawrence put his violin down and bowed. During the applause (and there was some) I handed electronic music specialist Hugh Davis, who was in the front row, a postcard which announced that he was now playing *Postal Piece* by Sam Richards and would be doing so until further notice. A few weeks later I sent him a card saying that the performance was over and thanking him for his cooperation.

Many evenings Lawrence and I planned performances, wrote music, and listened to records in the shed. This was how I first heard electronic music in the form of Stockhausen's *Kontakte*. I was very impressed. As soon as one record was finished we'd play another. This time it might be didgeridoo music from Arnhem Land, then perhaps some Cage, pioneers of the Mannheim school of classical music, street music from Bengal, glass harmonica works by Mozart, mechanical music, sitar.

There was a recording by The Watersons, a family foursome from Yorkshire who sang unaccompanied English folk ritual songs. The only instrument used on the entire record was a pounding bass drum which punctuated the choruses of one song. A cautionary note on the record warned that this might make some needles jump. For us this was a plus, and we played the record to hear the jump.

The songs were associated with seasonal customs: wassailing, Christmas, May Day, souling, harvest, pace-egging at Easter. But in truth it was not so much the songs but the roughly harmonizing voices which found their way to a spot that was waiting to be touched. That *sound* articulated discontents and questions, oppositions as well as pointers. They opposed the refinement of much contemporary European music. They counterposed its obscurantism with earthiness. They implied an already existing audience. With the avant-garde one was obliged to cultivate an audience. Even then you tended to see the same faces. The folk harmonizers proceeded in ignorance of academic music training. Effectively.

Academic training represents the way music is taught to one social class, perpetuating one tradition. Highly influential though classical training is, its participants (composers, performers, critics, audiences even) account for a very small proportion of the world's population. Folklore, so it seemed, is what everyone else does — with one proviso: once formalized into institutions it would be destroyed. Was there any reason why it shouldn't form as good a training for the composition of new music? Or perhaps even better because it resists institutionalization?

Lawrence and I began to experiment with these simple melodies and basic harmonies and found we could do it — after a fashion. The thought of us in a garden shed in Teddington singing: "We gets up in the morn and we sounds the harvest horn" didn't strike us as the least incongruous. Just before I left London in 1968 I had one foot in the avant-garde and one in the folk revival.

My move from a London music college to Dartington in Devon was initially motivated by the fact that I felt stifled in the academic milieu. Skills that I saw no real necessity to master, such as harmony and counterpoint or becoming a virtuoso pianist, had been presented to me as defining features of a real musician. *Ergo* I was not a real musician. It was not that I regarded such things as damaging, although in retrospect I think I do. It was more an absolute certainty on my part that as they were techniques which could be learnt by anyone with a modicum of music in them I could learn them if and when I needed to. The idea of filling the greater part of my youth with matters which seemed inessential appeared insane. It was many years later when I discovered an interview John Cage had given in 1965 in which he said: "Conventional music education is something that can only infuriate anyone who is at all interested in living. No matter what aspect of it you think of you get angry almost immediately." This exactly summed up my reactions. Folk music appeared to sidestep the devil I knew.

As a student at the Guildhall School of Music I had elected to study with a particular composition teacher who happened to work in a certain building. Once I got there I found that I had also to study with many other people who taught things I wasn't interested in. This was a financial agreement, a condition of receiving a grant. As a youngster I felt guilty about that. I *ought* to be interested. And so I got less interested as a consequence of the struggle to be interested. The nail in the coffin was the fact that I was not allowed to take composition either as first or second study because it was 'not examinable'. True though this was I saw it as a virtue, not a disqualification. I would be examined, and presumably my future decided, on the basis of my piano-playing plus one other instrument. As I couldn't play any other instrument and had no desire to do so it was time to review the situation.

I had been on two Dartington Summer Schools as a member of the composition classes taken by the French avant-gardist Michel Decoust. These were far more inspiring. And, one has to admit, the beautiful surroundings of the Dartington gardens were seductive compared to West London. So, in relative ignorance of what exactly I was opting for, I transferred from the Guildhall to Dartington, taking two major interests with me: avant-gardism and, as yet less manifest, folk song. If anyone had asked me at the time I would have said that the idea of the move was to place myself in a situation more conducive to experimental music-making. By the time I left college I was absorbed in folklore.

At first folk singing was a diversion. I poured my main energies into improvised, or semi-improvised, performances.

The Great Hall at Dartington is a restored medieval building with winding stairways up to a Solar and a Supersolar. Its atmosphere is indescribably antique, its acoustic resonant. On one occasion I invited the entire music department to play a guided improvisation in and around this hall, using the stairways, three rooms, and the ancient lobby leading on to the courtyard. Whether I had expected self-discipline and responsibility from all these players I don't know, but clearly the minimal instructions I gave them were interpreted as a chance for riot. They honked and screeched their way through an evening of aural hooliganism until some of them were literally screaming; a few delicate souls had a rather hard time. There were a few tears, hallucinogenic-type visions, and a lot of running up and down stairs as if possessed. I reflected at the time that this was thoroughly depressing, and credited the lack of responsibility to the inanities of conventional musical training.

In which situations could musical and social responsibility be found? Were they situations which trained musicians generally inhabited? I had begun reading about folk music initially as a back-up to my second interest. Old style folklorists writing at the turn of the century had referred frequently to the spontaneity of the unlettered. It took me a while to puncture this myth.

Variations on English Folk Themes

The Folk Revivals

PROGRAMME NOTE

Folklore provided the research and experience necessary to test my own stance. Why was musicianship tied up with virtuosity, concert halls, masterpieces? Why did music history only cover a tiny proportion which focused mainly on Western Europe for four hundred years at the most — not a drop in the ocean in terms of human evolution? Even within this limited time and space why did it concentrate only on music specific to certain social classes? What did aural tests prove? (Real musicians could sing any note in a six-note chord played by the teacher. Could people always do that, and if they couldn't were they deemed not musical?) Why musical analysis? Why no improvisation other than extra-curricular with Alfred Nieman? Why did colleagues and tutors regard Cardew and Cage as off the wall, but perhaps not Boulez? Worse still, what did examinations, graduations and pieces of paper prove other than the fact that as a student you had failed to ask such questions seriously? Or if you had you had failed to act on your conclusions?

More interestingly, why was it that students of the visual arts, dance and theatre concentrated on their own work and the twentieth century whereas in the Music Department the bulk of the time was taken up with other people's work of an earlier period?

I was an academic disaster. I opposed virtually everything that came along, not on principle, please understand, but because I was never given satisfactory answers to my enquiries.

What was required was a framework, a course of learning and participation which would eventually lead me back to composition, but which dealt with some of the questions I had no hope of answering in the academic music world. The ideology and mythology of 'folk' was the most powerful contender, although from the first I had to admit that its sounds were less exciting than those I was used to. Its exploration of social relationships, the mix of trained and untrained, and its opportunities for performance were crucial.

I now consider that, despite being a college dropout (I didn't finish any course) I had as thorough a musical training as any, lasting far longer than most. My campus spread over most of the Westcountry, my tutors were a handful of folk revival singers and a rather larger number of sheep farmers, Gypsies, children, labourers. Whether or not they would award me a pass I can't tell and wouldn't regard it as important. I assessed myself continually. There were many times when I reckoned I was failing miserably. And sometimes I awarded myself honours. It was always an intention to get back to composing. This didn't seem possible for at least fifteen years.

If you stood outside Exeter St. David's railway station on any Tuesday evening between about 8.30 and 11.00 you were likely to hear the sound of men's voices raised in an atavistic harmony wafting across the car park.

'Tis true my love's enlisted and he wears a white cockade
He is a handsome young man likewise a roving blade
He is a handsome young man and he's gone to serve the king
And my very
And my very
And my very
And my very heart is breaking all for the love of him

It was a massive, compelling, joyous, bibulous sound. I always felt a shiver of excitement as I walked across the car park to the Jolly Porter pub. It was particularly evocative in the winter with your topcoat collar up and the clean cold Devon air slicing through your jeans. I encountered the Jolly Porter folk club in 1970 when I was still at college.

The singers gave forth in front of a fireplace. A few tables were arranged in a loose semicircle around them. There were seats but you had to arrive early to get one. The mass of people stood behind. On a packed night they would be shoulder to shoulder as far as the bar, which was at the back of the room. It was like an initiative test to get a drink during the interval.

One of the local singers acted as MC. He did a few songs to kick off. This was the least enviable spot. But the following week, when someone else was MC, he'd go on later.

Floor singers were called up in no particular order, but it worked out that the noisier singers were generally left till last. The floor singers were variable. Some were painful, others inspiring. Some weeks a guest singer, for a fee of around £30 to £40, would finish off each half of the evening. Legends circulated like the one about the time Paul Simon got paid £10 and was glad of it. (And he wasn't much good either – so the tale went.)

The full title of this folk club was a laborious bit of pedantry: The Exeter Traditional Folk Song Club. Club policy was not to welcome what it lumped together as 'contemporary folk'. This was confusing at times. The singer Cyril Tawney, for example, ex-naval, bearded, with a guitar, did guest bookings which were a fifty-fifty mix of 'traditional' songs and his own compositions. The difference between his new songs and many others was that his sounded a bit 'traditional'. I knew someone who took his guitar along and played blues numbers by Big Bill Broonzy. It was none too gently pointed out to him that this was a *traditional* club, and that if he wanted to sing again would he please leave his guitar at home and sing *folk*. I was never able to work out what was not folk about Broonzy and the blues.

The standard repertoire was dominated by two forms of song — sea shanties and hunting songs — but it was obvious that the words of the songs were far less important than the musical opportunities embedded in them. Sea shanties were work songs from the days of sail. They were easy to remember, easy to join in on, and easy to harmonize. The hunting songs came from local traditions in which gatherings of people at the end of a hunt would drink, sing and be merry. They were both *choral* traditions. Although the words were important (after all they did express a world view), in the conscious mind of the folk revivalist they took second place to the invitation to bawl your head off in rough and ready harmony with a pub full of mates all intent on doing the same thing.

There were other types of song. Folk ballads of all kinds made their way into the repertoire. Women tended to go for slower, quieter songs, and were generally awarded a false reverence. Guest singers were expected to come with broader repertoires.

For all its inconsistencies The Exeter Traditional Folk Song Club held my interest for a few years over a period when I increasingly shelved experimental music. It wasn't the only folk club I attended, but at that time it had the strongest corporate personality.

It was a strange experience going over to Exeter on Tuesday nights after a day at college. Sometimes I went on the train. Other times I hitched the twenty-five miles. Probably during the day I had been working on a new graphic or indeterminate score, rehearsing student performers, attending lectures. In any music department one is continually surrounded by the sounds of practice — scales, arpeggios, the classics, warbling singers who always sound faintly comic at a distance. You live with these sounds to an extent that they begin to define your world.

Then to get off the campus and out into a working-class pub where a completely different set of values are being enacted by the folk singers — it was a disorientating but enlivening experience. It was my version of the O Riada story. I began asking: which? — not realizing that I could have both. One of the reasons that folk music scored a temporary but long victory was that it addressed and appeared to answer many of the questions I had asked to no avail in academic music circles. I liked the music, true, but the feel and ambience of a bar full of people excited about what they were doing, utterly committed and involved up to the hilt, seemed preferable to the polite bourgeoisery that ran through the European concert tradition like Blackpool runs through rock.

The people were friendly. There was an unpretentiousness about most of them. They created an atmosphere not so much by hard work; they did it by enthusiasm. Which isn't to say they didn't work hard as well.

The club provided all those who wanted it with an opportunity to develop themselves as a singer, albeit within the acceptable repertoire. If you sang well the response was audibly encouraging. If you sang very well you brought the house down. By this time I was shelving John Cage's concerns about the ego and rather enjoyed the appreciation of others. I hadn't been singing that long myself and was glad of the chance to perform.

Folk clubs were an example of a kind of quasi-democracy at work. If the folk revival introduced anything new into our musical life it was this. Musical innovation was never its most remarkable feature. It adopted a deliberately conservative approach to music which, in the end, I was to find stifling. At the time, though, there was some merit in having boundaries set. Within these confines it was assumed that everyone had an equal right to do a floor spot once in a while. While no bones were made about who were considered good singers (there was a hierarchy), those whose experience of singing was limited were rarely openly criticized for having a bad voice, a quiet voice, or anything else.

Where did the folk clubs come from? In the nineteenth century a handful of song collectors had blazed the trail, publishing their findings in edited versions. They focused their attention on rural areas and were fascinated by what they considered to be the old songs.

Recent evaluation of this work has proved how selective they were. It was a fivefold deception at least. Firstly they selected rural backwaters, secondly they selected the older inhabitants, thirdly they asked for old songs so they generally got what they wanted, fourthly they selected for publication what they considered to be the most interesting items. Finally they edited, censored, bowdlerized, and generally tampered with what they did print. The early folk song collectors manipulated into fact an ideal repertoire which came to be taken as the yardstick. I didn't see all this at first.

There were a number of pioneers — John and Lucy Broadwood, Frank Kidson, The Reverend Sabine Baring-Gould, Anne Gilchrist, Mrs. Kennedy Fraser and others — but the real revival of folk music found its greatest champion in Cecil Sharp whose first encounter with folk song has been retold so often it has become a folk legend in itself. He was staying at a clergyman friend's home in Somerset when he heard the appropriately named gardener John England singing *The Seeds of Love* — not an entirely innocent song, but delicately put. Apparently it was only one of many songs that John England knew, but it took Sharp's fancy more than the others. Sharp then got the collecting bug and spent the rest of his life gathering songs and proselytizing on their behalf.

A major impetus behind Sharp's work was his desire to reinvigorate English classical music via folk music. Grieg had done so for Norway, Smetana and Dvořák for Bohemia; there were also the six Russians and the Spanish nationalists such as Granados and Albéniz. The theory was that the folk music of each race of people is distinctive. The composer who knew his own folk music and allowed himself to be consciously influenced by it would therefore produce music which expressed the character of his own nation. Among British composers who accepted this line, either completely or occasionally, were Delius, Vaughan Williams, Holst, Moeran, Butterworth and Britten. Percy Grainger, the most challenging, was Australian, but spent much of his life in England.

It was a half-truth which stemmed from the current within the Romantic movement in the arts and philosophy which elevated *innocence* (and, increasingly, *lost innocence*) to a high priority in its aesthetic and world view.

The idea of a *folk soul* belonging to each race of people was elaborated by the philosopher Herder at the end of the eighteenth century and rapidly became accepted wisdom. It is no coincidence that this is around the time when the industrial revolution in Western Europe really got under way. Much was apparently being lost.

It was also a time when large, powerful nations were gobbling up smaller ones, so, to an extent, the *folk soul* was a radical way of emphasizing local distinctiveness. More than that, the implications of the industrial age, which became obvious early on, had many Romantics scurrying for psychological shelter in ruralism, ancient mythology, 'popular antiquities' (the term which preceded *folklore*), golden ageism, sentimentalization of children (the nursery is largely a Victorian invention along with the songs that go with it), and folk songs. It is almost *passé* to point out that this was really a middle-class trick. It was generally done at a safe distance much as Wordsworth wondered what the song of the solitary reaper consisted of. At least the folk song collectors had the grace to ask. If it was possible to claim that the folk culture represented what was essentially a better age of Man (before the Fall represented by industrialism) then one could avoid getting too involved with the realities of the present. Left-wingers have made much of this in recent critiques of the folk song movement.

There are more subtle layers to the Romantic necessity of folklore. The nineteenth century in Europe was an age of rapid change. Old certainties were questioned by the capitalist revolution. Even the very landscape was transformed in less than a generation. Folklore was one way of asserting, perhaps clinging to, a continuity from past to present. It was a refusal to jettison everything that had gone before in favour of the new, uncertain, threatening age. To be able to chart where we are going it is sometimes necessary to remember where we came from. Naturally this is a selective process — you select your past by the questions you ask of it.

The folklorists, and later the folk revivalists, created an origin myth. The folk past became an Earth Mother. It pointed to original Oneness, the birth of Us as we are and therefore as it is natural that we should be.

As an example plucked from thousands, consider the Arnhem Land aborigine myth of Eingana.

"That first time, the creation time, we call Bieingana. The first being we call Eingana. We call Eingana our Mother. Eingana made everything: water, rocks, trees, blackfellows; she made all the birds, flying foxes, kangaroos and emus. Everything Eingana had inside herself in that first time."

The Earth Mother contains in her belly all that is to be. Applied to music, the Earth Mother becomes, in the title of Curt Sachs' popular book on ethnomusicology, "the wellsprings of music" — where it all came from. All can, or could, be explained, by reference to a common source. For the myth to work, however, it has to be manipulated to confirm the ideological position of those who believe it. Therefore the early folk song collectors tended to make certain assumptions: folk music was the product of an oral tradition, it was anonymous, rural, those people who sang it were 'unlettered' and, most important of all, it was 'natural', 'simple', 'sincere'. The whole clutter of sentimental ideas is summed up in this passage from the Introduction to Sharp and Baring-Gould's *English Folk Songs for Schools*.

"Folk-song is in verity the product of the people, rising as naturally out of its consciousness, expressing as truly its feelings and its aspirations, as the song of thrush and blackbird and ouzel expresses the longings of the little hearts, and their rapture in spring sun and zephyrs."

It is interesting that the analogy compares folk song with the song of birds. This takes us back even further than the emergence of Man into a primal state of innocence untainted by the need to make a living, social organization, sexuality, and any form of premeditation. We are reminded of a statement attributed to the folklorist Grimm that "folk song composes itself". Folk song, really, is the womb — warm, mysterious, feminine — and its birth, even as itself, begins the Fall which, in the nineteenth century, culminates in the unmusical clatter of industrial machinery — the very thing it was designed to rebel against. Neat.

It is also interesting, but utterly consistent, that folk song has never been adequately defined despite the determined efforts of its champions from enthusiastic individuals to the International Folk Music Council. It has not yet been noticed that it evades definition because it is mythological. Definitions deconstruct myths, after which the myth no longer functions as myth but as previous incomplete knowledge. In the case of folk song a kind of collective necessity brought it into being as an origin myth — warm, mysterious, feminine. The whole process of collecting folk songs from old people in rural backwaters is like a wooing. Tact, offerings, determination and loving care are required to seduce the victim onto the symbolic sofa (usually a tape recorder on a kitchen table) until eventually the pursued can no longer resist and they reveal their most intimate secrets — a few songs. It's a very male pursuit.

This myth is the *anima* at work. The urge to definition is *animus*. Therefore the folk song pioneers, unscientific by today's standards, brought into being the undefinable, the part of themselves they could not locate and therefore had to project, and that was its mystery. It had to be known by intuition but could never be clearly seen. "No one can see Eingana. She stays in the middle water", as the Aborigines say. By their efforts to define it they attempted to bind it, own it, and make sure it really was what they assumed it to be. Any sensible person would wriggle out.

One powerful reason why the myth of folk song could never be clearly seen was built into its complexity: it was dying out. Therefore it could only be assumed in the distance. Culture was changing so fast that these particular old songs would soon be forgotten. This was true, but the facts become mythological by our attitude to them. Generally speaking the attitude of the folk song collectors was one of regret for the passing of an era coupled with a missionary zeal to preserve it. Most saw ideological, moral and nationalist reasons to revive it. Few took the view of Alfred Williams, a lone voice in many ways, who wrote in his *Folk-songs of the Upper Thames* (1923):

"The songs themselves, as far as singing goes, are practically defunct. There is no need to revive them. To do so, in fact, would be impossible. It is also undesirable. We live in a new age, almost in a new world. Life has changed. There are other amusements. We move at a quicker pace. Time and custom decide what shall or shall not continue. Fashions in everything accept modifications. It is the same with morris-dancing. Where a desire to sing or dance does not exist naturally, and is not spontaneous, no amount of artificial activity will suffice to restore the practice. Though you should resuscitate it for a time the life would not be permanent.''

Williams' view has a strangely prophetic ring to it for, indeed, there was a wholesale attempt to revive what he considered to be unrevivable. It did re-emerge for a while, particularly in the 1960s and '70s on a popular scale, but eventually splintered.

Sharp and his generation elevated folk song in certain ways. They got the songs into schools — something which generations of schoolchildren including my own didn't necessarily thank them for. ("Singing singing buttercups and daisies" — adolescent boys — I ask you!) They provided composers with raw material in the form of melodic ideas for symphonies and rhapsodies or songs to arrange for the concert platform. What stayed dormant were the democratic issues that lay around what they had brought into being.

In the first decade of the twentieth century Percy Grainger had recorded on cylinders singers encountered in his fieldwork, particularly in Lincolnshire. Grainger argued strongly that the song was not simply a matter of melody and words which could be reduced to a simplified form of notation. He insisted that the element of *performance* was paramount. The Lincolnshire singers were not mere 'carriers' of musical curios. They had a singing style which was subtle, had its own complexities, its own traditions and conventions. In Grainger's day this idea was revolutionary. It implied that the 'unlettered' had technique, aesthetic and, most importantly, consciousness of these matters. This didn't fit the myth. Whatever else could be projected onto the singers, conscious art remained taboo.

But Grainger was right and had the evidence to prove it. In the 1970s an enterprising record company, Leader Records, issued a selection of his archive recordings. Fighting through the scratches and crackle which inevitably make pre-First World War recordings specialist listening is a grace and style, decorative technique and rhythmic idiom which, to say the very least, is hardly random. Rustic singers could no longer be taken as the human equivalent of birds twittering.

Grainger transcribed some of these performances. His notations were printed in the pages of the *Folk Music Journal*. They look every bit as complex as some of the more advanced twentieth-century atonal works with irrational time values, changing time signatures, slides, trills, bleats, ambiguous uses of scale degrees and so on. Grainger had hit a truth which could hardly be overstated: what *was* disappearing fast out of English rural musical life was not an unconscious 'artless art' as one folklorist described it. Rather, no matter how selective the song collector had been, here was the evidence of a sophisticated performance style. Yet it was not formally taught. It was this particular style, along with the repertoire itself, which was being buffeted into history by the changing century.

Grainger was not the only folklorist to make recordings. Grieg had done so in Norway, Bartók in Hungary and Rumania and Sharp to a certain extent in Britain. The very technology that in some ways made the myth necessary became the most vital tool in the preservation of some of its details. But it took half a century before the recording of field singers became the recognized way of documenting their songs.

One of the most ambitious projects was initiated by the BBC in the early 1950s. It aimed to collect on tape the folk music of Britain. This was centrally the work of Peter Kennedy. He enlisted the help of regional enthusiasts and built up a huge sound archive. The important lesson that this taught, mainly via radio exposure (*As I Roved Out*, Sunday mornings, Home Service), was that singing folk songs was a live art, much as Grainger had said.

This alone was not sufficient to create a popular folk song revival. It was also necessary to have platforms for performance and at least some committed performers leading the way.

The post-war folk revival was a meeting of pioneering spirits, political activism, fieldwork and research, and fortuitous coincidences. Equally there was some public readiness to embrace the ideology of 'the people', its music, and direct participation.

Just as British folk song pioneers had chosen a repertoire which they regarded as 'folk', so in the United States a similar process was enacted. The Americans were broader based, their fieldwork ranging over white and black, Child ballads and cowboy songs, blues and white spirituals, gospel and chain gang work songs. Neither did they necessarily exclude songs of known authorship. These differences with the British model are explained by the brief chosen by the folklorists. In Britain it was retrospective, alienated, motivated in large part to replace something that was thought to be missing from national life and music. In America folklore served a different purpose, posed different questions and got different answers. It documented the building of a democratic nation. Built into this national identity was a melting pot of Afro-American, British, Spanish, French, Dutch, Italian (the range is huge) as a constant reminder of the new world's diverse origins. Just about the only group rarely mentioned in early American folk song collections was the native Amerindian.

There was a radical slant to the early American folk song movement. Singing groups such as The Almanac Singers or later The Weavers had latched on to the campaigning union songs and sang them in union halls to audiences of workers.

Union miners stand together
Do not heed the owner's tale
Keep your hand upon the dollar
And your eyes upon the scale

The American revival expressed radical patriotism. Many songs gave voice to an idealism of equality and fairness, qualities which trigger American history from the Rhode Island Convention of 1641 to the New Deal. American singers, some of whom like Josh White, Burl Ives, or Pete Seeger toured

Britain in the 1950s, presented a ragbag of Anglo-American songs, blues, radicalism, and froggies going a-wooing. The songs were simple. Many had choruses. They were popular in youth hostels and left-wing circles, and sold well enough to make the catalogues of major record companies.

In the 1940s a young English communist, A.L. Lloyd, during a spell of unemployment, had written a short book entitled *The Singing Englishman*. He later compiled *Corn on the Cob*, a book of American songs. Lloyd had been to Australia droving sheep, had taken a trip on a whaler, and was self-taught in folk song and Marxism. He took over some of Cecil Sharp's notions but added a basic Marxist historical perspective of folk song as a reflection of the circumstances of the common people. Folk song was passive, not proactive, in this view. In addition Lloyd could sing. He presented songs without the frills of the concert hall. He attempted a style which owed more to the traditions that Grainger had documented than to the composer's poshed-up arrangements.

Around the same time, Ewan MacColl, a communist playwright, actor, singer, activist had become disaffected with radical theatre and decided that folk song was the vernacular language that theatre lacked. MacColl was actively seeking people and places to start folk clubs.

Lloyd and MacColl were introduced to each other by the American folklorist Alan Lomax. Lomax had a strong hunch that this mix would be dynamic.

One of MacColl's earliest moves, in the early 1950s, was to form a folk club in the Princess Louise pub in High Holborn. (MacColl's club was not the very first. I believe that honour goes to the Bradford Topic Club.) The resident singers at the club included MacColl and Lloyd, plus Seamus Ennis and Fitzroy Coleman. This all happened before skiffle became a popular music craze.

The history needs to be stated in this order because it has been commonly believed that the folk revival was an outgrowth of skiffle. What in fact happened was that MacColl, Lloyd and others had established their base *before* skiffle and were looking for the means to grow into a popular movement. At this point skiffle emerged, gave them a means, but also brought with it the seeds of constant tensions within the revival.

The skiffle craze was a strange accident triggered by one man, Lonnie Donegan, over a couple of years in the mid-1950s. Donegan was the banjoist in the Ken Colyer Jazz Band, New Orleans revivalists. The skiffle group, led by Donegan's vocals, played interval spots. When the trombone player Chris Barber left the Colyer outfit to form his own band he took Donegan and the rest of the rhythm section along with him. This was in 1953. The following year a skiffle song *Rock Island Line* appeared as one track on a Chris Barber Band LP. A couple of years later Decca issued this track as a single, backed by the Donegan version of the black folk ballad *John Henry*. It stayed in the hit parade roughly half a year, peaking to number six.

The skiffle movement raised issues that have recurred constantly in most of the guises musical democracy has assumed. It suggested that participatory music needs a degree of simplicity in execution if it is to be picked up quickly. It was built in to the ideology of skiffle that everyone had a right to equal voice, needed to pass no test or audition, and didn't even have to improve. This meant that, skilled and committed interpreters apart, there was always a significant amount of painful stuff belted out.

As the folk revival began to meld with what the skiffle craze had created — informal settings for music and song — it inherited this discrepancy. MacColl's personal solution was to establish a Master-Disciple relationship, with himself and later his third wife Peggy Seeger as Master(s).

By the mid-1960s there were many elements to the folk revival. Those who sought the traditions where they were still traditional (in London Irish bars, East Anglian pubs, Gypsy camps) early realized that Sharp's ideas needed revising. The local performers did not conform to the myths. Their repertoires included, alongside the 'folk' songs, Victorian tear-jerkers, parlour ballads, music-hall songs (tragic and comic), and even some modern popular songs. Reg Hall and Mervyn Plunkett, both of whom had considerable knowledge of skiffle and trad jazz, produced an excellent periodical entitled *Ethnic* in which a more honest view of local traditions was attempted. *Ethnic* was counterposed to the Sharp-plus-industrial song mode derived from Lloyd.

Ewan MacColl's stance was, from the outset, more overtly political. He insisted that what he regarded as the folk disciplines should provide a framework for the composition of new songs which generally dealt with social and political matters. He also built up a theory and practice of folk revival singing based on detailed listening to British and global field recordings.

MacColl made a rule in one of his early folk clubs that singers should only sing material from their own ethnic backgrounds. This was his way of encouraging people to look to traditions close to home rather than rely on the American folk and gospel which formed most of the skiffle repertoire.

The American influences remained, however. Many folk clubs featured blues- and skiffle-derived music. Some of the blues players were channelled into the growing rhythm-and-blues movement which fed the pop scene. When fused with British folklore the blues produced a school of guitarists (John Renbourn, Bert Jansch, Davey Graham) which provided an interesting and genuinely original synthesis of styles. Musically it was one of the few real innovations of the folk scene.

There was a missionary element in the more 'traditional' and 'political' elements of the folk revival. Modern popular music was often cast as an enemy which had a downgrading effect on contemporary cultural life. The preselected folk repertoire was seen, consciously or otherwise, as both a corrective and an opposition to the inanities of commercial popular song. In MacColl's case this opposition was explicit.

There were the folk clubs like the one at Exeter which laid down a hard line in favour of 'traditional' material. A clear plus here was that certain areas of repertoire — the sea songs, ballads, hunting choruses, folk lyrics — had platforms to themselves. On the other hand such clubs generally excluded new, and particularly political, material. 'Traditional' could often mean conservative with a small 'c' as well as a big one.

The standard varied wildly. At the Exeter club a group of four young men formed a line-up called Isca Fayre. They had strong voices with a dynamic range from forte to fortissimo and sounded very impressive when they let rip in four-part harmony. At the other extreme was a chap in Exmouth who was practically tone deaf and utterly embarrassing to listen to. As is often the case he was one of the most enthusiastic. He sang a version of *The Derby Ram*. As he was unable to distinguish between pitches the audience raised the choruses by a tone each time they occurred. The result was that halfway into the song the pitch had risen impossibly out of his range, to which, blue in the face, he exploded: "You bastards! You've done it again!"

Less hard-line clubs than the Exeter one admitted into the folk canon what was then called 'contemporary' song, which really amounted to anything that wasn't 'traditional', neither having any clear definition. A newly-written song which pastiched old styles was generally regarded as 'traditional'. Along with contemporary song came the hearty chorus, guitar-bashing element partly derived from skiffle and partly from the ensemble Irish groups such as The Dubliners or The Clancy Brothers, both of whom had achieved considerable commercial success.

'Contemporary' song also included blues and gospel, and that whole area of new song represented by Bob Dylan at the more aggressive and Leonard Cohen at the more suicidal. Conceptually speaking, the whole scene was chaos. Nitpicking arguments went on all night about what was (or wasn't) 'folk'. Picking one's way through the factions, coping with club prejudices, and touring to earn a crust were, shall we say, exhausting.

At the time I entered the folk revival, as singer and collector, I had neither the experience nor the framework to see it as mythological. Nor, in truth, did I really care. It was only participation which insisted on throwing up questions which couldn't be answered within the given framework. The myth, in the end, was not sustainable.

My experience of the process was helped by some fortunate circumstances. At the beginning of this phase of my musical journey I came into contact with Peter Kennedy who had done so much collecting of songs in the 1950s and '60s. Through him I briefly met Maud Karpeles who had accompanied Cecil Sharp on many of his collecting expeditions. I got to know Peggy Seeger and Ewan MacColl whom I regarded as folk revival performers *par excellence*. Also, I was in the Westcountry, classic hunting ground for song collectors and therefore with accessible precedents — the Baring-Gould collection in Plymouth City Library and the work of Sharp in Somerset.

The main reasons I gravitated to the folk clubs had little to do with the sectarian polemics of the revival. The clubs provided a handy platform which was regularly and reliably available. It put you in touch with a community of interest. It had an underlying ideology of participation, immediacy and intimacy. Many clubs were run according to a direct democracy which extended to anyone who wanted to be involved.

Running a club was fun, if demanding. Trying to channel creativity into the ideology and mythology of the folk revival *and* maybe earn a small living from it was fraught.

The folk scene parodied the star syndrome that many of its founders theoretically opposed. This was obviously so in the case of electric bands whose methods of hype and aspirations were not dissimilar to rock bands. But it was also true of 'traditional' singers and even singers with a political slant.

It was partly economic. To put together and keep fresh a repertoire of sufficient interest to sustain singer and audience to at least the value of a return booking took time, commitment, research, energy, rehearsal. It was ideally a full-time job but fees were never really adequate and, of course, you constantly needed bookings.

Thus the would-be folk singer was forced into publicity drives, chasing record companies, hassling the media and press, dealing with agents, haggling over fees, producing posters with the right image, and so on. It was scaled-down commercialism, but commercial nevertheless.

There was a subtle code. If you looked too commercial your evil motives were sniffed out as if by ethnic bloodhounds who, once they found a bone labelled 'sell out', were apt to chew it to bits. Yet bookings were necessary. The balance was hard to find.

There was (and still is) a festival circuit where would-be professionals learned to whore for future bookings and established performers took the best spots. (Having done both I assume I have some right to this view.) But the real sessions, as was repeatedly heard, took place in pubs outside the scheduled festival programme. This was a contentious truth, but it left me wondering, if it were the case, whether there was any point in working hard at a repertoire only to be told that the real 'folk' happened when no one was trying. At the time I put it down to a folk revival cult of amateurism.

Musically and socially the mythology of folk was spread widely. The bedrock was folk song of a type that traced the line from Sharp to Lloyd. New songs either rested somewhere in that continuum or they derived from recent American models — Bob Dylan, Joni Mitchell, Leonard Cohen. Experimentation was rare and misunderstood. Political songs, for all the leftists' protestations, were taboo in all but a few places.

One of the line-ups I performed with was taken to task after a booking at a northern folk club. We sounded too much like certain other groups, took certain songs too fast, and didn't do enough chorus songs. Our accuser, a large beer gut with a bearded head on it, was, despite his refined state of intoxication, accurately voicing the real ideology of the 'traditional' wing of the revival: stay within stylistic limits but do something slightly original within them; don't get too close to someone else's sound (that's OK for floor singers); treat the repertoire in a musically conservative manner; above all encourage participation rather than too much listening. As the beer gut was the organizer of the club I felt obliged to take his criticisms seriously. It was only later that I learnt that he hadn't been in the room until our last song.

In the 1980s a magazine called *Folk Roots* managed to do something no other folk periodical had done for long. It survived, expanded and began to have influence. It did so by exposing contradictions within the folk scene. It broke the taboo on commercialism, showing it up as a double standard. It affected an upmarket style. It came clean about the constant tensions between 'traditional' revivalism on the one hand and the American influences which had been present since skiffle on the other.

All this was welcome but there was a less endearing side. Within a few years *Folk Roots* had a full-colour glossy cover, top thirty folk charts, house cult figures, flavours of the month. It could only have happened in Margaret Thatcher's era. Folk could be marketed too.

The title of the magazine is clever. It embraces any type of music which has even the most tenuous links with the mythology of folklore. It accepts a welcome degree of internationalism in response to the 'world music' fad.

It became the most powerful single influence since Ewan MacColl and A.L. Lloyd, but it sounded the death knell to their kind of folk revival. Now we were no longer building on traditions because they were efficacious. We were involved in entertainment. *Folk Roots* admitted what anyone in their right mind knew all along: the folk scene was slightly radical but not leftist, interested in musical traditions when given an accessible surface, and not in the least bothered about musical polemics. In its roughly thirty years of life the folk revival had traced a path from revolution to safety.

Although I could not identify with the implicit positions barely concealed in *Folk Roots* I had to admit that it spoke a truth of its time. Folk was now a free-for-all within undefined yet curiously tangible boundaries. The tactics of the pop scene were no longer taboo. For a short period in the mid-1980s I found myself caught up in this, but I knew my heart was elsewhere.

The Jolly Porter pub where The Exeter Traditional Folk Song Club met in front of a fireplace is still there. But now it's a wine bar. You don't find railwaymen in the public bar now. After nigh on twenty years hunting the hare, rounding the Horn, and harmonizing the glee of spring the singers had to find somewhere else. (This also coincided with the Thatcher years.) The club is now in one of those pleasant city pubs with heated food bar, bare floors like wot they used to be, a selection of real ales, and a somewhat dressed up young clientele. Although the club is still good, the change in tone is typical.

Rhapsody in Red

Ewan MacColl and Political Song

―――――

PROGRAMME NOTE

By the mid-1970s the suspicion had arisen that the optimism of the previous decade with its visions of transforming the collective psyche was just a little illusory. The building of tower blocks stopped, hem-lines came down, hairstyles shortened along with a new awareness of the real possibility of global disaster. The next few years were marked by mourning: the hope of the 1960s had deserted, leaving only uncomfortable facts and unanswerable questions.

The 1960s had unleashed energies, smashed barriers, offered freedoms. But they began to seem like a fantasy. There was no way the people could rule even if they were prepared to. Events were showing that political systems were too resilient, too devious to allow such a democratic thing to happen. So it was necessary to find out why. The 1970s was an era of politicization and smart new studies like semiotics and structuralism which aimed to penetrate the mythologies of what we took for granted. Perhaps these held the key to our dilemmas.

In music and the arts modernism (and with it its naughty but necessary child, avant-gardism) collapsed. It had eschewed the past. Now artists wanted history back in their work. The alienated artist as an individual had produced silences, blank canvasses, absurd theatre. The 1970s rejected such gestures. They looked as though they were destroying art. They also appeared to be a luxury that a political world could not afford, had no relation to.

Artists seemed to become aware of the need to understand the social and political nature of their work. Was it necessary, for example, to function as an individual? Could anyone own music? Collectives became an important option. The London Musicians Collective, for instance, acted as an umbrella for all kinds of music from free improvisation to pre-postmodernism. Personal-political relationships between people began to matter on a wide scale.

Another form of politicization was more agitational — to state creeds unmistakably in music. And as music cannot, at best, do more than imply political ideas by association, this meant that musicians had to turn to song. Cardew had taken this path. Many followed. My contact with political song was largely via the milieu which clustered round the MacColl and Seeger Singer's Club. It wasn't entirely satisfactory, but like that folk club in Exeter it held my attention.

Telling the truth in song had one logical problem. It assumed that the songwriter had the truth. If he or she were wrong there was nothing left of the *song. I was to find that this path was more likely to end in silence than John Cage. Whereas Cage's silence was enlightened, this silence was potentially full of the emptiness of disillusionment.*

In early 1985 the miners' strike was still on and Ewan MacColl was seventy. These two events collided at the Royal Festival Hall, London. MacColl's birthday concert was attended by Norman Willis of the Trades Union Congress, and Arthur Scargill, President of the National Union of Mineworkers. Scargill presented MacColl with a miner's lamp. He and Willis made eulogizing speeches about MacColl. You would hardly have known that Scargill and Willis were in bitter disagreement about the strike.

In the dressing rooms a portrait gallery of folk singers invited on the strength of their association with MacColl tuned and spruced up, passed round cans of lager, checked over repertoires. In some corners guitars twanged; in others there were Irish pipes, concertinas and fiddles. From Ewan MacColl and Peggy Seeger's dressing room came the sounds of vocal warm-ups — a clear 'Ah' flowing through an uninterrupted column of air, tone formation, breath control, relaxation — techniques MacColl had carried with him since his days in the theatre in the 1930s and '40s.

I wasn't half as nervous as I'd assumed one ought to be at the Festival Hall, although the group I played in, Threeway Street, had been programmed directly after Scargill's speech. But what was of most concern was a compelling feeling of no longer belonging to the folk scene.

The last time I'd been in the Festival Hall was as a member of the audience for a performance of Stockhausen's *Gruppen* in the late 1960s. Having moved to Devon I'd kept well away from the London concert halls. I was reflecting on how, a decade and a half earlier, I had met Ewan and Peggy, and how their approach to music now seemed like a necessary stage on a journey, but increasingly difficult to relate to on a creative level. I even experienced some distress. They were very warm people.

By the early 1960s there were a number of differences in approach in the folk revival. Not all of them were self-consciously radical but in essence all derived from the apparently radical idea that 'the people' (that is, you and me) had songs, could make songs of their own without the help of classical or mass popular traditions. One frequently heard the sentimental 'folk is people' doctrine bandied about clubs and festivals.

How the various factions acted in accord (or otherwise) with their approaches can only be summarized here. It is, however, important to emphasize that although MacColl and Seeger earned themselves a reputation for hard-edged politics they were not the only folk revivalists who saw a broadly political connection with their work. The work of Reg Hall is a good example. Hall, a melodeon and piano player with a great devotion to what was actually happening in the music of traditional communities (London Irish, East Anglian, Home Counties) represented an approach that aspired to an honest appraisal of roots music rather than revivalist theories. His piano accompaniments to Irish musicians can be heard on many a Topic LP of the time.

Hall and his close associate Mervyn Plunkett were largely responsible for the revival of what became known as English Country Music in the 1970s. Theirs was not a campaign of proselytizing, more of simply getting on with the music that appealed to them and making a few recordings *en route*. It was an edited version of one of these recordings that eventually had influence. The LP *English Country Music* was issued by Topic Records in 1976 but the original tapes were made by Bill Leader in 1962.

Mervyn Plunkett had met the East Anglian fiddle player Walter Bulwer in 1958. Bulwer was a mad keen local musician, known in his village as a one-man band, with a lifetime of experience of playing for dances in his locality. He introduced Plunkett to other local musicians and, with Reg Hall and another revivalist Russell Wortley, they formed a band to record some of the old tunes. Plunkett's description of the recording session that was eventually issued gives some of the atmosphere.

"We met at Walter's cottage on the Saturday of August Bank Holiday weekend and settled down to play in the living room. Some of us sat on dining-room chairs and others on chintz-covered armchairs, while Daisy (Mrs. Bulwer) sat on the piano-stool. Billy Cooper was only able to come on the Saturday because of family and other commitments so we got down to it immediately after lunch and played through till 8 o'clock without stopping except for Daisy's high tea with home-made bread."

These 1962 recordings were edited to form an LP issued by Reg Hall and the singer Bob Davenport. Ninety-nine copies were pressed and they sold out in a fortnight. Thus *English Country Music* remained something of an almost secret cult until the Topic reissue of 1976.

The music was rough and ready, exuberant, lively, decidedly unpolished, sometimes out of tune, and terrific fun. It had no political content (it was all instrumental) but implied a connection. This was working-class music made by working-class people (with the help of their folk friends), and whether one liked it or not it could be argued that it represented the state of the tradition.

This element of the folk revival had to wait until the mid-1970s before it had its day on any wider scale. More public in the 1960s were those approaches which, in one way or another, reached the mass media. This was the time of the rise of the Irish singing groups The Clancy Brothers and The Dubliners. It also saw the beginnings of guitar / banjo / mandolin-type line-ups such as The Spinners. In these cases the link with skiffle was obvious. The Ian Campbell Folk Group achieved great popularity with a catholic mixture of Scots and English folk songs, Bob Dylan numbers, and a number of contemporary British songs including those of MacColl.

MacColl himself was not satisfied with the approach of other revivalists. He argued that by courting popularity, and compromising the material, the political edge could be almost forgotten. It was 'easy', he once told me, to sing in favour of peace and the CND, less easy to maintain a political integrity. What was the point of singing anti-bomb songs if you didn't somewhere point out the political truth of why we had bombs in the first place, who manufactured them, why, who profited, how the whole thing was organized, in whose interests? MacColl was militantly opposed to wishy-washy humanitarianism.

Then, of course, there were those who saw in the folk 'boom' a chance to make money and insisted on folk as pure entertainment. This was not, at the time, a position even worthy of consideration for those who regarded themselves as political. In the event it produced some music of genuine value.

In the wake of beatniks and the stirrings of hippiedom a number of folk performers, motivated by that peculiarly unacceptable criterion of what they happened to like, stayed close to the blues and forged an Anglo-American style, often linking British folk songs with bluesy or jazzy accompaniments. Guitarists John Renbourn, Bert Jansch and Davey Graham were in the forefront of this style. It was commercially successful but it also produced what was possibly the only really original *musical* evolution of the entire revival. Its political wetness did not appeal to MacColl. He tended to obscure genuine musicality when it was not obviously linked with leftist politics. Later in his life he considerably softened -- not so much his political ideas, but his degree of tolerance.

Ewan MacColl, Peggy Seeger and others dissociated themselves from the rest of the folk revival, formed their Singer's Club and trained young singers as the London Critics Group. Their activities were partly informed by an oppositional attitude to popular culture, commercialism, capitalism.

One Saturday in 1972 the group I then performed with, Staverton Bridge, was recording in London (the record was never issued). Bill Leader's studio at that time was set up in the basement of Cecil Sharp House. On that occasion Cornelius Cardew and his associates were rehearsing The Scratch Orchestra upstairs. I remember someone saying, with a degree of anger, that the English Folk Dance and Song Society shouldn't be hiring their rehearsal space to these loonies. I registered this as an example of the folk scene's narrow-mindedness. It also put my own search in some kind of perspective.

In the evening we went to two leading folk clubs, the MacColl-Seeger Singer's Club, and the more entertainment-based The Troubador, to do floor spots and, frankly, to get noticed. We had been advised by Bill Leader that we would be unlikely to be well received at both. Unaware of the nuances of folk revival politics we unwittingly walked into the heartlands of each sect.

MacColl and Seeger were effusive about our two songs at the Singer's Club, and offered us a booking on the spot. At The Troubadour, which went on after hours, we went down like a lead balloon. It didn't take much thought to work out which way our wind blew.

After our Singer's Club booking we spent a number of weekends at MacColl and Seeger's home in Beckenham, absorbing their philosophy of folk revivalism, learning techniques and, incidentally, being offered some very good cooking in the process. I failed to understand the anti-MacColl smears that we occasionally heard in folk clubs. I found Peggy and Ewan generous, stimulating, dependably friendly, dedicated. Ewan was also a terrible autocrat, quoted fiction as fact, and had a streak of vanity. He talked working-class politics while he matched up the correct wine with his cheese. So he was human.

Ewan MacColl (real name Jimmy Miller) was brought up in Salford, and as a young man was a fiery working-class intellectual. In those days that generally meant communist. He gravitated to street theatre and what is now called agitprop with a number of groups, the most flamboyantly named being The Red Megaphones.

This led to his meeting with Joan Littlewood, who became his first wife, and Theatre Workshop. This was theatre committed to the working class and socialism, opposed to bourgeois traditions. It was originally part of the company's policy to take on extensive touring to industrial areas far from the influential nerve centres of straight theatre such as the London West End.

Littlewood and MacColl poured new ideas into this touring framework, MacColl himself writing some of the plays. Pieces like *Uranium 235*, an early anti-nuclear play, were remarkably innovative in their time. With a refined sense of theatrical possibilities MacColl had the cast simulating atoms and neutrons on stage, showing their orbits and paths and what happened when one of them was split. On his own admission he knew nothing about nuclear science. He mugged it up for the play. It also proposed a straightforward Marxist analysis of the politics of nuclear technology. It was strong stuff for the 1940s. In its use of space, physicality, polemic, it was progressive theatre in the sense that it was ahead of the game and few others were doing it.

Having reached a level of theatrical refinement, and perhaps questioning the long-term possibilities of permanent touring, there followed a split in Theatre Workshop. One faction, which included Littlewood, argued that they should establish a London base. If they were going to be influential they had to be where the important critics were. MacColl argued that their aim was to create a theatre of the working class, not to court critics. In any case, if the performances were doing their job the critics were unlikely to approve.

MacColl lost. Theatre Workshop established itself at the Theatre Royal, Stratford East, London. The move precipitated a wholesale re-examination of aesthetic for MacColl. When I interviewed him about this period he confessed that at the time he was in despair. His plays were being performed all over Europe, translated into many languages. He had been hailed as one of Britain's most important theatre-makers by good authorities, Shaw amongst them. Yet this acclaim wasn't even flattering.

As Confucius said, "The superior man seeks the Way, not a mere living". This is also the hallmark of a genuinely creative artist, and it was what MacColl faced.

A similar kind of bleakness to that which we sensed in Sean O Riada the musician now hung over the dramatist Ewan MacColl. His output and the acclaim it earned did not suffice.

Most artists' aims can be summarized very simply: to create works or fulfil projects, to see them performed, find an audience, and have influence. MacColl had all this. What else is there?

One way of framing a possible answer would be: a sense of authenticity. This has nothing to do with the pedigree of the influences pressed into service in one's art. It concerns personal honesty, integration and integrity. It links the artist's *being* in the world with his work.

To artists (and MacColl was no exception) the problem presents itself as one of aesthetics, politics, direction, and the relationships between these. So MacColl saw it that the trouble with theatre (even his own) was that it had "failed to find a language embedded in working-class experience". A lack of language is a serious matter and a powerful metaphor. It implies dumbness, incomprehension, impotence, choking. A lack of language signals apprehension about oneself.

Modernism, whatever its details according to era and fashion, provokes this difficulty sooner or later. It takes the courage of a John Cage or a Samuel Beckett to follow it into and beyond apparent nothingness. Individuals and social movements are prone to examine other avenues first.

One of the problems of modernism inheres in its evolution from the alienated Romantic artist. No longer an integrated cog in a social milieu like J.S. Bach or the ploughman who knew some good songs, the artist becomes free to exercise imagination, individuality, freedom. Breaking new ground becomes a necessity in order to distinguish one individuality from another. With no certain audience, patron or support system this is an alienated position. Who or what are you producing your art for?

Many artists are aware of this. They feel different and talk about this difference. Beneath the arrogance that some people affect as a defence lies a fear, a fear of being so different that they will eventually have to confront who and what they are. And there is the suspicion that we might as well be waiting for Godot, for on our own we are nothing. It takes a very special training to accept this fact as joyous.

Anyone opting to be a committed artist in modern society is by definition an outsider, accepting all kinds of insecurity as a permanent possibility, conventional (or mainstream) perceptions as partial, popular culture as, at best, inadequate. There must be some antidote to this painful but voluntary wounding. Fortunately, as with the nettle which stings and the dockleaf which soothes, in close proximity to this alienation is one potential cure — the myth of democracy.

MacColl, as a leftist, was not particularly enchanted by what he saw of democracy. Yet socialism could be seen as a rationalized and yet contradictory way of dealing with an otherwise vague idealism. At the heart of democracy lies the idea of equality. If people are equal then socialism claims to organize for this fact, tying itself up in knots because organization implies hierarchy and inequality. To pre-1956 communists this could be explained by the Marxist prediction that the dictatorship of the proletariat would eventually lead to the withering away of the state and the realization of true communism. What you had to do to reach this point was pure expedient, and inevitable.

Within democracy's vague outlines lies the myth of *Kratos*, the people who are going to rule. Most artistic traditions known to us are bourgeois. One of the few serious contenders for an art of 'the people' was folk art — mythological though it may be, mediated through bourgeois conceptions undoubtedly. Yet, say what we may in theory, something does (or did) exist which looks very much like people's art, even if the people concerned wouldn't have given a damn how someone else saw it.

The artist who experiences a crisis of direction, language, identity may choose the available option of following a path marked 'folklore' — open brackets: 'the people' — close brackets.

Ewan MacColl solved his problem of language by invoking the big ballads, sea songs, love lyrics, broadsides and bothy songs of folk tradition as he saw it. With A.L. Lloyd he extended Sharp's field to include what they disingenuously called 'industrial folk song'. It didn't matter that this was a contradiction in terms according to the folk song model articulated by the rest of their repertoire. It allowed proletarian heroism to enter the repertoire alongside the gentler graces of dairymaids and ploughboys.

Neither Lloyd nor MacColl were trained musicians. In his singing Lloyd had an emotional range from erotic jolliness to grand passion. MacColl was always theatrical. Left to his own devices he composed colourful, sometimes gauche, sometimes powerful texts to folk-inspired tunes. His later marriage to Peggy Seeger, who is more musician than actress, produced a genuine collaboration in which each partner's strength balanced the other's weakness.

As he explained it to me MacColl's philosophy of folk revivalism was as follows. The folk traditions needed reconstituting. The handful of genuine source singers still to be encountered were the last surviving representatives of a long and distinguished tradition. Even they were restricted in their range of tonal qualities, vocal effects, decorative techniques, and maybe even repertoire. Still, they were required listening because they demonstrated some features of traditional style, not least of which was an ability to pace or 'tell' a sung narrative.

Alongside the field recordings of British singers MacColl also introduced a degree of internationalism. He claimed that British styles were part of an Indo-European tradition, citing Alan Lomax's comparative global study of cantometrics (song measure) as proof. This, plus A.L. Lloyd's occasional radio talks throughout the 1960s and '70s, introduced many people to what is now imperialistically called 'world music'.

New urban platforms for folk music demanded new approaches, new techniques. MacColl used his theatre experience for this purpose. He used Stanislavskian methods in his analysis of texts, inviting singers to identify closely with characters in the narrative, to 'know' who they were in a song, to know 'why' they were singing that particular song — the most acceptable reasons were often political.

He transposed Rudolf Laban's theory of efforts from movement to vocal sound. He learnt to affect a number of British regional accents (it has to be said not all that well). In one song he was a Scot, the next a Mancunian or an Irishman, and sometimes himself. He was, after all, an actor.

Having dealt with matters of technique he went on to inspiration. What gets you through a heavy touring schedule, opens your mouth to sing when you're weary, provides you with the greatest creative joys? MacColl's answer was unequivocal. These songs had been produced by generations of working people. They expressed their fears, aspirations, struggles, consciousness. He, as a singer, was in the privileged position of acting as a vehicle for this cultural, historical, creative expression. In short MacColl was fired by his sympathy with working-class people. His singing expressed his political stance in life.

The folk songs and ballads partly answered MacColl's creative impotence sensed in Theatre Workshop. He had now found a language. The folk language was still spoken, he claimed, by working people. The metaphors, openness, phrase construction and style of workers' speech to this day is founded on the same linguistic patterns as the songs. He cited his extensive recorded interviews with railwaymen, fishermen, miners, prize fighters, Gypsies as proof. These he had done with Seeger and BBC producer Charles Parker for a series of radio ballads for which he had written the songs.

This analysis contains some truth but it misses one salient fact. In the mid-1970s white-collar workers, whose speech MacColl had found deadly dull, just peaked to 51% of the workforce. If we were going to speak the language of the people we'd have to assimilate that fact. I chatted the BBC into the idea of a radio programme based on office workers and started the fieldwork. I began in the huge Prudential offices in Holborn, assisted by Terry Mackey, lecturer in Industrial Relations at the City of London Polytechnic. MacColl was right. White-collar speech was dull — no metaphor, no colourful phrases, just a whole lot of impersonal pronouns, initials and jargon. I abandoned the project. Clearly we wouldn't be able to speak for all the people. We'd have to restrict our efforts to a workforce that was rapidly disappearing off the industrial scene.

MacColl was not interested in what he saw as the antiquarianism of the English Folk Dance and Song Society and could be scathing about it. His was a political folk revival. It referred to the past for its moral authority. If it was to be of the present new songs needed writing constantly.

The folk revival songwriter needed to know the poetic and musical styles of the ballads. These formed the basis for all creativity. MacColl often spoke of the filmic quality of the classic ballads. He was impressed by the economy of the language, despite the fact that some of the ballads he sang could last twenty minutes. They still told their tale in basic language.

Folk songs were specific. Lovers, for example, were not anonymous abstractions such as 'my gal', 'babe', or 'honey'. They were Johnny, Molly or Mary and they had jobs — ploughmen, sailors, milkmaids, miners. The heroes and heroines had social location. They were not objects of drooling fantasy typical of the pop song, especially since rock and roll. I took all this in, not remembering that for at least a short period in my childhood Little Richard ("I got a gal, named Sue, she knows just what to do") was the last word in music. In order to follow Ewan's line you had to deny a great deal.

One experience among many which convinced me that matters were not half as simple as the political song scene made out (whether MacColl-inspired or not) was my work with white-collar trade unionists. Terry Mackey frequently asked our group, Staverton Bridge, to present programmes of Labour songs to his students as part of his day release courses. Sometimes we attended weekend courses too. He insisted on discussing repertoire. He was introducing staff representatives to trade unionism and wasn't having them scared off by leftist sloganizing.

With very few exceptions I began to notice that the older songs we sang to his groups presented few problems. They were historical documents of significant moments in Labour history — Luddism, the formation of agricultural unions, working-class poverty, the strike for the dockers' tanner, and so on. Then there was a gap. The history of twentieth-century labourism in Britain produced few songs until the folk revival. Then matters became contentious. Many revivalist songs were confrontational pieces written by well-meaning leftist sympathizers and had to be ditched. The fact of the matter was appallingly obvious: those songs written by insiders, or broadside poets close to the inside, had authenticity. Although they were partisan they were ethically accurate. The folk revival songs didn't have that ring to them. They peddled a political line from a point of ideology. The old songs proceeded from experience. There will always be a huge difference between these two.

This contrast was even more marked when it came to songs on current political issues, strikes and disputes. They generally presented only half the case, stated prejudices, rendered highly complex issues down to a few lines. Heated arguments with Terry and some of his trade union friends eventually convinced me that leftism was exactly what Lenin had called it — an infantile disorder.

Experience was beginning to suggest that politicized folkies were an embarrassment to the trade union and labour movements. They were often people like me who had to mug up on political and industrial issues and probably misunderstood the strikes and disputes they sang about so forcefully. There were two standard reactions to such singers: knee-jerk approval or the kind of resignation one senses when the vicar makes an obligatory speech after an otherwise enjoyable day out. There was something colossally patronizing in the need to tell workers about socialism (theatre groups did it too); furthermore it had a detrimental effect in *music*. If the political message were the only really important thing music and poetry were reduced to the status of vehicles. This introduced a hierarchy of parameters which left the artistic ones impoverished.

On a personal level this was serious business. As the artistic parameters were the only ones I had real confidence in (I knew how to write music, words a little less, on politics I was unsophisticated) I was manipulating myself into the ludicrous position of putting my worst foot forward. Musicianship took a back seat.

It was unlikely, I began to argue, that a political aesthetic in response to the modern world could be as black and white as the ballad MacColl and Lloyd (much edited — we might even say ideologically bowdlerized) sang about a coal owner and a pitman's wife. The pitman's wife has been kicked out of Hell because the Devil is turning all the poor folk out.

This is to make way for the rich wicked race
For there is a great number of them in that place

This was clear Them and Us, good and evil, with us or agin us politics. It made less and less sense as I tested it out against experience. It led to some real *faux pas*.

I wrote a song in response to a pit tragedy. On 21st March 1973 there was an underground accident at the Lofthouse Colliery in the West Riding of Yorkshire. It was an old pit surrounded by many disused underground workings. The men working on the South 9B face were suddenly confronted by a deluge of water which flooded through a point in the coalface. It seems that they were working dangerously close to the disused workings, this being the cause of the flood. Although some of the fifteen workers managed to escape via three and a half miles of underground passages, seven of their mates were missing. A huge rescue operation took place, exciting the interest of the national media and the leftist press. The National Coal Board employed a team of new frogmen who were actually due for one more practice session before finishing their training.

It was a hopeless task. The whole area was filled with mud, both gates to the face were full of wreckage, air was giving out. Refusing defeat a local miner and father of one of the trapped men devised a courageous plan to dig a tunnel by hand. For days this and various other desperate attempts were put into operation. The men were not found in the area of the mine where they were presumed to be. Eventually it had to be assumed that the miners were dead.

Widows' appeals were launched. On the 29th March the Coal Board made the official announcement that the men were indeed dead. Then followed the awful business of bodies being recovered.

At the Inquiry which was held in Wakefield it became clear that the cause of the accident was indeed the proximity of old workings from the disused Bye Pit shaft. The Coal Board's surveys of the old workings were shown to be inaccurate. (They had been unaware of some field notebooks compiled by a nineteenth-century geologist which would have pointed to the danger.) It was the job of the acting secretary of the Yorkshire Miners branch of the union, Arthur Scargill, to criticize the Coal Board and suggest tightening up the training and procedure of Coal Board surveyors.

My song went straight for the jugular. I saw it as a straight Us and Them situation. At a time when the Conservative government of the day was fuming about 'greedy workers' this was just the ammunition needed to show how clear the class lines were drawn. Prime Ministers didn't end up in industrial accidents, did they?

Most of the song was a straight poetic description of what I had learned. Day began with a rising mist while our proletarian heroes hacked away down below. Then the historical bit: one needed to point out all those desperately unpoetic facts about disused workings, naming the old colliery to establish authenticity. Next the water floods in with the accusatory "No one knew of the disused workings, Seven men died for that crime". So we knew who the bastards were. Then came the inevitable verse, underlined in red, which pointed out the correct class line in case one's audience was too thick to work it out for themselves.

Keep on working, get the coal out
Safety takes up too much time
There's seven of those greedy miners
Lying in a sea of grime

A thousand and one subtleties were conspicuously absent. There was the uncomfortable fact that the men may have been working for 'wet money', which was a system of bonuses awarded for working in wet or demanding conditions. What did the song have to say about the fact that human beings would risk their necks for a little more cash? What, for that matter, did it say about the incredible heroism of the Coal Board's newly trained frogmen, the volunteers who laboured in vain to rescue their friends? Did it have anything to say about a society in which any form of shitty job is reckoned better than unemployment? Did it really believe that the Coal Board *liked*, or deliberately engineered, the situation out of negligence for the welfare of the miners? Was anyone pleased — including the Prime Minister? Who were these heartless bastards who couldn't give a damn about a handful of expendable lives?

No, the line was simple, to the point, and direct enough to be understood by a child. With Staverton Bridge I peddled this dope around the country with predictable results. At political meetings it brought the house down. Folk clubs on the whole felt uncomfortable with it unless they happened to be organized by the leftist fringe.

One folk club tour in 1974 took us to West Yorkshire. Although I didn't know it one of our venues was very close to the Lofthouse Colliery. Like lambs to the slaughter we trotted out the song. There was muted applause at the end. I wondered why. During the interval a middle-aged man spoke to me. It wasn't that simple, he tried to say. He was moved by the fact that someone from outside the area had written a song but, as politely as possible (but not without passion) he tried to explain a few facts. For all I know he might have been a miner, a Coal Board employee, a union official, or a manager. I was less aware of his words than of the way he was gently warning me off. I felt awful.

It became clear in a flash that making political capital out of tragedy was not only tasteless, it was politically naive. There is no issue in the world that can be reduced to a straight Them and Us analysis. Seeking to apportion blame outside ourselves is tantamount to refusing responsibility. As we are all capable of responsibility (the ability to respond) refusing to take it amounts to perpetuating the very matters we claim to be against.

Although I continued to sing, and even write, such songs for a while I gradually began to experience an embarrassment which went deeper with each predictable response. In fact what became startlingly clear was that my audience, political or not, folk club or union conference, was happiest when I did what I was best at – being a musician.

I began to see the role of the artist as one of asking rather than answering questions. The most important questions were not the ones you felt you had to ask in order to conform to an ideological position but those you posed as a consequence of your musicality. These were what challenged people because in asking them I was challenging myself. This put me on a level equal with those who chose to listen and questioned the implicit assumption that the performer knew best.

Yet in the folk milieu it was the *musical* element that was most lacking. The excitement that I had experienced when improvising with Cardew, the compelling sound of John Cage's cacophonous events, or the pre-political days of our group Staverton Bridge when we banged hell out of old drums and sang loud close harmonies without a care in the world — these had become forgotten dreams.

It took me some years to understand one stunningly simple fact: in formulating his theories MacColl was actually talking about himself. This is inevitable. Artists function through their experience of life. When they take the step of placing themselves in leadership positions they need to do so cautiously.

The Master-Disciple relationship no longer suits the Western world, if it ever did in the sense used in Oriental religions and practices. It involves too much denial. It is simply not true, not provable, and not neutral to claim that the creative mind necessarily needs an imposed framework from individuals, techniques, or schools of thought.

MacColl confused his personal quest for a language (something which enabled his development into a powerful performer) with a desire to universalize his own position and thereby to lead. He has been accused of adopting a Stalinist (or Maoist) style of leadership but that is merely a matter of which pet devil one wishes to invoke. MacColl was an autocrat, and those whom Wilhelm Reich would have regarded as having an authoritarian temperament followed willingly enough until their developing maturity obliged them to part company. This was true of the young singers and musicians who formed the London Critics Group, MacColl and Seeger's project which involved their theories of the revival, songwriting, politics and theatre. By 1972 when I met Ewan and Peggy the London Critics Group had folded in predictable acrimony.

Then there was the music. On a musical level I found the folk revival deadly dull. In their highly influential song book *The Singing Island* MacColl and Seeger attempted to lay down ground rules for accompanying folk songs. On the basis that "the song is more important than the accompaniment" would-be performers are taught that chords should be kept as simple as possible, "diminished, augmented or non-triadic forms" are not advised. "Even 7th chords should be used sparingly as they are extremely lush and need thoughtful placement." Songs should ideally be learnt unaccompanied first, occasional chording or picking out of the melody being regarded as a 'crutch' which singers "should discard ... as soon as possible". In *freely sung songs* accompaniment should not "cut across the basic free rhythm of the song", and in constructing a countermelody "as it is usually the tendency of a competent instrumentalist to use to full capacity his skill and imagination, take care that such improvisation does not over-balance the voice-instrument equilibrium".

As far as instrumental resources went: "The traditional instruments most commonly used in accompaniment of British folk music are the fiddle, pipes, concertina, and melodeon. Guitar and banjo, so recently become widespread in Britain along with jazz and popular music techniques, are foreigners to this tradition. Generally speaking, the traditional instruments above named accompany by following the song melody, occasionally offering sporadic chordal comments. Only when they accompany in ensembles do they even begin to approach the block-chordal type of accompaniment characteristic of guitars and banjos. However, these latter two instruments *can* be moulded stylistically to suit British tradition but must be used carefully, with an eye to preserving both their own integrity and that of the songs."

It didn't occur to me at the time that I hadn't read anything quite so restricting since I rebelled against the inanities of harmony and counterpoint in academic music training. Indeed, these rules make Bach chorales look like free jazz.

The folk club and festival touring I did with Staverton Bridge, and later with Tish Stubbs as a duo, taught many lessons by experience.

It seemed to me that anyone wanting to build up a case for sexism, imperialism, racism or nationalism could just as easily do so without even extending the boundaries that Sharp had set himself. References to 'old England' abound in the sea songs. William leaves his lover to "fight the blacks and heathens on the Banks of the Nile", and the ballad of *Adam and Eve* (much loved by the resident singers at the Exeter club) just about stitches up the feminist case by asserting Biblical authority. Adam, as we know, was created 'Lord of the Universe' but was not happy until a helpmate was found.

As Adam was resting in slumber
He lost a small rib of his side
And when he awoke 'twas in wonder
To see a most beautiful bride
In transport he gaz-èd upon her
His happiness now was complete
He prais-èd the bountiful donor
Who to him has given a mate
She was not taken out of his head sir
To rule and to triumph in man
Nor was she took out of his feet sir
By man to be trampled upon
But she was took out of his side sir
His equal co-partner to be
So united is man with his bride sir
Yet man is the top of the tree

In fact, the position of women in folk song is generally so simperingly outdated that up-and-coming feminist singers had a hard job to isolate that part of the repertoire that best fed their myth. So few songs present women in a non-passive, non-domestic role that the exceptions tend to be sung by just about everyone. The rollicking tale of the three drunken maidens who got blotto on the Isle of Wight joyously losing their maidenheads in the mayhem (a good song, true) has been so done to death that one could be forgiven for wishing they'd been a little more demure and thus not worthy of record. It could equally be said that the song was fun because it was about sex, and may have been a male fantasy. (It was always collected from men.) Or maybe it was repressed sexuality on the part of the feminist singers. Nothing is ever that clear.

The same could be said, not to quite the same extent, of any modern ideology looking for support in the folk repertoire. The fact is that such ideologies were not consciously manifest at the time many of the songs were written. How can we expect ploughmen who have never heard of socialism to sing socialist songs?

My point is this: once you begin to select your repertoire to reflect your part of the myth in a consciously ideological way you inevitably get involved in a mass of contradictions, self-deception and manipulation. The reason for this is simple: one song is as good as another. I am not referring here to whatever aesthetic criteria each individual might bring to the songs. We are all entitled to our taste. But in terms of the documentary record, even allowing for its basis in mythology, all the songs reflect some aspect of day-to-day life experience.

Or put it like this: all the songs were collected from *someone*. For those singers, less stuffed up with folkloristics (in fact not stuffed up at all unless the folklorists got to them), the song was learnt for many reasons: they liked the tune, the words, father had always sung it, the story illustrated a point of truth, it went down well in the pub — whatever. And yes there may have been the occasional political animal who liked the way the story got at the bosses (whoever they were at the time). And yes there's a case to be made to say that, like the blues, many of these songs expressed implicit opposition to social mores of the time. However we look at it, then, for those singers it is fair to assume that the songs were functional and consistent with life experience. It is in this sense that one song is as good as another. They all reflect something.

Now, how are you going to choose your repertoire? Well, why not choose it just as the source singers did – by whatever happens to take your fancy? This, in fact, is what much of the folk revival did. With less of an ideological axe to grind the repertoire opens up. How far?

The source singers didn't discriminate between areas of material. Anyone who has done a modicum of reasonably honest fieldwork knows that without prejudice local singers take into the repertoire anything that suits their purpose. This includes (and research shows that it *included*) all the flotsam and jetsam from popular song forms. Modern recording technology did not invent popular song. True, it has had a decisive effect, but so, for some centuries, did the growth of popular printed broadside ballads designed for mass circulation. In addition there was church music, band music, dance music. By today's standards it was not a very wide palette, but evidence shows that local traditions could and usually did make an informal choice from whatever was available.

It is self-evident that the selection of repertoire left to its own devices is influenced to some degree by belief or world view. Social class can be shown to have some relation to aesthetic preference although it may not be decisive. (It doesn't account for uniqueness.) But these matters are subtextual. They are as importantly related to the subconscious factor as the conscious one. Mass orientated popular culture in large societies could be defined by its direct and ruthless appeal to the unconscious. So we will take all this as read. The point is that without *conscious* ideology staking a claim in the area of artistic sensibilities people appear to act as they always have done: they choose what they like from whatever sources are available.

The folk revival singers and audiences who used folk clubs as a form of

direct, informal participatory music and song could do likewise. For some years
the lines were carefully if tenuously drawn — we've seen one example in the
Exeter traditional club. Singers used to make quite clear in the *Folk Directory*,
for example, whether they were 'trad', 'contemporary', or 'mixed' and got
booked or not according to the labels. It was a form of whoring — I will do it
to your taste or advertise in advance what I specialize in so that we all have a
good time. Woe betide anyone who went too far. But actually, peddling the
MacColl-Seeger line was taken by some clubs as transgression.

A folk club in Torquay had been running well enough for some years until
we arrived. The repertoire had been a catholic mix of whatever happened to be
around. The resident singer, Martin Scragg, had a preference for traditional
material and was an admirer of various revival singers including MacColl. He
gave his preferences a weekly airing but took a soft line on what floor singers
did. On his guest list were a fair number of contemporary and blues singers.
But he also liked the Singer's Club model and fancied trying it. We dutifully
drew up a 'resident's rota', held weekly workshops to show the uninitiated how
to sing (they'd been doing alright till then), and made sure that the
non-traditional felt less welcome.

The week the Americans were defeated in Vietnam we wrote some new
songs and trotted out some of MacColl's. This was the final sin. I have a
picture of the woman who used to take the money on the door pulling Martin's
hair, yelling "Can't you see what's happening!" as if the Vietcong were about
to take over Torquay. The club folded soon after.

It took me years of painful experience to work out where the dysfunction
was. I was in absolute misery the morning after a booking on some occasions.
If the evening had gone well more often than not I had reservations about why.
If it hadn't this could probably be put down to the club's total ignorance of
Important Matters. When we did political benefits I generally fumed at the lack
of interest in any song other than the one that hammered the current slogan —
Free the Shrewsbury 24, the Pentonville 5, the Heinz 57 or whatever.
Politically motivated audiences were generally uninterested in the older folk
songs and talked through the love affairs of farm workers, the tragic voyages of
sailors. But they woke up if you sang about stringing a "rope across the way to
catch the throat and break the spine of the dirty blackleg miner".

The rationale which hovered in the background was this: the very term 'folk
revival' implied that something was already moribund. We have seen that what
in fact was dead was a certain construct which had been introduced into our
understanding of local singing and music-making. This came from Romantic
nationalism via the folk song pioneers through to Lloyd and MacColl into the
folk revival. Implied with this was a loss of mass creativity, a death, if you
like, of viable art forms which could serve the people. This had been taken
over by a snide popular culture which wasn't much use to anyone except a few
stars and those who made money out of them.

This fits very well into the classic political revolutionary myth. I have
written elsewhere that "It may not be fanciful to see the resurrection and
rebirth theme in the central theoretical moment of revolutionary socialism.
Capitalism would be seen as bringing about the temporary death of the human

spirit. This is a partial death, and the human spirit is to be reborn in nobler form in the rising of the proletariat. The period of death is usually conceived as a sleep, as explicitly stated in many a socialist song, the *Internationale* amongst them.''

> Arise ye starvelings from your slumbers
> Arise ye criminals of want
> For Reason in revolt now thunders
> And at last ends the age of cant.

In the more missionary elements of the folk revival, explicitly political or not, this theme plays a major part. The folk revival was not only about reviving folk songs. It was equally importantly about reviving the folk. This assumes that they *have* been sleeping since the Industrial Revolution. The Marxist can account for this by reference to 'false consciousness'. The less political blame the telly.

One evening in South London in 1984 (let the club be anonymous) I abandoned the folk revival. We had driven from the Westcountry with a car full of instruments. Having found the pub the bar staff looked blank when we asked where the folk club was. I reasoned therefore that the club was not a dynamic force in community life. Eventually someone let us in to the club room. There was no one on hand to help us carry instruments up two flights of stairs. The organizers turned up late, the audience even later. There weren't very many of them anyway. After the club we were whisked off to the usual uncertain accommodation. As I tossed and turned in someone else's bed I vowed that I would never ever do another folk club booking. The repertoire was strangely incongruous in the 1980s; scholarship was showing how mythological some of the revival's most basic positions were; musically it was stifling; and, as the club in South London made obvious, nobody cared.

In a short-lived group I played with in the 1980s we managed to experiment with songwriting which opened its ears to rock, jazz, blues, ethnic styles, introducing Lewis Riley's excellent tabla playing, synthesizers, folk instruments, and some pure rock and roll. I was never very happy with the disparate feeling of this ensemble, but it had the virtue of casting off some pretty strong chains. It was this line-up that played one song at Ewan MacColl's seventieth birthday concert. It was accompanied by synthesizer, Appalachian dulcimer and tabla — an almighty mix of cultures which, at the time, I found appealing. I sensed that MacColl didn't.

When MacColl, Seeger and their family got on stage there was the old magic at work. It was obvious why MacColl had been influential. He was skilled, dedicated and charismatic. But as they swung into some of their new songs in support of the miners I began to sense that my changing direction implied no loss. It was clear that our paths had diverged.

MacColl was fond of quoting a story attributed to George Bernard Shaw. After a critic had mercilessly slated one of his plays Shaw said, ''I can't understand the man. I never did anything to help him''. I would rather put it another way. In order to criticize sincerely you first have to admire. Much as I found MacColl's way insufficient, I definitely admired him.

Pastorales

The Village Singers and the Mud

PROGRAMME NOTE

Long before I developed any workable critique of folk revivalism it was evident that its ways had very limited connection with what could be encountered in fieldwork amongst local traditions. MacColl's approach was a case in point. It was a theoretical relationship with tradition which was enacted in his particular practice.

In terms of music neither MacColl nor the folk revival in general answered the questions I had asked as a composer and improviser. MacColl in particular had created a discipline every bit as formalized as any I had rejected. Furthermore, the whole field was now complicated by self-conscious ideologies. These obscured two vital matters. One was the original one I had set out to confront: What do people do musically when left to their own devices? The second — What is folklore anyway? — became an issue which was raised by fieldwork.

I began 'collecting songs' (as I would then have called it) in 1971. By the early 1980s I was spending far more time in field research and community arts than in touring as a performer.

- 1 -

It is axiomatic in all research, folklore included, that if you look long enough you will find what you want. It took me three weekends trudging around the villages near Totnes in South Devon to find my first singer. Enquiries in pubs, post offices and vicarages led me to Broadhempston, a ramshackle village with a Church House Inn, a few old cottages and some council houses. One Saturday afternoon an old chap called Harry Smith unfolded his life story. At one point he mentioned songs. He'd known hundreds when he was in the navy but couldn't recall one right now.

Using all the techniques I'd learnt I started prompting with first lines of songs. "Did you ever hear one that began *As I roved out...?*" He didn't. "Did you know one about the leg of the mallard?" (Peter Kennedy had some good versions of this from Devon.) Harry's face lit up.

"Yes I do know that."

Pause.

"But I shan't sing it to 'ee.''

It turned out that *The Leg of the Mallard* was his neighbour's song and it wouldn't do to give strangers someone else's song, now, would it? I had heard of the informal copyright between local singers and here it was.

The neighbour, a big man in his late fifties whose flannel trousers flopped over a huge leather belt, was Henry Mitchelmore. He was a council worker and the village sexton. It all fitted the stereotype so well that I was utterly convinced by it.

Henry allowed me to record the song. It had more of a chant than a tune, and followed the pattern of *Green Grow the Rushes O*, each verse getting progressively longer. The final rundown was:

Oh I've ate I've ate and what've I ate
I ate the bill of the mallard
Bill and bill
Head and head
Neck and neck
Wing and wing
Breast and breast
Side and side
Thigh and thigh
Leg and leg
Foot and foot
Toe and toe
Toe nippens and all
It all went into the pillagy-o
Most bittaful [*beautiful*] leg o' the mallard

Then he gave a slight cough and spoke the last line over: "Most bittaful leg o' the mallard'' — rather matter-of-fact.

Soon after recording Henry I was given a hot tip by a local journalist which led me to a retired farm worker, Sid Parker, who also lived near Totnes. My sessions with Sid, aged 72, brought up the whole issue of the selectivity of the folklorist.

Sid had been in the First World War. He recalled eight songs and I recorded them all. One of them, *The Young Sailor Cut Down in his Prime*, I took to be folk material because it conformed to the model and I had seen other versions of it in printed collections. His other songs included music-hall comedy items, sentimental tearjerkers, and songs that had meant a lot to his comrades in the war. One of these was positively mawkish. It was a tale of a returning soldier who was greeted with the awful "my lad your mother's dead''.

Sid's aesthetic was different to mine. His eyes watered as he sang this doleful tale, his lip visibly trembling. He told me that it *was* a bit sentimental, but that sort of song had meant a lot to his mates, many of whom he never saw again.

For me it was a raw experience. On the bus home I turned matters over. Artistically I had little sympathy with the song. Its tune was predictable, the words were emotionally manipulative. No doubt, I guessed, songs like this confirmed some pretty reactionary ideas which would have been rife in the war. Yet the man's tears stayed with me. He had identified with this song far more than he had with the one I prized. Something was wrong. I was entitled to my own taste, yes, but did I have any right to impose it on the record?

- 2 -

On the tiny Channel Island of Sark spring comes early. In February you can feel the sun. You can sit out. You can see the even smaller island of Herm. In the distance is Guernsey.

I was touring with Staverton Bridge. The year was 1972. On Sark we played to the Music Society. It was light years away from the folk revival, avant-gardism, political song. The remoteness of Sark meant that any gesture, musical or otherwise, would go no further than this miniature universe. We had to communicate entirely in the here and now to human beings as we found them. There was nothing else.

The chairman of the Music Society was posh, old school, retired. He advised that anything we sang would go down well – except protest. In fact that very week some chappie had been on BBC Southwest radio and played a song in support of some damned hooligan strike in Shrewsbury. I didn't tell him he was talking about me.

We had loaded our instruments on the quay at St. Peter Port in Guernsey and then had to wait for the tide. On our arrival on Sark a tractor and trailer had chugged our gear up the steep hill. We walked. No motorized transport is allowed on the island. Except for tractors. You can hire a bike. They reckoned they had a traffic problem — sixty tractors in three square miles.

We stayed a couple of days after our concert, awaiting the tide and the ferry back.

We were introduced to Jack Le Feuvre, the island butcher. Jack was in his seventies and he lived with his wife in a small house with few amenities and some very natural smells. Neither of them ever went off Sark, not even to Little Sark, a minuscule island linked to Sark by a natural causeway. Mrs. Le Feuvre had been to Guernsey once, years ago, for a shopping trip. She found it tiring. Jack knew dozens of songs.

We begged a cassette recorder and fixed a session for Sunday evening. Jack had been visited by folklorists before, Peter Kennedy among them. He was used to being recorded.

His tough, clear old voice was hacked out of the rocks. Phrases echoed the landscape, the coastline — jagged, gnarled. He used little ornamentation. Just clear narrative.

As his songs were mainly in Sark patois, a French dialect, none of us could follow them too well. That didn't matter. Hearing a stylistic local singer with a huge repertoire, totally at ease with every note, no battle with technique or words, led me to believe, by unlogical extension, that there were good singers still around everywhere if you looked hard enough.

- 3 -

We called him Little Bob. That distinguished him from Big Bob who was married to his sister Ellen. Actually they used to be called Petrol Bob and Belcher's Bob but I never worked out which was which. Little Bob was the one who knew songs, but he wouldn't sing them in Big Bob and Ellen's chalet or even let us into his little caravan parked alongside.

They were Gypsies by the name of Small, in their late fifties perhaps. To hear Little Bob sing you had to follow him round. The first problem was to find out which pub he was in. The barmaid at The Fox in Newton Abbot would tell you he'd just gone to The Seven Stars, but they hadn't seen him in there. Perhaps he was at the Union Inn in Denbury with his mates Charlie and Archie. Eventually you'd catch up.

Then it was: "You good people. I enjoys your company" and a few songs, often tantalizing scraps. A small group of us, mainly the members of Staverton Bridge folk group, took him to Bridgwater Fair, Bampton Fair, Priddy Fair, around the pubs, out to friends. At the fairs we'd hear Gypsy step-dance tunes played on 'cordions' as they called melodeons. After a while we had a network of contacts as long as your arm.

On one occasion at Bampton Fair I stood with a young Gypsy man listening to the spiel of a barker flogging blankets, shirts, clocks, china horses. Suddenly I felt a large soft bundle under my right arm. As I stood wondering what it was I became aware of my friend nudging me and muttering, "Quick, quick". So I moved away from the crowd only to discover a bag full of stolen shirts under my coat. I had been expected to pass them down a line but had nearly blown it.

It was impossible to ignore social and historical contexts in trying to collect music from Gypsies. The more unfamiliar the culture the more obvious it is that its music is its exact expression. This helps to de-normalize our own viewpoint. I felt it necessary to learn as much as I could, and pieced together a history which began with migrations from the Hindu Kush in the tenth century. By the fifteenth century Gypsies were in Britain where there is some evidence to suggest that they were fashionable novelties. Their popularity was short-lived. By the time of Henry VIII it was a crime simply to be a Gypsy. The punishment was hanging. From then onwards they were marginals in an often hostile host culture.

Many Gypsies told me of their recent past. Eddie Holland, in a recorded interview, said: "We had to pinch our 'taties, pinch our swedes whenever we could to get something in the pot to eat. And they days there were more chicken around. We used to have a chicken when we wanted it — provided the farmer didn't catch us. And this is what we called survival. It was hard times."

Those of them who had been to school recalled having to stand for abuse, and generally hitting back. Brian Holland, a settled Gypsy and brilliant melodeon player in North Devon, reckoned: "When I was at school I can remember being called 'Gypsy' and all this here, and you was, sort of, cast out of it a bit. But I mean you fought your own battles and they respected you for that really. The only hounding I did have was when I went to school, but if anyone said anything they got a smack in the mouth."

Older Gypsies had more dramatic tales. Daisy Small of Newton Abbot remembered: "I've seen policemen come in Sussex and kick the kettle right over my brother-in-law's mother. And she was just lucky that she had thick clothes on and it was pulled off her quick 'cause she would have been scalded".

In view of this marginal history it struck me as curious that Gypsies preserved an area of song and music that the mainstream society had already begun to cast off at the time of Cecil Sharp. Many folklorists seemed to have gathered huge numbers of otherwise unheard songs from Gypsies in various parts of Britain, and I was no exception.

As with the elderly village singers I had encountered the Gypsies immediately presented me with the problem of sorting out the bias of accepted folklorist's wisdom.

Little Bob had a kind of signature song. He'd gulp a mouthful of beer, sway back on his stool, and with a disarming grin that would sell fridges to Eskimos, would sing:

Now when I was a young man I took great delight
In a drinking and smoking from morning to night

It was a song I knew from printed collections and therefore offered no challenge to the frame of reference that had been handed down from Sharp to Lloyd to MacColl and beyond. In the next breath Bob would introduce "a real old song" and sing: "You called me baby doll a year ago..." and a few other items from his youth. Younger Gypsies, dressed anachronistically in the fashionable style of the late 1950s, sang Elvis Presley numbers ("There goes a-my honley po-sess-shons, there goes a-my hevery thing"). All sang Country and Western cowboy songs, especially those of the late Jimmie Rodgers who, they all claimed, was a traveller by descent.

The Orchard Family live in North Devon surrounded by a huge scrapyard, dogs and loads of kids. Old Tommy plays a melodeon, talks the hind legs off a donkey, and sings cowboy songs. His yodelling is a thing to behold. His son, also Tommy, is a brilliant step-dancer and plays the melodeon better than his father. When I first met the family there was also young Carol, probably about six years old, who also step-danced.

I watched Carol grow up. As she entered her teens she became a powerful singer of Country and Western songs — Patsy Cline, Dolly Parton, Billie Jo Spears all rolled into one. Proud father lifted her onto pub tables and called for the best of order as his protégée swung into endless streams of redneck songs she'd learnt perfectly off records.

So although the folklorists were correct — you could find Gypsy singers who sang old ballads and broadsides from an earlier era (and often sang them very well) — it was the modern popular songs with a Nashville twang to them that had the highest profile.

I wrote in an academic article in 1987, "If the intention is to collect and publish certain kinds of texts which conform to criteria established by the folklore then a selective approach may be appropriate. In the last analysis, however, this tells us more about the folklorist than about the travellers. If the researcher wishes to view song as folklore amongst modern travellers *and by doing so gain valuable insights into their culture as it is lived* the selective approach is of very limited value." What I meant was really more blunt. Looking at a social group's music in order to confirm one's own preconceived viewpoint is not just limited, it's downright dishonest.

With this constant thought I tried to be as unselective as possible. Although I preferred the older songs I saw no justification to impose my taste where it hadn't been asked for. Carol was an innocent in the world of popular music, passionately attached to the charming possibility that she might be 'discovered'. She was young and pretty and certainly made a good stab at imitating her role models in her singing. She took to me because I encouraged her and sometimes took along an electric keyboard and played accompaniments which sounded more like the records than her old man's squeezebox.

One day she told me that she was going to make a record — not a single, "a proper LP", and I was going to lead her band. She wanted to know how to go about it, how much it would cost, and who to send it to. This presented me with a considerable personal crisis. I could see that her dream was fuelled more by innocence than any knowledge of the mucky scene she wanted a passage into. I sensed failure: her singing was, after all, derivative, although good of its kind. I could see her giving a lot of money to a lot of people who would be all too happy to take it off her. Furthermore I didn't want to be the leader of a Country and Western band. Somehow this didn't seem to be the logical conclusion of the questioning which had led a young composer away from the musical establishment.

I explained that it was a hard business, full of sharks, plenty of knocks, more failures than successes. She took it all on board. She was ready for this scene. It was exactly how would-be stars had been advised in those film biographies. ("Well, kid, the chances are small and the rewards are big. Why doncha jess settle down and git yo'self a nice guy who'll look after yo'?") I had the stupid thought that probably she would become a star on the strength of her innocent persistence while I was still trying to convince arts funding bodies that the people had a viable culture of their own.

Carol had to pursue her dream as far as it would let her, so I ended up gathering a band of professional musicians (guitar, harmonica, bass, piano, synth drums), and taking her to the best recording studio I knew. We recorded two songs for her 'demo' and had a nice day which she paid us for. I discovered that my early love of rock and roll had given me a kind of feel for country riffs on the piano.

I provided her with a list of addresses. She didn't get a peep. Despite the fact that I had warned her I felt rotten about it. She was philosophical. "I won't be able to say I didn't have a go when I could, will I?" And that was true.

But what was happening to me? A combination of my early questioning of the European concert tradition, unlocated reservations about the avant-garde, rejection of the folk myth, community arts funding, and some damn fool desire for anthropological accuracy had led me to playing — well, let's be honest about how I felt — bullshit.

In any case, the older Gypsies who knew the songs I was originally interested in were dying off fast. Little Bob went out and got boozed one night, drove home, had a heart attack, and was found dead in his car. Everyone was upset. His sister Ellen still talks about it.

- 4 -

After these introductions to some local singers allow me to invite you to The Rockford Inn on the Devon side of Exmoor. It's sometime in the week between Christmas and New Year. This is one of the slacker times of year for the farmers. Come in April or May and they'll be lambing night and day. June-July is shearing. There's not a lot of energy left for singing at these times, although it does happen. But around Christmas is ideal.

It's about half past eight, a bit early for singing. There's not many in yet. The young couple standing by the bar I've seen before. The man sings.

The people who run the pub are friendly, and there's a few families sitting round. They're staying at the pub for a few days, and there's one little group that have a holiday cottage somewhere, I'm not sure exactly where but they were here this time last year. So there's a few people around to exchange pleasantries with.

At around nine o'clock Farmer Dick French, his wife Lorna, and an entourage of friends and farm hands swell the numbers drastically. Dick calls up a round of drinks, offers us one, and puts it all on the slate.

There's a lot of Dick French. Everything about him is huge — his farm, his flock, his figure, his personality, his silences, his love of singing. His trousers reach way up past his huge belt. Despite the belt he always wears braces. For work he wears old shirts and jumpers with holes in. But for going out he has a shave and puts on something dry.

Over the next half hour the pub fills up. There's a few friends who have driven over from Porlock on the Somerset side. Delwyn does contract work. He's turned up with his wife April. Delwyn's Dad, Donald, will be on his way later. Jim Sanders, a wiry tough farmer from out on the moor, has turned up with his daughter Kathleen and her husband Jim White. By half past nine we're all talking, telling jokes, chewing over any gossip.

Now we're aware of Dick hovering, starting to direct the traffic. He's forthright about his intentions. Better start playing that squeezebox, he instructs me, else it'll get too late. Got to get people in the mood a bit early. Get some foundation.

I play a little game with him. Alright Dick. I'll strike up when I've finished this pint. Never mind that, he explodes, he'll buy me another. Just get playing.

So it's the usual concertina medley of music-hall songs to kick off — *Daisy Bell, She Was One of the Early Birds, Two Lovely Black Eyes*. The purpose is to create atmosphere, not to be listened to, but it's nice to hear a few voices mouthing over the choruses.

Now someone ought to sing. Who's it going to be? How about Jim Sanders? No, he'll have a go later. And Dick rarely sings this early. Rather than wait around too long I decide to give them a couple of chorus songs that I

sing just about every time. Now people are listening, joining in the chorus. I
get a little applause and pass the ball to the young bloke I saw at the bar.

Then Jim Sanders decides to give it a go. He has a loud penetrating voice,
pitched a little high. The muscles of his neck visibly strain as he belts out an
old Doris Day hit song *Que Sera Sera*. This includes powerful chorus singing
from many of the drinkers and a fair amount of repartee from his mates. The
song concerns a young boy asking his mother what he will be when he grows
up. On the line "Shall I sing songs?" the whole bar roars out NO! but Jim
carries on.

There's a couple of other squeezebox players there on this occasion. They
rattle off a few faster tunes. One middle-aged, very healthy looking chap
provides a percussion accompaniment by rattling an empty beer bottle on the
table top. It's very clever and neatly adds some excitement to the rhythm.

And so the evening goes on, passing from one performer to another.
Sometimes there's a serious song, often a sentimental Irish number popularized
by Foster and Allen or Val Doonican. But most of the songs either have
choruses or are funny. Many of them are quite vulgar.

Many people ask me how I got to know Dick French. In 1975 the Beaford
Arts Centre in North Devon employed the three members of Staverton Bridge
to research folklore in the area. A trail of enquiries led us to The Rockford Inn.
We were hotly recommended to visit Farmer Dick French just a mile up the
road. Follow the road uphill, past the church, round two sharp bends, first left
and straight in the farmyard on your right. Can't miss it. Ask him to sing *This
Old Jacket*.

Dick, then in his mid-fifties, was cool about this request, but he showed a
certain interest and hospitality. He invited us into the kitchen. They were just
having tea. He ordered us to sit down.

The long farmhouse table was overflowing with piles of toast, bags of sliced
bread, cheese, pickles, tomatoes, huge jars of beetroot, a few cartons of clotted
cream, jam, cold sausages, cold meat. Around the table were various labourers
and friends, Dick's wife Lorna, and a white-haired white-skinned old man. I
sat next to him. Little was said. The click-click of cutlery was deafening.

I took a slice of *Mother's Pride*, smothered it with clotted cream and jam,
and reflected on the culture clash. Cream tea with sliced bread...

The white old man sitting to my left suddenly slumped. I was sure he had
died. What should I do? He slowly overbalanced then fell on my shoulder.

"Shove 'ee back up, will 'ee?"

I did.

It happened three times. It turned out to be one of Lorna's aged uncles.

Dick was intrigued by our request to hear songs. "Come back in three
weeks. We'll see what we can do."

Would he sing *This Old Jacket* then?

"We'll see."

Three weeks later I returned. We had our sing-song. It was unforgettable. I
went back countless times, and still do.

Dick sings:

The turkey cock is a very fine bird
He's bigger than any crow
I saw him come striding along
Playing on the old banjo (Now the chorus. Join in, mind.)

Now Jim Sanders launches into an epic dialect piece about an unlucky farmer.

Dick French 'ave asked me to sing 'ee a song
An' I ban't gonna keep 'ee too long
For as sure as you see me, you'll please to forgive me
Vor I'm certain to zing 'ee all wrong

The song goes on and on. Young Sally runned off with a tramp, the hens won't lay, the prize bull died with a mangold stuck in its throat, and the day's rabbit hunt ended up with "I never shot nort but me dog".

Later in the evening Dick really warms up. He insists that everyone who so much as knows half a verse sings, anyone with an instrument plays it, no matter what the standard.

Suddenly he shouts to the crowd that he's going to do the oldest song on Exmoor. He may not remember it all but he'll have a go. It begins like this:

This old cap I have wore since the day that I was born
And it started going to pieces
For I spent all my tin on the ladies drinking gin
And upon the brimey ocean I may wander

Then, as everyone joins in the chorus, he throws his old cap on the floor.

In the next verse it is the turn of the old jacket. That ends up on the floor. Then the jersey, braces, belt, shirt, two vests, trousers, long johns, shoes, socks. As he draws his pants down in the final verse he grabs a beer glass and puts his plonker in it.

Eighteen stone of naked wobbling flesh is neither sexy, suggestive (there's nothing left to suggest), nor even rude. It's just plain vulgar. When I first saw this performance my sides ached. Tears rolled down. It was agony.

He had once performed this piece in front of a prim old lady. He grabbed a pair of stag's antlers from above the mantelpiece, covered his willy with them, and said to the old dear: "'Ere missis. I bet you never seen one with 'orns on!"

Some years later someone held a stag party (the male-only type — nothing to do with hunting) and booked two strippers who came all the way from Bristol. They went through their routines, showed their charms, got men to eat marshmallows off their breasts. Dick, not to be beaten by city folk, followed with *This Old Jacket* and stole the show. The girls' minder told him he could get a job doing that in Bristol.

"Well I thought about it. After all, 'tis a job in the dry."

- 5 -

This is a good place to pause and reflect. What was the quest beyond the theories, ideologies, revivalist practices, the community arts tag which funded much of the work? And does it follow any pattern? How does it relate to contemporary music-making whatever its form?

We have seen how the Romantic era brought about the notion of folklore contrasting with the challenging new world of industrialization, proletarianization, expansionism, imperialism, capitalism, technology. The late nineteenth century watched the decline of the old order as it saluted the Empire's finest flowering. Two world wars, significantly the first, gave it the boot.

Despite the poverty widely attached to these changes the dominant and rising culture became increasingly refined, technological, specialized. Collective experience suggested that this was not always an unreservedly positive process.

By the time I was a young child in the 1950s Erich Fromm, in *The Sane Society*, was quoting alarming statistics showing that the incidence of homicide, suicide and alcoholism was highest in the most affluent countries. Jung had referred to modern man in search of a soul.

The refined technology had made war more costly and wasteful than ever, even before Hiroshima. In my teens the CND took off. One of my major formative experiences was being splashed across the local paper holding the banner for Ealing YCND when I was fourteen. It displeased the local vicar so I'm told. His kind, his belief system, were another victim of the changing world view.

Alongside these social challenges were more neutral if not positive changes. The world was getting smaller or 'imploding' as McLuhan said. Without moving we could sample international cultures, ways of life, music. Meat and two veg was no longer a good meal. The potential for refinement was vast.

In the arts and the sciences new views of the universe were developed. These were remarkably congruent. The new refinement would require spiritual development if we were to control what we had brought about. It is not necessarily the skilled computer operator who is in control: it is the highly developed person.

The response of the 1960s is now legendary. The determination to break down barriers on all fronts, including the arts, reflected a spiritual need. I took part in many a musical happening before I was twenty. Yet only now can I begin to locate a feeling (that's all it was) of fear, of something incomplete, unsatisfactory, lurking incomprehensibly even in the most triumphant moments of playful anarchy.

To locate that fear in words is difficult. But having begun my work I took an archetypal journey away from it in order to get back and, eventually, to confront it.

This is alchemical. In order to recognize the relationship which exists between various ingredients (of experience, of music, of material) one has to separate them. For progress to be made there comes a time, often soon after the work has started, when vital aspects of it have to be abandoned. At a later stage there re-emerges an openness to a wider range of experience. Tom Chetwynd, in his *Dictionary of Symbols*, says, "This often involves reclaiming part of your personality which was originally exiled by your own dominant conscious Ego". Precisely. And it is the categorizing Ego which originally experiences the fear of the unknown and tears away from it.

By following this route relentlessly the questions I was forced to ask were bold ones. What was I part of? Although individual psychology is important, I was always aware of being part of something.

It was an impulse to find the mud. It was to seek and experience the raw; to try to discover what the gross substance is before it was refined. It is an overwhelming necessity to find the *prima materia*. Lévi-Strauss made structural categories of the raw and the cooked. Artists in the twentieth century have displayed an astonishing urge to discover the raw for the very good reason that a good meal never comes cooked. Conventional music teaching brings you in at a high point of refinement — harmony and counterpoint, classical tradition, and so on. It's not raw at all.

The mythologies of folklore, the common stream, the proletariat, people's oral history are calculated to allow this comparison between the raw and the refined. They are made into pseudo-sciences by 'ologists' who in time question their very existence, as folklorists have. Then follows the desperate scramble to redefine the field or adjust the myth so that it fits a new supposed reality. Cecil Sharp, Baring-Gould, Percy Grainger, and later Lloyd and MacColl *did* select what they wanted — the in word is 'mediated'. They did so because, if they were honest, they were conducting their research as artists, not social scientists. So they had every right to go for the nice tunes, rewrite material or skew the evidence.

Ideological constructs rationalize what otherwise seems irrational. Cornelius Cardew did this at a point when his personal quest altered. He too needed his mud in order to continue. So did Bartók with his folk music collecting. So did Cage with his Orientalism. So did all the composers in Europe from the nineteenth century onwards who consciously injected authenticity into their work by referring to folk music. So did Steve Reich with his studies of African drumming and Balinese gamelan. It continues.

This mud is chameleon-like. It is village singers to me, something else to you. As each generation is the final product, the summation of its ancestors, it also depends on where you come in as to what is your mud. AMM improvised music was mud to 1950s integral serialism. To me, ten years younger than most of its members, it was high refinement. To some people the mud might even be harmony and counterpoint.

The mud is the basic material. Life moulds and shapes. The old song *Sixteen Tons* begins "Some people say a man's made out of mud", recalling the ancient myth. Tom Chetwynd says: "Mud is the malleable substance of our being, full of potential for growth and transformation". The folk, the people, the proletariat, the popular culture, the fading tribe — all are mud. Or they were my mud.

The search for the mud is profoundly democratic, although as it is archetypal it has also been a feature of predemocratic worlds. Democracy, the dominant political myth of our age, is founded on the notion of equality. The search for what is common, what's left when the refinements of class, gender, race, age, epoch, are stripped away is part of the democratic quest. We need to know what life is. We need to know in what sense we are equal. We need to know about the mud.

I found my mud. Actually it was shit. Cow shit. I stood in it frequently in Dick French's farmyard on Exmoor. And Dick showed me as much literal and symbolic mud as one life will ever need with his uproarious, wild, anarchic performances of songs which had me laughing as I'd never laughed before.

Dick French stands as an example for many of the village singers in his ability to express the totality of his life experience in a five minute song. Although his songs are picked up from here and there, like driftwood, they all end up with remarkably similar melodic contours, high but undulating.

His rhythm is elastic. He pulls four-square tunes about like chewing gum. He has the same attitude to time in his daily life. Certain regular events are roughly set — dinner anywhere between 12.30 and 2.00, lambing, shearing, pub at 9.00 most nights. He hits these flexible targets without fail. What happens in between is variable. Urban singers 'keep' time more strictly. Our sense of musical time echoes our lifestyle.

Dick's subject matter doesn't have to be agricultural to be similarly expressive. (It often is, though.) Textual matters do not tell the whole story. His imposing confrontations with his audience put his stamp on the situation just as they do on the moor. Survival is at stake. An imposing jerk of the arm commands attention. The upright posture, eyes slightly raised church-like, heralds a serious song. The clasped hands mean effort, concentration. At the end of a song he never acknowledges applause. He's back on his bar stool before his friends have finished the last chorus. He instructs, grabs strays, imposes, goes with the weather, seizes the best moment in song and farming. He never revels in momentary glory. There's always something to do next.

This totality of performance and life began to concern me more. A person who can express everything they know of life in one song seems to render modernistic concerns about the barriers between art and life as somewhat obviously intellectual. But of course this is not so.

If you looked around Dick French's farmyard you would see old walls, sheds, timbers that appear to have been there since the year dot. You would also see implements made of modern plastics, breeze blocks, new machinery bought as necessary. A line of old stone outbuildings which might make a picturesque photograph is followed by a huge barn of corrugated iron. All these are the working materials and it is the same in the song tradition he is part of. Whatever comes to hand is useful material, whatever takes his fancy. The practice of singing is not frozen in an ideal moment, nor does it conform to anybody's idea of how it should be. Dick occasionally expresses regret that he can't recall some of his father's songs, so he sings something he heard on a tape last week. So there is a similarity of attitude to singing and the rest of life.

The village singers are not exceptional. Everyone from Dick French to Pavarotti encodes their attitudes and values through performance. But this isn't always clear. You have to find your mud to see it. You have to see it on an unfamiliar small scale, in different surroundings, so that it surprises you. You have to be an outsider. To the insider it is not noticeable. To you it is folklore — or whatever you like to call it.

For some years the raw had seduced and hypnotized me. It stripped everything bare. The sight of Dick's big bum said it all. We wear make-up in the form of musical preferences, ideologies, theories, get heated about arts policies, get depressed when no one listens. We forget that we are born, get along somehow, procreate, and get old and die. Underneath we're all the same and that, my friends, is funny.

The older Dick gets the funnier he becomes, and he shares this comedy with everyone until they get the point. This is really the mud. There's nothing undignified about it. To write music you have to begin from this fact.

- 6 -

Our evening at The Rockford Inn is eventually over. It's outrageously late, we've had a good few drinks, and taken part in a kind of direct communication that we might agree is rare.

The following day we walk on the moor and reflect. What do we make of that experience?

Folk music, if the term has any meaning to me, is a matter of attitude. It is not amateur music, but neither is it professional. It doesn't recognize the distinction. It is not necessarily old music, but it may be. It does establish some continuity between past and present. It doesn't need specialists but it can accommodate them and benefit from them.

It doesn't call for years of training, but training nevertheless takes place — in public before a supportive group. On the other hand, if you've had some training you can turn it to good advantage. If you are a complete beginner you are no less in the face of the music than anyone else.

The attitude which distinguishes folk music is this: we can do it now. We don't have to wait till we're good enough, till we get a booking, till we have enough material, till someone offers to pay us, till we're famous, till eight o'clock. But if we do have these things that's OK too.

The local traditions answer an important question. If a group of us decides that we want to make music we can do so with what we've got. We can provide percussion with a beer bottle and an old mouthorgan. If one of us has a good singing voice that can be featured. As to repertoire — we sing what we know, and what we know is what we sing. What we happen to know will be an accurate expression of our lives because it is what we have casually encountered. If we don't have an audience we sing for ourselves. If we don't have a concert hall, well the local pub is better anyway. It is a typically rural, small community way of problem-solving, looking to our own resources rather than calling in outside arbiters.

This may sound like a romantic picture but there is plenty of counterbalance. Within a local tradition innovation is unwelcome. In particular the *sounds* of folklore are severely functional. A tradition is what it is because it is narrowly proscribed. The content of the songs avoids controversy and frequently underlines conservative social, sexual and political attitudes. The local traditions are *raw* but they are raw because they are restricted. That is why they are raw.

So now we can begin to sense where the experience of Sean O Riada failed to add up. The urban-trained composer expects to explore, to go further, to challenge. In the local traditions such self-expression is not given a high priority. Although it is true that the performers do express themselves, and very effectively, they do so in a manner which reveals inherent values to a community. Such revelation is afforded higher priority than expression.

Similarly, the local singer shares rather than performs, the 'audience' commits rather than appreciates. So let us just agree that at one end of a performance spectrum the 'folk' / rural / small community model is one of problem-solving from within, using resources to hand. The other is the popular or 'classical' / urban / large society model of feedback which includes conflict, innovation, challenge, looking out.

These polarities imply a huge challenge for the artist who becomes aware of them. Cardew's work is illustrative. In his avant-garde work he looked out. In his political work he attempted to root his ideals in specific groups, not exactly to look in, but to contextualize what he offered in a way that admitted more issues than the European avant-garde seemed capable of.

The irony is that both ends of the spectrum from time to time gaze at their opposites with a degree of envy.

Popular Medley

Bill Hingston of Dittisham

PROGRAMME NOTE

Local singers were unconnected with the cash nexus; they rarely sang for money, and when they did it was peanuts. They had neither the desire nor the means to market themselves. They didn't dress up in silly clothes to look trendy. Their world didn't collapse if no one listened. They ordered another pint and talked about something else.

But there was more to discover. To gain even a sketchy understanding of musical values, how music and song worked in this local context, it became increasingly clear to me that merely collecting songs and maybe singing them was tantamount to imposing on them the values of another musical context. Even to glimpse the singer's context it was necessary to focus attention on them in detail — how they learned songs, where, why, what they used them for, what values were attached to them. I was fortunate. I got to know a real old Devon charmer, Bill Hingston of Dittisham.

I had been told that an old man with a squeezebox could be found at the Ferry Boat Inn at Dittisham. A crowd of us went down one Friday night. A few locals sat round a table playing euchre, an impenetrable local card game. There was a wood stove — very warm — a few lads chucking darts, a fruit machine in use, some old men.

Was Pop Hingston likely to be in? That was him on the fruit machine, and his squeezebox was perched on a little ledge behind the bar, where it always sat.

His enthusiasm was immense. He wanted to know if we could play too. I could knock out a tune on my concertina. Pop joined in immediately. I was convinced he knew the song. It wasn't so. He heard my rendition once and played by ear.

From that day in around 1972 to his death in 1986 I tried to visit him every week. I inhabited the pub, knew the locals, his home, his family. Once I drove him and his wife to Essex to see their son. I loved him.

Dittisham (pronounced Dit'sum) is idyllic. It lies just up-river from Dartmouth, with its wide expanse of water, a picture postcard view from any angle. It used to be famous for plums but fewer orchards remain today. Newcomers, usually well off, have bought up cottages, kept the old-style exteriors and done a Habitat job inside. There's an occasional murmuring about holiday cottages and second homes. They have changed village life irrevocably. A local man, Perce Andrews, still alive in the 1970s, commented: "All along here — all these houses are summer houses. But back in they days there was *people* in 'em.''

Sixty years ago Dittisham was isolated and almost self-sufficient. Part of the village is on a steep hill that plunges down to the River Dart. The river is deep and wide at this point, and the village road ends abruptly at the water's edge. Roads into the village used to be rough tracks of stone and rubble rolled flat.

There used to be a ferry, bringing a butcher every week and transporting cattle to market. Four or five bullocks at a time would be taken across by ferrymen whose only power was their muscles and enormous oars. Older locals remember the fun they had as children when the animals decided to jump overboard and swim back to shore.

Some men fished for half the year and worked on farms the rest of the time. Everybody gathered driftwood, went cockling. Some ran boats and navigated for visitors. Many men worked in the shipbuilding yard of Philip and Son in Dartmouth, taking the boat to and from work every day. By the 1950s the yard had ceased building ships. Today it is a repair yard.

Employment prospects being what they were in the late 1950s, the displaced workers either moved, went back to the land, or found other local employment. Change occurred but life lolloped on.

Mechanized farming changed another thread of village life. Communal harvesting faded into history alongside unlocked back and front doors, and by the early 1960s the scene was set for further alterations. Wealthy newcomers, a smattering of the famous amongst them, have given the place a look of prosperity. Go a few miles away and you'll hear certain parts of the village referred to as 'Millionaire's Row'.

Whatever the truth, Dittisham has got used to seeing a lot of new faces. The Royal Naval College nearby has its effect in this respect, royalty and the upper ranks being no strangers to the neighbourhood. Then there are the fly-by-nights who come and go, having made a handsome profit on their houses, and the yachting fraternity — in evidence for much of the year.

And of course there are the summer tourists. Before the Ferry Boat Inn was altered the two small bars were often a heaving mass of T-shirts, bare flesh, and lager for four months of the year.

Another smaller group of new faces was that of younger musicians, some of whom had regular contact with the folk revival, and others who had been influenced by it. They, along with many other visitors, were attracted by the music, songs, and personality of Pop Hingston. With his Devonshire accent (which he called a burrrrr), inventive turns of phrase and ability to attract a crowd he was one of the Ferry Boat's biggest assets.

Bill was not strictly speaking a local. The usual joke in Westcountry villages is that you have to have a granny in the graveyard before you can be considered a local. Bill was born in 1914 in Modbury, some twenty-five miles away. He had been in Dittisham for much of his adult life, although older locals still thought of him as 'one who came later'.

I interviewed Bill many times, usually in the living room of his council house. His wife, Lucy, would bring cups of tea, cakes or whatever (sometimes pasties) while we chatted. The view of the river from their window was the sort that people would pay thousands for. It always amused me that it was a council house.

"Will you believe me," he said "if I tell you I can still remember being breeched? Having bloody trousers on for the first time. On a Sunday night. Gospel truth! I'll tell you — it came from a bet in the Exeter Inn in Modbury, and I was hauled out of bed and carried to the tailor's shop and stood up there. A little boy! And I stood up there and me nightshirt was hauled off, and I had hairy trousers put up me arse, and a hairy shirt that itched worse than any bloody grey blanket in the army. Crying me eyes out! That happened over a bet!"

Bill clearly recalled the corner of Poundwell Street and Brownson Street in Modbury, his first home. There was a printer's shop, a cobbler, the Hingstons on the corner, then a stable and harness room, pigs' houses, a policeman's house, a pumphouse and a big slaughterhouse. The slaughterhouse indirectly influenced Bill's early knowledge of songs.

His father worked as a drover, taking sheep, bullocks or pigs on the roads from Modbury to Plymouth just after the First World War. Bill, with a good perception of the workings of oral transmission, believed that the drovers were important in spreading songs.

"I think a lot of these songs came from cattle coming from Ireland to Liverpool, or else going across to Bristol. And then the drovers from the Southwest and the South going up and meeting these and exchanging a night with the blokes in the pub and picking up their songs and bringing 'em down this way.

My old Dad, as a boy, see, he was a drover. He started off as a butcher's boy, nine year old. And he was driving cattle about the roads, and one thing and another, and he sang a lot of songs from all over the damn place."

From his father Bill had songs such as *The Young Sailor Cut Down in his Prime, Where Are You Going to my Pretty Maid?* and *The Country Carrier.*

Bill's mother also sang at home. He remembered her singing a song with the chorus:

Hi dicky dicky doo ra
He's lost his fidoora
Hi dicky dicky doo ra
Dicky doo ral aye ay
Hi dicky dicky doo ra
He's lost his fidoora
Never marry a poor old man

This is a version of *Maids When You're Young.* The only complete song that Bill had from his mother was *When I Was Single.*

"I got that from my mother. So long ago as I can remember singing. My mother sung that one because her brother-in-law sung it at his wedding when he married my mother's one and only sister."

Given the words of *When I Was Single*, its performance at a wedding is notable. The singer complains that when he was single his pockets did jingle, and he wishes to be single again. He wife takes a fever, dies, he rejoices, but marries another far worse than the other. We can be sure it was sung in good spirit, but what was the song saying that would perhaps have been unacceptable in direct speech? That marriage is, after all, an economic contract? That once married you should be content with your spouse because there may be many worse? Was it the last bravado of a never-again-to-be-single man? Or inverted male chauvinism — whatever you do the woman will gain the upper hand? Whatever the case, this element in the conventional wedding celebrations is startling.

Also from his earliest days Bill remembered *Camborne Hill*. The song is said to be about a steam locomotive constructed by Richard Trevithick in 1801. As it puffed its way up a hill in the Cornish town of Camborne the horses, perhaps ruefully contemplating the implication for their future employment prospects, stood still and watched the wheels going round. The song is often heard in Cornwall. Over the years it has gathered a number of nonsensical verses. Bill learnt it from a second uncle living in Saltash, which is just in Cornwall.

Bill often told me that he went "blind with the measles" as a young child. His parents gave him a mouthorgan to play, the only musical instrument they could afford. He learnt quickly. He listened to the street musicians, many of whom were wounded during the 1914-18 War. Some went round in gangs, some on crutches played old battered squeezeboxes. There was Lancashire Jack the clog dancer and there were the Gypsies who step-danced at Modbury Fair every year. In the streets you would hear the old war songs like *It's a Long Way to Tipperary* (which Bill knew right through) or *Keep the Home Fires Burning*. From the Gypsies came the step-dance tune Bill called *The Back Hand Shovel*. On fair days there would be revelry in all four of Modbury's pubs and the Gypsies would dance on the flagstones outside. Of the more regular street musicians Bill recalled: "They'd go play in the streets with their tin cup out. Or else a bloke with one arm would have his cap on the stump, walking round. Knock on the doors. For a few coppers."

Bill's blindness did not last — probably chronic ophthalmia after the measles — and before leaving school he had worked part-time on a few farms near Totnes, having moved from Modbury. By then he had already developed a repertoire of tunes, many being popular items of the day, and a good ear for picking up songs.

Bill left the school at Staverton, the village where his family now lived, when he was thirteen, and his first full-time job was as messenger and errand boy for a dairy in the nearby market town of Totnes. After a short while, though, he settled, aged seventeen, for farm work, and took jobs on various farms for some years. His descriptions of farm life were rich in detail, often amusing, and certainly not always rosy. It very much depended on who you were working for. Bill often refers to the well-known song *The Farmer's Boy* as a "bloody fairy tale". The song tells of a wandering boy desperate for work who is eventually taken on by a kindly old couple at a farm. When they die they leave him the farm and their daughter as his bride. It has a grand tune. After one performance in a local pub Bill addressed the audience.

"Bloody fairy tale. It never happened. It never happened. Cor bugger me. Fairy tale. When I was a boy in farm houses, one place I worked at I wasn't good enough. I was good enough to milk 'is cows. Good enough to do his work when he was up bed or at market drunk. But I wasn't good enough to eat at his table. I used to 'ave to eat at a little table in the corner. I thought about making a wooden trough an' takin' it in one night. [I might have said] 'Here maister. Yer bloody pigs ate out of a trough, I might just as well ate out of the bugger'."

After a little more invective Bill remembered that my tape recorder was still running.

"You haven't bloody well recorded that 'ave 'e? Well who cares? Old bugger's dead now." He stamped on the floor and yelled out: "Can you 'ear me down there?"

If you were fortunate enough to be working for a good sort, though, the picture was different. Some of Bill's most vivid memories, as well as many of his songs, come from the period in his teens and early twenties when he worked for Tom Baker, an old Dartmoor farmer from Walkhampton who took one of the biggest farms on the Sharpham Estate. Six people — Tom, his wife, their two sons, a serving maid and Bill — lived together in a close-knit unit which seems to have been harmony itself.

Many an evening the young lad and the old man would pass together by the hearth fire. It was on such occasions that music and singing would unite them across the generations. The old man would tell tales of the moor, sing the odd song and call on the youngster to play to him on the melodeon.

"Oh yes. He'd ask me to play the squeezebox by the hearth. All the wood sawed up with a big circular saw. Didn't matter if I burnt half a copse a night as the saying goes."

I often had the feeling that history was repeating itself. Now I was sitting by the hearth with Bill. I encouraged him to tell me as much as possible. Although I couldn't have explained it, I felt that I was now finally learning about *music* in a new way, the way I needed, even if we spent the evening talking about other matters. The questions I had asked as a student composer were finally being confronted.

Songs and tales surfaced at work, as did many other types of folklore. In the normal daily round of jobs on the farm information, skills and wisdom would be passed on in traditional ways. Old Man Baker knew the importance of teaching the youngsters. He showed Bill how to make spear sticks for thatching ricks and recited a rhyme to help him remember:

To split a stick and split it well
You start at the end where the bird doth dwell

Chopping wood with an axe was done rhythmically with the aid of a cautionary cry:

Bacon and eggs
Mind your legs
WHACK

Bacon and eggs
Mind your legs
WHACK

Old Tom would potter about, changing buckets in the dairy, singing above the noise. When one of his sons told him that he could be heard all over the farm, old Tom would retort, proverbially "Better they 'ear than let 'em be deaf!"

A favourite song was *Tavistock Goosey Fair*, which Bill claimed to have picked up word for word, note for note in Tom's version. It originated as a Westcountry music-hall piece with exaggerated dialect and pronunciation, and was written by C. John Trythall and copyrighted in 1912. Along with William Weekes' slightly earlier *A Mortal Unlucky Old Chap* it has become an accepted classic of its type, known to most Devonshire singers. The original tune, with its modulations and shifts to the minor key, is difficult to sing unaccompanied, and singers have ironed out these features in various ways. The words have also changed from singer to singer, so we may say that it has become absorbed into the main current of orally transmitted songs in Devon. Tom Baker's version was more individual than most, and different from Bill's father's. In later years this became a source of amusement. "Bill don't sing the proper words," his old father told me emphatically.

Another song that Bill gathered at this time is the one variously known as *The Capable Wife, Old Father Grumble*, or simply *The Old Man in a Wood*. It tells the tale of a farmer and his wife who dispute who can do the most work in one day. To find out and settle the matter they swap roles. The man gets in a complete pickle and vows never to criticize his wife again.

A version of this song was printed in *English Folk Songs for Schools* edited by Cecil Sharp and Sabine Baring-Gould. Bill was adamant that he had never seen it printed, although he had a dim recollection of seeing it on a blackboard at school. We worked out one night that the way he sang it was his own composite version.

While working for Tom Baker Bill palled up with Bert Edmonds. Bert worked on a nearby farm, knew many songs, sang at home, less usually in the pub, and loomed largest of all in Bill's recollections of local singers.

As a younger man Bert had been a sailor and had picked up most of his songs at sea. He left the navy after losing some of his fingers when a hatch smashed down on his hand. Invalided out, he went back home and found farm work. Bill was fascinated by Bert's tales of the sea, and visited him at home to sit and listen to his songs. Bill learned how the singing sessions, known as Sing Say or Pay (or show your arse), took place on board ship:

"Probably Panama or somewhere like that. But he told me that they used to have nothing to do, and there was no drink except for the tot in their grog. Then they used to get up on top of the fo'c's'le and they'd all be lazing about, and one of 'em used to take off his buckle strap. He'd double it up and slap 'un down and, if it was given to you, you'd have to sing or tell a story. And if you didn't within a given count they'd get the strap laid on 'em."

Bert had ribald words to *The Sailor's Hornpipe* (Bill couldn't remember them) and he'd hum them through as he demonstrated the dance. Then he'd sit down again, perhaps get some playing cards out or tell another tale of the sea.

"He used to sit at home. Mostly beside the fire. And light up his old pipe, and sit there and sing away. I've heard him sing in the pub, but very rarely."

Bill described how Bert distinguished between the different types of songs and contexts.

"The songs he sang were all the sort of songs that you would get sung on the fo'c's'le of a man o' war. And some he sung were songs he picked up from people that came from other places. But if he was in a pub he wouldn't sing that type of song."

On those rare occasions when Bert did sing in the pub it would be items he had picked up off sixpenny records from Woolworth's.

Predictably, most of Bert's songs were about sailors and the sea. *Bring Me Back the One I Love* is a young woman's thoughts about her sailor lover far away, with a realistic verse showing that she expects him to be with "some other one" but consoling herself with the thought that he only thinks of her. The ubiquitous *Young Sailor Cut Down in his Prime* — he dies of VD but is given a full military funeral — was another of Bert's. So was *Give Me My Rum and Tobaccy*, a jolly effort with a good chorus, and *The Sailor's Grave* written in the style of a parlour ballad by Eliza Cook and John C. Baker and published in 1859. Bert also knew a few rustic songs such as *Buttercup Joe*.

One night as we were recording some of Bill's recollections he moved on from Bert Edmonds to Jack Norrish (nicknamed 'Doney' — why?). He gave a detailed description of the man and his songs. After a couple of hours we took a break and switched on the telly. It was showing one of those mad-things-we-have-filmed efforts that local stations are prone to. As the picture came in focus Bill shouted: "That's him! There he is! Old Jack Norrish!"

Doney Norrish had been filmed some years earlier by Westward TV doing his party piece — eating live snails. The film showed him winkling them out, holding them up so they unwound, then plopping the long slimy creatures into his mouth and swallowing them whole. He then turned to the camera and grinned.

He was elderly when the film was made. He had a waxed moustache, a wrinkled face, and a broad grin. Bill had described him as a rough old bugger. He looked it.

After a few years working for Tom Baker Bill moved off to take a job stone quarrying. His workmates were Dan Tucker, who owned the quarry, George Mathews, a staunch Chapel man who never swore, and Jack Norrish, who had been a soldier in India. This rough and ready quartet quarried the stone for the roads of the parish. The rock was drilled by hand with sledge hammers and a drill. Bill described the entire process from blasting, hammering down to size, loading on to a lorry, tipping on the roadside, and rolling in to make roads.

The process was tiring and not without minor injuries, but the old men took little notice. They couldn't afford to. It was a job of work when work wasn't plentiful. In the 1930s there was always somebody waiting for a job. The job of splitting stone had its own folk wisdom:

"There's an old saying that when you go breaking stone you look at 'un first. You size 'un up. Size the grain of 'un up, see. Then you split 'un like you would a bit of wood. There's an old saying: 'Small end of a stone, big end of a woman'.''

The initial process of drilling was a long grind in which communication was difficult. From then on, especially during the 'napping' (breaking the stone into small pieces) Jack Norrish frequently sang.

"Bugger yes. Well you had nought else to do. Spin yarns and sing, Old Jack would. 'Twas something to take the monotony off the job. What more monotonous than napping stones all day long? Oh blimee. Click clack click clack. All day long.

He'd been in India you see with the army and that, and he used to sing old songs. Old load of nonsense. Lots of words to 'em that you wouldn't be able to repeat, but that was what helped to pass the time.''

Bill applied this idea of songs to lighten a heavy job on the land as well as stone breaking.

"I'll tell you where I learnt some of these old songs. That was from soldiers who'd done their time in India and had come home. And there was only one place for 'em to go. On the farm. And you'd get hoeing in the field. Three or five of 'ee. Hoeing all in a line.

Well one of these blokes would burst into song, probably after they'd got a good quantity of cider down 'em. There was always bags of cider in the fields in they days. And they'd burst into song. It was only to pass the time away when you was hoeing. Because I mean, you could hoe bloody turnips and mangolds with your bloody eyes shut. Like using a sweeping brush. Just fo'ard and back, fo'ard and back. Us used to hoe half an acre of mangolds a day. Well you'd sing then, you see. Somebody'd start singing. Well, 'twas to pass the time away. Stop you thinking 'bout the backache probably. But the likes of Jack Norrish and they — I've heard them cracking stones and heard he sing. He used to sing a lot of they old songs.''

Doney was the main singer during stone-napping. He would sit up on an old straw bag and sing away, perhaps not realizing that much of what he sang was lodging permanently in the mind of his younger workmate.

Other noted times for music and song were just after dinner, or walking home from work in the evening. Work rarely stopped for bad weather, but in those cases where "it belted heavens hard, there was an old grove barn handy. And you'd get in the old barn out of the rain... Well then all these old yarns and songs would come up, see. As you know, I always played an old mouthorgan and squeezebox or something.''

Bill painted an endearing picture: the group of them sat around in their overalls in the old grove barn, the rain chucking it down outside, the clatter on the roof, and the Chapel man who never swore presumably not singing the risqué songs. The youngest provided the music on his squeezebox and the oldest regaled the company with his yarns and songs of army life.

Some songs stand out as Doney's — *The Soldier's Prayer* for pay, beer, the Murree Brewery, and wenches, or *Nobby Hall* ("who only got one ball but it's better than bugger all blast your eyes"). His other songs included *One of the Rakish Kind,* and a music-hall innuendo song *Let Go Eliza.* Doney Norrish also sang in the village pub, especially if his brother-in-law Dicky Reed was present. Bill waited till Lucy was out of the room before he sang some of Doney's songs. Then it was:

She had a dark and roving eye
And her hair hung down in ringlets
She was a nice girl and rakish girl
But one of the whoring kind

Pub singing was a highly democratic activity. Every song was afforded the best of attention and if someone got up to sing you could hear a pin drop. Singers also respected one another's material and operated an informal agreement not to poach songs.

Confusingly, Bill knew two pub singers with the name George Lamble. One, from the village of Cornworthy, was an old thatcher and sheep shearer who had a large repertoire. He was nicknamed 'Chainey' and had only one eye. He sang many cumulative songs such as *The Farmyard Song*, a sort of English *Old MacDonald Had a Farm* complete with animal imitations.

Another local man, Harold Turner, sang *Herring's Heads* which was also cumulative. Its final rundown goes:

Now what shall we do with the old herring's tail
Make 'em in ships and set 'em a sail
For it's herring tails, ships that sail
Herring's belly, girls called Nelly
Herring's back, boys called Jack
Herring's fins, needles and pins
Herring's eyes, puddings and pies
Herring's heads, loaves of bread
And all such things as that
For of all the fish that live in the sea
The herring is the fish for me
Ri fol lol laddity, ri fol lol laddity
Ri fol lol laddity oh

Harold worked on the next farm to Bert Edmonds. Bill remembered Harold as having very poor eyesight ("glasses like beer bottle bottoms") and he would always sing *Herring's Heads* at the drop of a hat.

"Little old short man with his breeches and leggings on, boots about two or three sizes too big. Half a pound of barley straw in each boot to keep his feet warm. Funny little man he was."

Bill was amused by the posh accent Harold affected when singing.

"Curious. Only a rough old farm labourer. Probably never been anywhere. But he seemed to put on a bit of an accent. And the blokes in the pub at Bow Bridge would echo the old chorus when it came to 'and hall sich things as that'. Because although he was an old country bloke and probably never went to school after he was nine, and yet he used to sing in a rather posh voice. Like the squire would talk in them days."

Most of the songs Bill picked up from pub singers were chorus songs, mostly funny pieces.

Lest the picture painted seems to portray a thriving singing tradition of some permanence, one which was perhaps only wiped out by the Second World War, it is worth reminding ourselves that ragtime had invaded England before Bill was born, and that the golden era of the music halls had faded in Bill's father's youth. Bill's old man had helped to set up the first moving pictures to be seen in Modbury, and the movies developed into an important source of songs. The Original Dixieland Jazz Band had toured England in 1919 when Bill was five. As far as the pubs were concerned in the 1930s:

"Jazz started to push the singing out of the pubs. Because, you see, you got people going to dance bands, you know, and the ballads sort of became too slow for the younger people that was drinking, see. And they used to say to me, even playing the squeezebox: 'Het it up a bit. Swing it.'"

The mass media had an effect on the pub repertoire in the tangible form of Woolworth's sixpenny records. Bill remembers buying his copy of the *Melody Maker* and reading through the lists of current records. Any song that was on the list could be bought in Woolworth's.

"You'd hear the song on the radio perhaps on a Monday night. You went to Woolworth's on the Friday, the pay day... I've had many a new song. Like that old ballad 'Oh I wonder yes I wonder, will the angels way up yonder'. I remember that one coming. Nipping in Woolworth's, getting the record, come home, have a wash, getting ready, put the record on to hear it. Put it back on again to hear the words, once more to hear the words. That was it. Didn't want the record after that. Go and sing it that night in the pub."

The pubs concerned were scattered over the fairly small area of South Devon between Totnes and Dartmouth where Bill flitted from job to job for a few years. Having finished stone quarrying he went back on farms for a short period and then started work on building sites, the work he stayed with until retirement. By this time he had moved to Dittisham, although site work took him over a wide area of the county.

He met his future wife in The Sportsman's Arms, a pub near Dittisham. She was working there at the time and liked many of the tunes he played. He used to play *Danny Boy* for her. They married and settled in Dittisham and raised three girls and a boy. Up to his death Lucy would ask, "Aren't you going to play tonight?" if it got past ten o'clock.

Dittisham had one old character that everybody knew: Sammy Coombes. He only knew one song, an old bawdy ballad — first written down in English in about 1620, but no doubt centuries older — about the lobster in the pisspot.

Sammy was badly malformed at birth. His photograph used to be on the wall at the Ferry Boat Inn but most of the deformities are carefully hidden from the camera. One hand was like a donkey's foot, "fetlock and all" according to Bill. The other had but one finger which was bent, and a thumb. One of his legs was so short that he needed a fifteen-inch built-up boot, and his mouth was slightly twisted with a hare lip. His response to these problems was remarkable. He worked as best he could on the river and, by all accounts, his best was first rate. Bill became almost lyrical:

"There was nothing he couldn't do in the way of steer a boat. Do anything. Except thread a needle. He could tie a trace on a fishing line quicker than you could with all your fingers.

There was no subject he couldn't talk about. I'll tell you this much — if anybody started about politics he knew it all. He was the most well read man I've ever met. And you could talk about any bloody port in the world and he knew it. You could talk about the history of the Great War — he knew it. Through reading. And swim? He could swim like a fish!"

Sammy must have been resigned to his odd appearance. He even drew attention to it. His fifteen-inch boot he called *The Ramilles* because the ship of the same name was the first to have fifteen-inch guns.

Sammy's skill with boats, his ability to navigate and his knowledge of the River Dart meant that he was never without a living. His song was usually requested on Saturday nights, and he sang it right through uncensored, although Bill reckoned that some of the earthier lines were slurred around the hare lip if strangers were present. That such a Chaucerian piece of honest vulgarity should be the signature of a man with so much to complain about as Sammy was a significant detail for Bill. Sammy didn't complain. He got on with life, learned to use what he had and made people laugh with *The Lobster Song*.

> He took the lobster home
> He couldn't find a dish
> So he put it in the pot
> Where the missus had a piss
> Singing ro tiddly oh
> Ro tiddly oh
> Ro tiddly oh tiddly oh toh toh

Bill's squeezebox followed him through the army and went with him on active service in India and Malaya. He recalled a lot of singing.

"Oh bugger! They was always singing. Everybody sung. You always had a singsong in route marching and things like that. In training you always had a singsong. And there was wet canteen. You was always singing. Sergeant's Mess singing."

A number of the songs were cumulative or number songs. At least two versions of *Old King Cole* circulated as well as a raw bawdy piece to the tune of *Scotland the Brave* ("I saw a lassie wi' a big hairy assie...!"), and the inevitable *Roll Me Over in the Clover*.

In Malaya the Devonshire Regiment lived alongside various Scots regiments, who were pretty high on obscene material according to Bill. There was also a form of barrack room Urdu which crept into some of the songs. *Chilli of Chowringee* was a parody of *Lili Marlene*.

The vast majority of twentieth-century army songs are parodies, either of old folk songs, or of popular hits of the day. Even the official musical repertoire is parodied. Regimental marches, such as the march of the Royal Engineers, became reworked as *Poor Bugger Jagger*.

"There's lots of marches got words to 'em, and if they haven't soldiers'll put 'em to 'em. There's a lovely tune called *Pageantry* which is played as an

inspection piece. I saw the Queen walking round one time. I thought to myself
— if only her knew what they blokes was singing in their heads!''

Although Bill's account of service in India had its amusing and warm side,
his overall conclusion was one of disgust for the grinding poverty and
ostentatious riches that he saw existing side by side. He had read a lot about
India in his youth.

"Used to read about these terribly rich sultans, Indian potentates and
whatnot, Maharajahs and all that. And then you see the other side of the story.
Utter poverty! My India was Kipling's India and all that nonsense. Bengal
Lancers and all that sort of stuff which you read. And then to see the utter
squalor. Bah! No!''

One evening Bill rummaged through some papers and found his regimental
photograph. It was odd to look at him there, thirty-five years younger, slightly
stouter, as his comrades knew him. And to sit with him as I knew him. He
looked at the photograph into a past I knew nothing about. "They were a great
bunch of blokes!'' There was a hint of a tremble but he admitted he was glad to
get back to Dittisham when he came out in 1952.

By then the older style singing traditions were coming under the influence of
records, the radio and, increasingly, television. In 1952 a singsong at home, at
work or in the pub was no longer a vital part of the pattern of life. At times the
surface may have looked the same. Bill recalled: "Perhaps we'd go play a game
of darts to a pub, like. And I might take the old squeezebox, like. And as soon's
you walked in they'd say 'Ah. We're going to have a singsong now. Come on.
Get going. Bugger the darts' — which would rarely happen now.

Over the top pub I used to say: 'Hingston's Half Hour'. Us used to have a
half-hour singsong. So we'd play the tunes, see. They'd expect you to play this,
that and the other thing. And sometimes for a bit of fun I'd think to meself:
'Ah. Let's go back a bit.' They'd say: 'Cor you pulled that one out of the hat'.''

The old songs were not so much on the surface. You had to dig them out.
They were becoming a *memory culture*.

Bill continued with building site jobs — laying water mains, building a
school, Paignton Festival Hall, a multi-storey car park, Torbay Hospital, and a
number of other jobs. For many of them he was the ganger on the site. The
blokes loved him. He in turn was full of praise for them. When they presented
him with a silver snuff box as a retirement present he got to his feet and thanked
them saying, "It doesn't matter who the bloody hell you've got in the office
giving orders. It's the lads that do the bloody work!'' And they cheered like
hell.

It seems that Bill learnt few complete songs in the 1950s and '60s.
Nevertheless, when he changed his loyalties from the top to the bottom pub in
Dittisham he took to leaving his squeezebox in the pub rather than taking it
home. He had a "bit of a blow" most Saturday nights. This normally consisted
of popular songs of the 1930s and '40s, community songs, and his two party
pieces *Tavistock Goosey Fair* and *The Farmer's Boy* — when anyone would
listen.

I knew Bill for over three years before I started to record him, by which time
I was getting to know his repertoire. In 1976 I recorded a handful of songs and

some background information. From then on I recorded his songs and conversation regularly. There were many times when I was unable to draw the boundary between fieldwork, research and friendship. We went to different pubs together, to Widecombe Fair, to see his daughter across the moor. In the end I gave up bothering. It was easier just to be friends. And I was learning as much.

Bill Hingston was a great communicator. I was always struck by his ability to put a song across, to compel listening, although it is true that a certain willingness on the part of those present was necessary. I had the sense that it was not only Bill that was singing to us. It was also the groups of people he had known — the work gangs, the family on the farm, the soldiers, the village pub characters. His performances gave voice to the life experience of all those who taught him the songs. Those communities almost became *our* community for the duration of each song.

Each song had a place in his mind. It was important to him that everybody knew that *The Lobster Song* — which he slightly cleaned up for general consumption — was not just a rough old tale about a daft lobster grabbing the old girl where it hurts most. It was also a celebration of Sammy Coombes. I never heard Bill sing the song without making a reference to Sammy at the end of it. Outside Dittisham he often simply muttered, half to himself, "Old Sammy". In the Ferry Boat Inn he usually gave a thumbs-up in the direction of Sammy's photograph and shouted "Alright Sammy?"

One evening I asked him whether he always thought of Sammy when he sang the song. "Yeah. Never fail. Tell you this much" — and he pointed to the river across the fields outside his living room — "I been going across here with a boat, blowing a bloody gale and the tide running, and I've heard him say: 'Keep up you bloody fool. What the 'ell you doin' down 'ere?' Bloody gospel."

Whether he knew it or not, his friends and workmates who taught him the songs exerted a powerful and audible influence. Poor old half-blind Harold Turner's funny posh voice always emerged in *Herring's Heads* on the chorus line. Bert Edmonds' songs came over with a sustained lyricism. Doney Norrish's were coarser, more comic. Tom Baker's songs were delivered in a broader Devon than the rest, and the army obscenities came forth with the plain, vigorous, unadorned style they were no doubt sung with during the War. All who heard him agreed that Bill communicated his songs exceptionally well. Why? Because unknown to today's audiences, the old farm hands, stone quarrymen and nappers, council roadmen, the Chapel man who never swore, the army comrades, Sammy Coombes, and maybe even the folk enthusiasts of the later years — all figured so vividly in Bill's imagination.

But I couldn't escape the difficult truth that were it not for the interest of people like myself, those with a conscious and ideological interest in folk music, Bill would have been virtually without context most of the time. The local pub may be a good place to dig up old songs, play the tunes to each other, but there were countless times when we played to ourselves; even Bill's peer group were not always particularly interested.

During the tourist season the bar was packed. Occasionally a group of holidaymakers would gather round fascinated by him, often assuming, incidentally, that I was his son. (I got plenty of pints bought on the strength of that.) But the days when you could hear a pin drop when someone was singing are well gone. Bill was aware of this.

"I've been down there when you haven't been down and they've said to me: 'Come on then. Aren't you going to play?' And I've sat in the old armchair playing away and I've thought to meself I'm bloody sure no bugger's listening. And I play the *Dead March* from *Saul*. And I've looked up and they've said: 'What've 'e stopped for?' I've said: 'What was the last tune I played?' 'Dunno, but you was playing.' Bloody true."

Bill had his own explanation. He blamed transistor radios and argued that people got used to music as a noise in the background. This means that music is subconsciously heard for much of the time instead of being consciously appreciated.

"I've lost count the number of times I've played a tune and after I've finished somebody's asked me to play it. They've subconsciously heard it so it's come into their head. They've heard you playing. It's just something that's rung a bell unto 'em."

So if anything gave him his life back, as he often said, it was those of us who clustered around the folk revival. He learnt a number of songs from folk enthusiasts, and made a few trips away from his home base to other pubs, folk clubs, local village hall functions, Women's Institutes, an Old People's Home, children's parties, local schools (where he was brilliant), local television and radio.

It wasn't a one-way friendship. He taught me to play the concertina. His method was disarmingly simple. If he played a tune I didn't know I used to stop and listen. That would never do. "Play up!" he'd yell. "I don't know this one" I'd say, to which he would reply "You will if you play it!" Tell that to the academies. Furthermore, it worked a treat.

At times I tried to convince myself that a renewal of local singing and music-making was not only desirable but possible. I based a lot of this on my close association with Bill. An honest evaluation would have shown that this was a vain hope. If I'd really listened to Bill I would have grasped this earlier. He once told me most forcefully that it's up to each generation to make its own music. "No good living in the bloody past" he used to say.

But it took his death to force me to be really honest. He went peacefully, telling a story to some local kids who thought he'd fallen asleep. The reason I was so upset at his funeral was not merely that I'd lost a friend. I also lost a myth, a philosophy. For all he had taught me about music and communication, I had perhaps relied too much on him being there. As the parson delivered a moving speech about the loss of a village character my own mind was in a ferment. It was going over the questions that originally made me decide to give up composing 'for a while' (it was now fifteen years). I was well aware that Bill's death was destined to be the creative shove that I needed. I was also remembering the many times when someone asked him if a knew a particular tune. He'd point to his squeezebox and say, "They'm all in there. It's only a matter of getting them out".

Suite

Con Moto / Band One / Band Two / Band Three / Prelude

PROGRAMME NOTE

Folklore and folk music, because of their supposedly collective nature, their suggestions of dark, forgotten, unconscious areas of experience, function powerfully as myths. They may convince us that we can recover areas we feel we lack. The appeal of allegedly pagan festivals is a case in point. Are there untapped areas of antediluvian intuition, sexuality, abandon, Saturnalian pre-structuring, which were destroyed by the successive floods of religious repression, mercantilism, capitalism, materialism, and poor old Descartes?

So we read the signs in the way we wish to. The hood-like mask on the Cornish Padstow Hobby Horse which roisters around the streets on May Day suddenly becomes a sign for comparison with mysterious African connections, which, of course, we can prove by reference to (selected) ethnographic evidence. The repetitive music and relentless drumming recalls the trance-like chants of shamanism. And so on. The way to rediscover the lost causes within ourselves is, for some, to construct and act out folklore. The outline is revived, peopled by our assumptions about its function.

The catch is that it is always someone else's folklore, never our own. It is this rural tradition, those Gypsies, a corpus of industrial songs, fertility rituals, proletarian ballads, a distant tribe, someone else's jazz. These are taken as nature (how things are) rather than myth. The reasoning goes: if only we could create in the manner of these models all would be well. It was Bartók's point in a monograph which Ewan MacColl was fond of quoting. We had to learn to create as the folk create. But why? What's missing? The fact that we feel a lack indicates that the potential is in ourselves. Surely.

Who are these 'folk'? If they really do create differently from the rest of us is there not good reason for that? How can we speak of 'folk disciplines' when the whole point is that there aren't any? (In twenty years of fieldwork I never met any 'folk' who knew of such disciplines.)

Is it merely by chance that traditions have been preserved in certain localities? If they are so basic, why have they been eroded elsewhere? Does their persistence in some places relate to other factors — economic, social — rather than a local desire to preserve some damn fool bit of sexy ritual that may or may not predate Christ? And finally, what do these expressions mean to the people who perpetuate them? Does it matter to them that the mask they

*use, or the steps of their dance, or the contours of their song recall something
that we know about but they don't? (Most of them have an ironically tolerant
attitude to an outsider's theories. When I asked the Minehead Hobby Horse
team why they continued with their custom every May I got the perfectly
logical reply: "If we don't who will?")*

*These realizations come slowly, painfully and inconveniently. Having
thought I had found my mud I seemed to need even more mud. I was stuck in
the mud. By exteriorizing I was still avoiding the issue.*

- 1 -
Con Moto

Dick French's singing friend Jim Sanders farms a high part of Exmoor. His
farm buildings present a ramshackle appearance but they are not uncared for.
The main house is an old building with a big kitchen. Electricity comes from a
generator outside. The layout of the yard has changed little for as long as it
matters. Part of the ground is concreted over. Some of the fencing relies on old
wooden stakes. These are often joined by modern wire mesh. There's an old
stable with a newish corrugated iron roof, and a tidy number of plastic bags,
breeze blocks, modern taps and troughs scattered around.

Allowing my eye to wander over this scene one afternoon I had the
sensation that I was looking at a visual representation of the local singing
tradition. Its basic structure had been shaped years ago yet it was not resistant
to new influences. Just as Jim would sing his Doris Day hit back to back with
an old dialect piece, so he would use old stone or new breeze blocks depending
on what he had available and how well they did the job.

This simple observation stayed with me for a long time. Dick's farm and
yard told the same tale: no sentiment, no attachment to the outsider's pretty
romances of the way life should be lived. And the same was true of the
musical repertoire and manner of presentation. What did it matter if someone
in London had dreamed up some theory about vocal style, even if it had been
based on painstaking historical and ethnographic research? Like the old stone
wall, if it didn't do the job in the present context it could go to hell. A few
breeze blocks would do just as well.

This simple analogy wasn't restricted to the work environment. It began to
serve as a model for the way people dressed or treated their tractors, cars,
cattle, pubs. If there were things that hadn't changed for decades this was only
because no need had presented itself. If there was still a pisspot beneath the
bed it was because it was a long way to the loo.

I noticed the same accumulation, discarding and adaptation in more abstract
matters such as local religion, values, attitudes, socializing. If it worked — use
it. If it didn't — chuck it. But if it *was* used it was used to the hilt. Every
ounce of value would be squeezed out.

And so it seemed with music and songs. Dick knew a couple of old songs
which I prized, but he rarely sang them, claimed he couldn't remember them.

If he dragged them out at all it was due to my insistence, not because he thought they got the maximum out of the situation in the pub. I had to admit that when he sang what he really wanted he was electrifyingly funny.

Now!
When (h)I was a lad and a farmer's lad
I looked after the farmer's pigs
And the pigs was weeing 'ere
And another weeing there
Here a wee
There a wee
(H)everywhere a wee
For to plough and sow, reap and mow
And be a farmer's boy
And be a farmer's boy

Left to their own devices without the intervention of even the most tolerant folklorist these local singers were uncannily capable of encapsulating their entire experience of life in each five-minute song. They didn't have to shift values or attitudes in order to sing.

I did. My singing involved a degree of selection, parody, denial. Ultimately I could only be an admirer, not a real participant. When I sang in their pubs I might fool others, but I knew I was for ever a visitor.

This was accentuated with the Gypsies. Their status as a marginal group doubly ensured that. Yet the same analogies seemed to hold good. Living in uneasy relation with the host culture they had, for centuries, established their way of life on the basis of reacting to what *gaujos* (non-Gypsies) determined. *Gaujos* abandoned cars. Gypsies used or recycled them as scrap or parts. *Gaujos* changed the rules about 'loitering' (camping). Gypsies had to respond. The Romany I heard spoken was a *lingua franca* rather than a genuine language. It substituted words within English syntax. (You got a *mooey* like a *grai* = You've got a mouth like a horse.)

Their song traditions likewise preserved many of the discarded ways of the host culture. They had preserved the many vintage classic ballads and broadsides long after the rest of society had forgotten them. The younger singers recycled the recently abandoned Elvis Presley, Jimmie Rodgers, Patsy Cline songs. This was consistent. Even in the Country music field none of them knew much of more progressive singers like Emmylou Harris or Guy Clarke. Like their clothing preferences their music was just out of fashion.

Yet with all these local singers it was not a simple matter of reacting mechanically to the dominant values. The material, once received, was hammered into shape creatively, making it distinctly unlike its sources. The Gypsy Country and Western singer would never fool anyone with half an ear. They always sounded like Gypsies. Tradition gave them boundaries but not rules. They still had to create, and in creating they both affirmed and remade their reality.

Were I content to be an anthropologist I could have left it at that, documenting other people's cultures with as few conscious value judgements as I was capable of. But this was beyond me. I began to think it was beyond anyone. It was obvious that any form of intervention was not objective, even when the observation was apparently passive. I was having an effect, influencing matters. I was glad to learn that subatomic physicists had to accept the same conclusion. Even mere observation is transformative.

Seeking the mud I realized that I was one of its most essential ingredients. I couldn't answer one of my original questions: what do people do to make music when left to their own devices? There were two reasons: culture and tradition *are* our own devices, and secondly I was always there. These realizations led to a crisis marked by inactivity.

For some time I had been part-funded by Southwest Arts as a community artist. This only contributed to the crisis. The local traditions, I argued, were community arts *par excellence*. They were locally generated and only the most ethnocentric bourgeois could claim they were not 'art'. My role as I saw it was to encourage, animate and document, all of which I did with some accomplishment. So I got funded.

But questions nagged. The local traditions seemed to prove that no matter how much an outsider may value certain creative expressions, if a group of people lost their need for them they would simply abandon them. It was patronizing in the extreme to claim that this was a shame. Why? What if people were just as happy without? What proof did we have that they were really happy with? By whose standards?

Then again, if you kept your ear to the ground and took note of the occasions and details of some modern folk celebrations you were in for some shocks — the Queen's Jubilee, stag nights with strippers, the church calendar, welcome home our lads from the Falklands knees-ups, *Jerusalem* at the WI. Some community artists I knew genuinely believed that it was part of their task to aid and abet. I didn't. But on the other hand I didn't see much need to oppose either. I certainly couldn't accept that the end of my quest was blowing up balloons in the village hall and calling it art, but it didn't matter much if someone else wanted to do that.

What I did not do until depression forced it upon me was to honour my own creativity. It seemed that all my work for the past decade and a half had been directed *outwards* via ideologies. To put it plainly, one took an action because it appeared to conform to what one believed. Actions that one might have wished to take could often be excluded because they were taboo according to the belief system. Self-conscious ideology is a poor motivation for expressive action. With it come morals, denials, taboos, funding, frustration, and self-righteousness. I learnt from observation and experience that the only ideology worth having was none at all. I am undisturbed by the contradictory nature of this proposition.

As my imposed (by funding) or self-imposed roles crumbled to nothing I sensed the screaming insanity of the whole situation. The folk revival singer had found the folk revival irrelevant to local folk traditions (it wasn't, but it felt that way) and staked his claim firmly in the village halls, farms and pubs. The folklorist became aware of the mythologies of his own position. How could you be a folklorist one minute and not the next? I could not view the people I worked with as informants. They were friends. Consciousness of one role implied observing the other. The community artist saw himself as phoney. When people have viable forms of expression which serve their purposes what need is there for artists to come in and redirect the traffic?

It might be objected that not everyone has a local tradition which meets their needs. My studies of modern folkloristics with its broadening of the scope of the subject at least taught me to be highly suspicious of such a proposition. Is it really true that the vernacular culture of the rural populations "suffered considerably in the course of the Industrial Revolution and subsequently received even more deadly blows at the hands of industrial and city planners" — as leading community artist, Su Braden, once wrote?

Put it to the test. In my areas of operation I extended the folklore concept to include any and every form of grass roots music-making. This meant anything outside the mainstream classical and mass-popular commercial axis. Although it was true that the older 'folk' traditions had had their day in most places, a modicum of research revealed an amazingly high number of handbell ringing teams, a thriving church bell ringing tradition, rock and roll groups, Country and Western singers, dance bands of many different idioms, a national movement of street bands, choirs, trad jazz in pubs, a developing interest in contemporary styles of jazz, brass and silver bands, and even folk revivalists, many of whom had felt the need to depart from the formalities of folk clubs.

This extremely healthy state of music at the roots (even the word 'roots' betrays a prejudice — what is the flowering?) raises questions. If, like the old-style folk pioneers — Baring-Gould, Sharp, Lloyd, Kennedy, MacColl — we define 'folk' by idiom it is perfectly possible, as some American scholars have done with greater success than their British counterparts, to say what its features are. We might list typical melodic formations, scales, formal and metrical matters, poetic style and so on. These could be taken as the blueprint, and anything which didn't conform (allowing ourselves some leeway) would be outside the scope. In which case we could virtually cross England off the folk map, for what little remains as 'folk', in this formulation, is part of history.

There are immense problems with this approach. It doesn't recognize that even in the past (recent or remote) the lines were not so finely drawn. Virtually every folk song collector who has taken this line has had to edit, one might almost say censor, each informant's repertoire. There are good grounds for smelling a socio-psychological projection here. Which takes us back to Romanticism and the search for the pure stream, the Holy Grail, that the lady with the copper boiler knew nothing about.

Or we can take another approach. We can look at the values, the context, the typical functions of this music. This was the way that was forced upon me by sustained experience in the field. People were not offering me 'folk songs' by the old definition — or relatively few of them. They were showing me how they used music and singing to relate to one another in their own environment, not in the least stuffed up by what folklorists thought they should do. Having seen this I automatically broadened the scope to include any and every form of music-making outside the popular and classical traditions. If I wanted to preserve a category for the old songs which had originally claimed my attention (many of which I still find beautiful — I'm entitled to my taste) I could muck about with words and counterpose 'folk song' to 'music as folklore' — which I did for a while. But essentially it made little real sense.

I sensed a danger. If every music at the roots could claim my attention as a folklorist, why was I making this distinction between 'roots' and 'not roots'. Didn't all music function in similar ways? Wasn't a string quartet at the Wigmore Hall just as contextualized, just as functional, just as capable of expressing all that needed expression? I got terribly confused.

I did work out a system for profiling events. You could apply it to anything from Wagner's *Ring* to a children's skipping song. It did allow me to make some apparently rational evaluation of musical (or other) events. But it was a creation of my mind. What it showed me was that no matter how I evaluated the categories of folk, classical and popular I was still left with two questions: how did I respond to the music? and what was it signifying? — neither of which could really be accounted for. All I really knew was that, as previously outlined, folk implied an attitude rather than anything directly measurable. And that attitude could be found in many of the musical forms I had not previously considered as folk.

It may be true that a sophisticated critic would detect within these forms of music limitations, attitudes and restrictions they would like to challenge, encoded ideologies which suggest a need for change (according to other equally fallible ideologies, incidentally). But apart from the fact that this would also be true of all folk, popular and classical music to date, how would the transformation be effected? Not, as I had discovered, by, uninvited, trying to reorganize or merely 'revive' what was already in existence. Nor by inventing new so-called vernacular techniques and frameworks and introducing these to the unsuspecting — the aim being to manipulate them (from the best of motives, of course). Nor, indeed, by arts administrators creating policies and casting round for appropriate, skint or ambitious monkeys to carry them out. No, funded and recognized or not, our grass roots (there's another myth for you) musical life is varied and rich and survives very well, thank you.

I began to sense that if I genuinely sought transformative experience through music, for myself and others, I ought to have the decency to own up to how I felt and get on with my own work and bugger the consequences. If I died in the attempt it would be better than never being born.

Although I regarded both the folk and community arts movements as useful phases I now floated in the chasms that I had allowed into my own creative life. Community arts in particular had been high on all those things that smack of patriarchy: ideological debate, missionary work, administration, organization, forging links (if critically) with existing structures, none of which, despite being male, I gave a fig for. With moral injunctions and taboos surrounding personal talent, artistic enquiry and individual vision it was becoming clear that the myth of 'the people', *Kratos*, could, if we didn't watch out, turn into a Frankenstein's monster.

It was soon to occur to me, mainly via contact with Jungians and Buddhists, that what I saw as contradictions had their roots in dualistic thought. There was assumed to be a 'people' *out there* which could be transformed by artists doing ideologically challenging things to / with / for them. But if the person *in here* felt compelled by denial, taboo or radical morals, then what was done *out there* would resonate about as audibly as a fart in a thunderstorm.

Platforms and conventions of practice (even radical ones) belonging to movements had to be thoroughly dumped. I was not quite ready to begin composing again, however. Just a little more observation was necessary. I became fascinated by street bands. The village singers had been soloists. I needed a handle on how larger groups could operate.

- 2 -
Band One — The King's Korner Jazz Band

Styles's Pewsey Band led the first Pewsey (Wiltshire) carnival procession in 1898. By the time the thirty-strong band made its first LP in 1982 it had been known as The King's Korner Band for as long as anyone cared. The instruments ranged over brass, saxes, a hose pipe, mouthorgans, recorders, accordions and melodeons, drums, cymbals, a dustbin and a tea tray.

The sleeve note proudly boasts: "Eighty-four years later, without break for war or tempest, King's Korner Band still marches on". During the 1939-45 War the band had been reduced to two drums and an accordion, but it still went out on carnival week.

The band has an abandoned attitude to music. Outrageous costumes are worn, including drag and many hats. One of the players was asked by a BBC interviewer what qualifications were needed to become a member. The reply was: "To drink gallons of beer and play out of tune". It is true that there are rough edges.

Tradition has it that the band goes out on a particular day before the big carnival. It sets out from the same pub each year, beginning with the same tune, the ironically titled *Cooper's Arms March Past* (they never march *past* any pub). There is a set route, certain tunes being associated with particular pubs and places.

The repertoire is a hotch-potch of well-known standards — *Waltzing Matilda, Scotland the Brave, The Happy Wanderer, Tipperary, Onward Christian Soldiers, My Old Man's a Dustman*, plus a few trad jazz / skiffle numbers such as *Down by the Riverside*. The full name of the band is now The King's Korner Jazz Band.

The formula is to belt out the tune good and strong with anyone who wants to playing parts. Although overlaid with military drumming styles the music swings. Occasionally one section is featured alone but there are no solos.

The line-up gives away the democratic ethos of the band. Some brass and sax players, for example, are competent jazz musicians. A handful of folk enthusiasts add weight, texture and a lot of melody with squeezeboxes. But there are also half a dozen mouthorgans and recorders, at least ten percussionists and a number of rhythm guitars. The mix is between 'posh'

instruments which generally cost a lot of money and homely cheaper ones that
hang around many a home and can be played with rudimentary technique.

The approach is not intimidating yet there is care and musicianship in the
playing. The band has a style formed out of doing rather than thinking. Those
who wish have plenty of opportunity to break away from the plain melody.

- 3 -
Band Two — The Grand Band

I regarded The King's Korner Band as an inspiring idea. I made a list of
everyone I was regularly in contact with in Devon who had a musical
instrument whether they could play it or not. I circulated a letter and invited
them to the first rehearsal of The Grand Band. Quite a few heard about it by
rumour too.

We met monthly over a period of about a year. On one occasion we had
twenty players: five piano accordions, a melodeon, a concertina, tin whistle,
three violins, flute, tea chest bass, two guitars, mandolin, clarinet, electric
organ, and two percussionists.

The idea was not to manufacture an imitation of The King's Korner Band.
The dynamics which constitute such a tradition elude deliberate creation. As
we had no annual incentive such as a carnival it was obvious that occasions for
performance would have to be sought out or invented. I had visions of The
Grand Band on the seafront, in carnival parades, playing for parties and local
hops.

I consciously felt the influence of The Scratch Orchestra behind the new
idea. The draft constitution drawn up by Cornelius Cardew, Howard Skempton
and Michael Parsons contained a parodying reference to 'popular classics'
which would become part of the Scratch repertoire. This would depend on only
some members of the orchestra being able to play the written parts from, say, a
Beethoven symphony. The others would busk along, trying to play as best they
could.

The 'popular classics' were from the concert tradition. In playing them
incompetently the 'right' way to play them was subtextually stressed.

If the ground was shifted from 'popular classics' to straight popular tunes
with no Ur-text the elements of parody and irony would recede, so I believed.
It should be possible to take a repertoire, popular and broadly 'folk', and
approach it non-meticulously. A few players who could play the tunes and
keep time would hold the large ensemble together. Gradually the others could
learn the tunes more accurately if they desired, although they would be under
no pressure to do so.

I made cassettes of the repertoire and sent them to everyone so that they
could familiarize themselves with the shape of the tunes. I also wrote them out
in conventional notation for those who could read music. There would be no
barrier to occasional tuition if required.

I could 'hear' an ensemble in which well-known tunes were recognizably
played. Highly skilled or adventurous musicians could contribute virtuosity and
ideas in improvising over the basic tunes. They might add parts, solos, play in

another key, whatever they liked. Yet even complete beginners would be important in providing outline and texture. Although there may be a hierarchy of skill there would not be one of value and function. I was still operating according to self-conscious ideology, and this approach suggested the situation I had seen amongst the village singers in their pubs.

Musicians would be told that if they couldn't play the tune they could play anything whether it appeared to fit or not. 'Wrong' notes indicated wrong thinking. Technical limitations could be made functional. If some could play three notes on an instrument that was enough for the time being, until they learnt a fourth. But the need to learn more would come from the experience of playing, not from textbook-style training.

It felt like the most democratic idea I had yet produced.

From the first meeting I realized that the idea was seriously flawed. With the exception of a brilliant jazz musician who came because his girlfriend did, no players of any developed technique attended at all. I was confronted with an ocean of beginners. Obviously (when you think of it) highly skilled players already have their outlets and ensembles they regularly play with. They also expect to be paid. My belief that even a few would be interested was naive. They were not being asked into music pure and simple. They were being invited to try out a philosophy of music.

So I had the task of creating the band from scratch. It was clear that these players wanted to read notes, play the tunes, or thought that was the way to make music. To a man and a woman they assumed that if you could play the notes you were doing it 'right'.

A typical session was that in the back room of The Three Crowns in Chagford in January 1985 when a complement of twenty players attended. We bashed through *The Black Velvet Band*, *The Keel Row*, *Early in the Morning*, *Drink Up Thy Cider*, *Cockles and Mussels*, *Little Brown Jug* and a few more. There were friends from the local pubs, the village postman, a few vaguely alternative types, and the inevitable teachers.

Attempting to broaden the scope of the repertoire I had included the Rodgers and Hart standard *The Lady is a Tramp*. The postman voted this one out because his single row mouthorgan didn't have the notes. Anyway, he didn't like it. He happened to be one of the best 'folk' players around with a sizeable repertoire of local step-dance tunes.

The attraction for most of the members of the band was the chance to play in a big group. In order to do this the repertoire had to suit everyone. Therefore the jazz-influenced tunes were ruled out because not all could relate to them. Tunes which demanded any degree of chromaticism or key-changing had to be avoided due to the limitations of melodeons and mouthorgans. Unfamiliar tunes, even within this narrower range, had to be taught by rote, a process which reminded many, including myself, uncomfortably of school. This left a set of restrictions which defined the style of the band. All tunes were sixteen or thirty-two bars in length. They were in 4/4, 3/4, or occasionally 6/8 time. They didn't modulate or include chromatic notes. If they went above a moderate tempo many members found them technically difficult.

On a few occasions I encouraged players to abandon the notes entirely and play anything that might fit. We tried this once with the music-hall song *Daisy Daisy*, chosen because everyone without exception knew the shape. It worked a treat. The members of the band claimed to enjoy the experience of loose cacophony but they seemed to regard this as private fun. They still wanted to learn the notes. I had brought into being an amateur band. Struggling with the influence of community arts philosophy I had been attempting an aesthetic which blurred amateur-professional distinctions. The amateurs didn't want that, and the professionals didn't turn up.

The Grand Band had one real success when it played in a barn for a party. Two of its members lived in a farmhouse with barns and outhouses in mid-Devon. They were regular party-givers. The Grand Band sat at one end of the barn, about a dozen strong, and bashed through its repertoire. I still have the tape. For that particular situation it worked well. The sound was joyous, a little like skiffle without the vocals.

It also stimulated a few of its members to learn their instruments according to the book, some of whom have since become quite accomplished. So it served its purpose. But the band folded. It may have been that many members had to travel a long way (Devon is a big county). Or that its limitations determined its natural life. Or that my enthusiasm began to wane. Probably all three.

The musical limitations of The Grand Band, particularly the messy sound of wall-to-wall squeezeboxes, forced me to look elsewhere. Having discovered how restricting the raw could be I was now prepared for a degree of refinement. I began to notice a local ensemble called The Ambling Band.

- 4 -

Band Three — The Ambling Band

'Amble': to move at a smooth or easy pace. My introduction to The Ambling Band was at a village fete in the summer of 1985. Having struck up their first tune they moved at a smooth and easy pace to a remote corner of the field. Saxes and brass wafted across, occasionally filling in spaces left in a gentle breeze.

Dave Murphy: "I have the feeling that it could fall apart. Or rather it doesn't exist until certain individuals get together and make it do something".

They smoothly eased their way back to the madding crowd and the bottle stalls, hoopla and roasting lamb. And carried on with their set.

That day they were a five-piece. Their minimum was four. They had been known to field a side of twelve. The most I saw was a nine-piece: four saxes, flute, trombone, tuba, two percussionists.

Sax player Mick Green: "As long as you cover a range of parts you're OK. The more players there are they simply double up".

The nine-piece band played at a folk club I was involved in running. Their music made no reference to what was generally accepted as 'folk'. People started to dance. They don't do that at folk clubs. Did I detect a nervousness amongst some members of the audience? If they admitted enjoying themselves physically where did that leave the standard folk club fare?

The Ambling Band included some full-time musicians, but most of its members were teachers or college lecturers of one kind of another. Its repertoire included some Renaissance dances, Latin and African dance tunes, a Gabrielli *Canzone a 4*, some jazz pieces, *Jealousy Tango*, and *Abide With Me*. They first played *Abide With Me* in 1984 at Torrington in North Devon, having been booked for the day by the local Plough Theatre. The band processed through the town, picked up stray instrumentalists who then came to a workshop, and appeared in concert that evening playing what they'd just learnt. Poor publicity and the FA Cup left them with a meagre audience. Truth to tell they played to one, a bloke on holiday from Kent. He was delighted.

The band was instigated by trombonist Andy Langford. He had picked up the basic ideas from the Bristol Musicians' Co-operative. People from differing musical backgrounds came together to share experiences and pool resources. The South Devon version started with the same idea.

Mick Green again: "Most people get together because they like the same sort of music — jazz groups, folk groups or whatever — but we actually got together because we played instruments — and then tried to find the music that we all liked. We came somehow from the other end. So we have all these people and then we're thinking: what can we play?"

The band defined its repertoire as it went along. Eclectic though it was there was unity of approach and a strong corporate identity.

Andy introduced the idea of rehearsals beginning with exercises: singing, humming, dismantling the instruments, discovery. Doing was more important than achieving. The band could integrate mixed skills from beginners to advanced players. Novices, at one time, breezed in and out of the rehearsals.

To begin with they played in the open air, experimented and improvised a lot. The challenge of street music appealed to Dave Murphy, one of the sax players: "Playing off the sides of houses and things when the street narrows. All that is very exciting."

Problems set in when the band was invited to play indoors. At a Labour Party benefit they shambled rather than ambled, had no clear programme, went on too long. They decided they needed to be more disciplined as a performance band. This was their response to the contradictions between an open ensemble playing when it liked, where it liked, with a non-discriminatory policy towards membership, and the need to offer a presentation for public consumption. The open democracy of the original had to modify.

The looseness of approach was compromised the more the band played in public. They had to say who was and wasn't in the band. If new people kept turning up for rehearsals the whole band had to start from the beginning again. On one occasion they asked a complete beginner to leave.

At one point Mick Green thought the band had gone too far in the direction of tightness. Working from parts and playing set pieces lessened the improvisational feel of The Ambling Band. "We seem to have tightened. Now it needs loosening off a bit." The members of the band mainly came from a jazz-contemporary background, and you could hear this in virtually everything they played. In their rendition of *Eternity* you were back at a New Orleans funeral — slurs, slides, inflections and all. There were many echoes of progressive and Latin jazz styles. Their rendition of *Abide With Me*-with-soul, often featuring some good free blowing from Murphy, always reminded me of Rahsaan Roland Kirk's treatment of *The Old Rugged Cross* — a number The Ambling Band also played.

The culmination of my experience with The Ambling Band was at a festival in Bristol in which bands from all over the country met up for a weekend. I had no idea there was such a widespread movement with a broad similarity of approach. Something like twenty bands gathered for a mass blow on College Green and although there was a fair amount of excitable honking the message was clear. These people had taken control of their music. They had done so by developing their own styles and repertoires.

They constructed repertoire on the simple basis that folk musicians had used for ages: by playing what they wanted to play, what seemed appropriate and enjoyable. There was no doctrine of 'folk' or 'jazz'. Most of the bands resisted such labelling. And, of course, it made them unmarketable, which was a plus for their philosophy. The only form of exchange they took on was musical.

But The Ambling Band seemed to have a natural life-span dictated to some extent by the contradictions in its approach. Having settled into a more or less fixed line-up the band suffered a crisis when some players moved on and there was no one else available to play bass lines. Those remaining had become so used to their arrangements that they didn't seem complete without bass parts. So the band folded. Had it still been following its original *open* democracy it wouldn't have needed to, but it had become a performance unit.

From time to time the band resurfaces but now it's a collection of players rather than a unit with an inner drive.

The Ambling Band was crucial in adjusting my vision. I argued that it was a 'folk' band if the word had any contemporary (as opposed to antiquarian) meaning. I was also aware that few people would see it that way, although some members of the band did. But this was really only playing with words and concepts.

The real impact of The Ambling Band was its non-doctrinal approach to music-making. It played Christmas carols in shopping precincts and village halls. It played progressive jazz, rock and roll, trad jazz. It embarked on an idea to provide music for village dances, playing its own music, thirties' standards for ballroom dancing, employing a caller for folk dances. Yet it was not eclectic. And this was the intriguing thing. It always sounded like itself.

I wrote out a folk tune, *The Boscastle Breakdown*, added a few countermelodies, a bass line, and left it to the band to work out how they wanted to play it. On one level (the analyst's) you could say it sounded like South African township jazz with an English triple stamp to remind us of where it came from. But nobody ever said that — it was just The Ambling Band. I called the result *A Trip to Boscastle*.

At the height of the band's career I wrote a soprano saxophone solo for Mick Green, one of the band's most regular players, to the accompaniment of a handbell ringing team from a local community, Kingskerswell, with myself on piano. It was based on a tune collected from MacColl and Seeger's published collection of Gypsy songs. It was a lightweight piece but it taught me what I needed to know — plus a lot about handbell playing. It was performed in a concert for the local arts society.

For the same concert I took the hymn *Abide With Me* (already in the band's repertoire) and arranged it for handbells. The band played from a gallery, with the bellringers on stage. It was wonderful.

Finally I wrote a full-length score for the band. It seemed that as the band itself had a corporate identity which pervaded any music it played, this identity, this attitude, could be allowed to inform a much more contemporary piece.

Fool's Holiday was based on a drum rhythm as used by the Minehead Hobby Horse musicians on May Day. This was played throughout a long first section with no variation except in volume. Woven over this were melodic fragments arranged on a large page like a game, with a system for getting round the 'board'. The system made sure that certain phrases would be repeated, but there was no attempt to arrange how or when the melodic fragments would occur in relation to the rest of the texture.

An inspiration behind the piece was the archetypal figure of the 'trickster' which Jung and others had written about at length. The 'trickster' is amoral and causes havoc because he doesn't yet understand social boundaries to behaviour; he changes form and challenges normality by disregarding it. (Charlie Chaplin is often held up as a twentieth-century example.)

The first section of the music worked by playing similar tricks. Players knew what they would be playing but they had no idea of who would be playing what alongside them. I made an effort to ensure that most of the phrases would counterpoint with each other but there were deliberately fuzzy areas which threw players back on their own resources — whether to pause, keep playing, or, as rehearsals developed, to improvise.

The second section of the music was all percussion. It took us into darkness, beginning sparsely and concluding in a climax of unison rhythm — the Minehead Hobby Horse motif. Finally a repetitive jazz-like phrase took the piece into a loud closing ceremony.

Almost from the outset I realized that the piece was theatrical. I spoke to a theatre director, Pete Kiddle, about the possibility of making a theatre/dance event from this music. He was fired by the idea and produced a show using his company, Theatre Of Public Works, plus a number of students. There were masked figures, characters on stilts, fire-eaters, tightrope walkers, jugglers, mime, and a beautifully constructed Hobby Horse, all of whom acted out a scenario which lasted about an hour. The following year the show went to a festival in Luxembourg. Theatre parts were shared with local young people who presented a new version alongside some members of the original cast.

- 5 -
Prelude

It is possible to avoid the issue all your life. You can spend years testing the water and never plunging in. It's a favourite pastime of intellectuals — getting

the theory right before taking action. Which can mean taking no action at all.
Or maybe taking evasive action.

Democracy. So whom does it refer to? Which people? Or person? What's
the nearest example you know? Exactly. So why have you been pinning your
hopes on theories, myths, other people? Not even a baboon would look for
permission to follow instincts. If society has one clear purpose it is to confuse
those who would be confused.

Bill Hingston died in 1986. A few other village singers had recently gone
too. A.L. Lloyd was dead. Charles Parker, who had produced the MacColl-
Seeger radio ballads, followed soon after. MacColl, after a battle with his
health, departed a few years later. Cornelius Cardew (tragically young),
Morton Feldman soon...

Soon after Bill's death my car spontaneously burst into flames in a car park.
By the time the Fire Brigade arrived it was a wreck. A huge crack was
discovered down the side of the house I was living in. The building was
pronounced unsafe.

With a generation of elders rapidly disappearing, plus a series of uncanny
disasters flowing gracelessly into one another, it was clear that something was
up. Interpret things how you like. My conclusion was clear: a lack of
attentiveness to life's processes spirals into forms of destruction. The
depression was acute and creative. I had obviously been propelling myself
there in order to proceed.

In the midst of what can only be described as personal agony I came across
a passage in a book by a Jungian, M. Esther Harding, that flashed across my
life with the intensity of tea with the Buddha.

"Such is man's inner freedom and hubris. Unless he accepts his own inner
guidance, he becomes a mere puppet of fate. If he sets himself up against the
inner voice, asserting that he is free to choose what he wants, he inevitably
becomes the victim of the dragon. *Only when he voluntarily chooses that
which he must inexorably do has he any free will at all.*" (my italics)

I kept a notebook in which I copied such short passages exhorting people to
be themselves — Jung, Gnostic teachers, Eastern sages. One of my favourites
was: "If you bring forth what is within you, what you bring forth will save
you. If you do not bring forth what is within you, what you do not bring forth
will destroy you". Amen.

Considering the implications of this collected wisdom it was clear that now
was the time to start composing music again, a process I had already begun
with *Fool's Holiday*. Immediately I was confronted by all those questions I
had been asking two decades earlier. But now, with those years of experience,
other traditions, other debates, I had the courage to rephrase the questions into
statements. Here are some of them.

✓   Notation is anything that causes music to be made.

✓   It is not always necessary.

✓   There are plenty of ways of making music. They are all OK.

✓   Academic disciplines are not necessary, although they have their place
      if and when they serve a creative purpose.

✓ There is good reason for believing that jazz harmony, electronics, studio techniques and improvisation are more useful today than classical harmony and counterpoint.

✓ Virtuosity does not define musical accomplishment.

✓ Rather than ask whether composition is examinable we had better ask why we need to examine. What does it prove? Who is excluded? Why?

✓ All techniques are best learnt if and when the need arises.

✓ The classical music of post-Renaissance Europe is one ethnic tradition amongst many, even within Europe itself.

✓ Art and theatre students spend most of their time doing their own work and relating to contemporary ideas and approaches. This should be true of music.

✓ Paying attention to life's processes is the most fruitful way of cultivating music.

I was astonished to discover the fact that *some* of these propositions had made tentative inroads into *some* music departments and colleges, although with the alarming proviso that they had been given an educational slant. Still, it was good for my soul to realize that I hadn't been entirely wrong all those years ago. If we would only challenge the educational world's obsessive desire to examine, we would be getting somewhere.

It was in 1987, just as composition was beginning to flow once more, that I visited the house of Sean O Riada and had the uncanny feeling that I knew this man. It seemed that he was striving for integration between a vast list of apparent opposites typical of the dualism of Western thought. Coming face to face with my own dilemmas was strange enough but suspecting that an apparent lack of viable solutions was what had killed O Riada was even more cautionary.

As it was clear that there were no answers, and that only by following your own path could you contribute to the next stage, I became fascinated by people who had done just that, including some musicians. I had earlier unwittingly assumed that by becoming a kind of follower I would inherit a Master's solutions; now the process was becoming more detached. Perhaps more mature. It was now possible to admire others independently of whether or not they appeared to offer ideas I could attach myself to.

It was on this level that I began to take an interest in a composer living only a few miles away: Frank Denyer. He works in ways which I would never attempt but still admire. A quality of enlightened humanism pervades his music due, I think, to his ability to be uniquely himself.

I began to suspect that his career had been influenced by some very familiar issues. So I arranged an interview.

Solo

The Music of Frank Denyer

PROGRAMME NOTE

It is dangerously clichéd to speak of musical and spiritual regeneration at a time when this might suggest the irritatingly tranquil drivel which passes for New Age music, most of which is neither particularly new nor musical. The same caution applies to any discussion of global consciousness.

Yet the less faddish aspects of these areas suggest an important alternative to the myth-making of both the old and the new ages. The musical and political debates of the latter half of the twentieth century have inevitably been conducted according to the rules of a game that was developing long before we were born. The classical tradition, the folk, the rise of mass-produced popular music — these are our precious birthright and our cross to bear. They reflect and create social realities as the West has seen them.

Global consciousness has been talked and written about for decades. A serious consideration of the musical and social matters suggested by ethnomusicology is a powerful way of demythologizing our own ethnicity, even including the way we attempt the task. One of the possibilities this path offers is the removal of taboos. Humans are human and they make music in any way consistent with their world view. This music does not only reflect its context. It helps to create it.

A *Monkey's Paw* (1987-88) by Frank Denyer is one of the most unusual and beautiful pieces of music I have ever heard. It presents unique difficulties that are not so much due to the technical demands it makes on performers (although there are these) as to the composer's insistence on reinventing musical resources.

The instrumentation makes interesting reading. Apart from a violin, tuba and vocalists, the rest is a glorious conglomeration of folk instruments and invented percussion.

The female vocalists make sounds with tree branches containing dried leaves and other accessories. The male vocalists play eunuch flutes which either have to be specially made or hired from the composer. There are parts for ceramic ocarinas specially designed for the piece. Tin whistle, banjo and melodica figure prominently. The list of percussion instruments is breathtaking: slate gongs, 'sea drum', rubbed glass, an ordinary furniture cabinet, friction drums, silver jingles, whistling tubes, rubbed tiles, steel plates, glass gongs, a Kenyan rattle raft, five fishing rods, sandpaper, mango-seed rattles, pea whistles, aluminium cooking foil, slapsticks, three planks of wood, glass marbles, anvil, wet slap, bass drum, iron bells, cowbells, junk rattles, and gunghuroo.

Not surprisingly *A Monkey's Paw* has not had many performances, although it was taken to the prestigious international new music festival in Darmstadt in 1990 where it caused a riot. It divided the audience: roughly half were fascinated, the others were audibly not. Well-known and respectable composers from the European new music establishment were heard to boo, hiss, shout abuse and generally look as daft as those (white) jazz critics who derided Charlie Parker's bebop. Denyer was accused of having something against form in music.

A Monkey's Paw begins with rubbing and scraping sounds, followed by a flurry of whistles shrill enough to wake the dead. Parts of the score combine conventional instruments (violin, banjo, tuba) with the composer's invented instruments. Voices hoot, glissando and growl. Deep drums punctuate. Ideas that seem to be fragments suddenly combine, only to splinter again.

Twice the violin takes over from the roars, rumbles and rustlings. On both attempts there are distinct echoes of the instrument's history and usage. The second solo in particular hints, but only hints, at a conglomeration of folk fiddle styles — Northern European, Celtic. But the ensemble takes over each time with its insistent aural cacophony which might suggest either a musical instrument museum or a rubbish tip, depending on how you're listening. One violin solo is followed by the deliciously violent sound of fishing rods swishing through the air.

Eventually a solo female voice gradually emerges from the busy texture. It sings a wisp of melody — it may be a chant, or a forgotten tune from a folk collection, or maybe it doesn't have to be anything at all. It meanders with direction. It is not deterred by the occasional instrumental sounds which would detract if they had their will. Some of the instruments pick up odd notes of this vocal melody. Previously they had the stage to themselves, clattering their colours through patterns the ear could be forgiven for not quite grasping. Now they are stilled by this quiet voice. After just under half an hour the piece concludes in a composed silence.

The reception this piece provoked in Darmstadt strikes me as baffling as I sit in my room repeatedly listening to the CD that was made over there under James Wood's direction. There is nothing shocking in the music at all. Strange in parts — yes. Genuinely innovative — yes. But why even some of the ears of Darmstadt, seasoned connoisseurs of plinks and plonks, should find it provocative is a mystery. Unless, that is, the piece gets to the heart of certain exclusive prejudices.

When Frank Denyer showed me the score I was almost disappointed. Most of it is meticulously written out in conventional musical notation. It is a thoroughly composed piece leaving little room for personal improvisation on the part of the players.

The monkey's paw of the title refers to a talisman the composer saw inside a small drum in East Africa. A traditional healer used this drum to accompany certain songs. The drum was the source of healing power because secret magical objects had been placed inside it. "In private", writes Denyer, "a female healer showed me one of these, always kept in the dark inside the drum. It was a hideously decayed monkey's paw. That this grotesque object, so like a human hand, should hold the secret of regeneration and renewed human health seemed to hold a profound meaning for me."

A Monkey's Paw, therefore, seemed a better title than the original Under the Waste. But it was the idea of waste that prompted Denyer to compose the piece on his return from Africa. Industrial society always produces waste. It encourages the abandonment of objects, food, glass, even ideas which a society less possessed by the having mode would keep or recycle. This includes music other than the most commercial. Music too is discarded, cast in the shadow of the waste. We may imagine the clatter of waste at many moments in A Monkey's Paw.

This music plumbs the unconscious. The ear is never quite sure what it is hearing — is that passage meant to sound like organum, folk melody, fiddle music, a lullaby, or are these illusions? There is form to it in the sense that it hangs together, but where is the glue, the system, the diagrams, the pre-concert talk? They are not what we hear in the music if we hear them at all. We have to listen to sounds instead.

Some years ago Frank Denyer turned up to one of Pop Hingston's Saturday night pub sessions. The folk club contingent outnumbered the locals by a good majority. In addition, some of Frank's students from Dartington College had decided to make the trip down the country lanes to the Ferry Boat Inn. At that time I had not heard any of Frank's own music. I knew him as an ethnomusicologist who occasionally asked me to do some visiting lectures on British folklore.

With Pop in good form, we had a splendid session that night. Frank Denyer commented that it was remarkable how the themes of the songs and the manner of entertainment matched those he had witnessed in East Africa. And when you think about it there isn't much else to sing about — the peculiarities of the people you know, love, sex, labour, food and drink, and maybe money and status or the lack of it.

My route to internationalism had been stimulated by British folk revivalists — A.L. Lloyd's many radio talks, MacColl's encouragement, Alan Lomax's study of cantometrics. In Frank Denyer's case it was the occasional LPs of non-Western music which excited his curiosity in the mid-1960s. Like many others, he first heard the Japanese flute, the shakuhachi, on a Nonesuch album — A Bell Ringing in the Empty Sky — the title of which is as good an invocation of the quality of the shakuhachi as one is likely to find. It was played by Goro Yamaguchi, visiting artist in the World Music Programme at Wesleyan University, Connecticut, USA. Its silvery tones and subtle intonations had an immediate effect.

Frank Denyer told me about his music over cups of tea and biscuits in an informal interview situation which uncannily brought back the ambience of folklore fieldwork.

He studied composition at the Guildhall School of Music and Drama with Alfred Nieman in the early 1960s. When we spoke about our mutual association with Nieman Denyer asserted that Nieman was "the only thing worth knowing at the Guildhall" at that time. "You could never do anything so wild that he would reject it. I had a score at that time that was made out of toothpaste on manuscript paper." Apparently Nieman didn't flinch.

Denyer was one of a small group of student composers who dedicated themselves to playing and investigating the new music of the time. Listening to him recall that time I could identify closely with his relationship to the European scene on the one hand and the American on the other. The Europeans (Boulez, Stockhausen, Pousseur, Berio, Nono) were vitally concerned with formal matters. They had inherited this from Schoenberg, Webern and Messiaen and they created from serialism a near religion of musical systematization. Although Denyer was "interested in the European avant-garde, but not in the theoretical superstructure" like many others, Cardew included, he found himself drawn to more radical approaches suggested by the Americans Cage, Morton Feldman, Earle Brown, and Christian Wolff. Later in the 1960s the names of La Monte Young and Terry Riley also emerged from America.

Whereas the Europeans used systems, calculations, mathematics and form to bind and order sounds, the Americans appeared to invent methods to free sounds. In the music of Morton Feldman there was a willingness to work in the free space of the intuition which made sense to Denyer.

For all the logic followed by the Europeans Denyer was unable to find answers to fundamental questions concerning form. What considerations dictate and prepare the end of a piece? Was it sufficient to say that when a system had been worked through the music ended? What if this only made sense in theory rather in music? What if the composer's intuition sensed moments that were not accountable via the system?

These matters were not black and white. Plenty of Europeans did relax their rigid controls. No one has ever composed music totally without intuition, but Denyer's first meeting with Feldman suggested approaches he could identify with. Feldman determined how long a piece should be by writing it. He maintained that when it was beginning to get tedious he looked for a way out.

Denyer was impressed by something Feldman said in a radio interview referring to his four-hour string quartet: "This is a natural clock of anxiety, not artistry, that tells you that you are three quarters in. If you have something to say you had better say it now". Denyer gives a huge laugh as he recounts this, but adds that Feldman knew exactly where he was in the long forms he employed.

As with Denyer's own music, formal matters in Feldman are not presented as of prime importance. In some pieces there is little system as such, but there is continuity. There are tonal hints, notes in common between chords which are separated by silence.

In the same year as he met Feldman, 1968, Denyer formed the new music ensemble Mouth of Hermes, using highly skilled virtuosi. There were problems as he introduced music they found challenging. The musicians were unsure about some of La Monte Young's radical ideas — chords held for ages, or Christian Wolff's music which, unaccountably, often got a bad press. Wolff's scores generally demanded explorative ways of approaching usual instruments, an important influence which Denyer now acknowledges.

In other parts of London Cornelius Cardew was experimenting with *Treatise, The Tiger's Mind, Schooltime Compositions,* and *The Great Learning.* Denyer and Cardew met and often had long conversations about music. On one occasion Cardew invited Mouth of Hermes to play with The Scratch Orchestra. This was at Cecil Sharp House when I was downstairs recording my first folk album. Cardew treated the professionals and Mouth of Hermes with kid gloves, making sure they felt comfortable, asking their opinions frequently.

It was at around this time that Denyer encountered non-Western music. As he spoke about it I became aware of a familiar path, one which I too had travelled, although the details were different. At exactly the same time as I had started my forays into British folklore Frank Denyer began to ask similar questions via an interest in Indian and other Oriental musics.

"Going outside Europe, but first to the Middle East and India, was a very important experience for me. I soon found that I was meeting a lot of musicians but thinking it was impossible to share with them my own music that I'd been working at. People might understand this experimental music in a few cities in the West, but in the middle of India it was, not suprisingly, very difficult for people to get a grip on it, and there was no earthly reason why they should. That worried me and led me to think seriously about what I was doing, what I wanted to do. It seemed quite wrong if I was a musician not to have anything to offer other musicians merely because they came from outside my circle. A very uncomfortable feeling. Obviously the music itself was terribly narrow and provincial."

This had been my experience too. Having seen at first hand a different approach to music-making (for Denyer in India and Africa, for me in rural England) it became uncomfortably clear that the huge potential of experimental music was in danger of being confined to contexts and assumptions which would ensure its isolation. The need to question this state of affairs is not necessarily linked to a desire for wider popularity for the music. The traditional music I heard in Devon was hardly aimed at majority taste but it did raise alternative views of music's function, aesthetics and context.

The irony was that some avant-garde musicians had begun to suggest that their efforts were in the forefront of an international, even universal, language which would transcend its culture of origin. Experience has shown that even if this dream is desirable it is a long way from realization.

"The problems of the European avant-garde," says Denyer, "melted away because they weren't addressing relevant questions." Ditto Cardew, ditto Sean O Riada, ditto Ewan MacColl in theatre and song, and doubtless many others. The need of many experimental artists at a crucial point in their development to investigate alternative contexts and attitudes seems perennial.

Denyer boldly comments that "Western culture today certainly does not like to see itself as ethnic", but that, of course, is precisely what it is to outsiders, and most are outsiders. The European concert tradition is the folk music of a

powerful ideology. It is not universal. Any assumption that it should or could
be is imperialistic. If any particular form of music has the edge it is Western
pop. And that is imperialistic.

Denyer's visits to India, travels in Iran and Afghanistan, ethnomusicology at
Wesleyan University in America (where he caused a stir by challenging the
orthodoxy of Cage's followers), plus fieldwork in East Africa opened up new
concerns. He knew from the outset that he could not use the musics he was
experiencing by direct reference. "That was too facile, too easy. Somehow
whatever one learned of the wider musical world had to be entirely rethought.
This process itself might result in something that was stylistically completely
different, but there would be certain attitudes, certain aims and approaches that
informed and infected the whole, or underpinned the results."

Three major concerns emerge in Denyer's work following on from these
experiences: a reassessment of the contexts to which he related possible
instrumental resources, a consequent need to deal with the attitudes of the
players themselves, and a fruitful partnership with Yoshikazu Iwamoto, the
Japanese shakuhachi virtuoso.

Iwamoto was an artist in residence at Wesleyan. Denyer's practical studies
of the Japanese koto gave the two men a chance to play together and this led to
a commission to write some shakuhachi pieces. The traditional solo style
associated with the instrument, which Denyer describes as 'seductive', might
be respected but had to be totally avoided if it were to avoid becoming a
Western parody. It was necessary to develop a new range of techniques and
sounds which would help the instrument transcend its "...Japanese context so
that I might personalize them in mine".

Denyer was helped immeasurably by Iwamoto. They both lived in London
for a while during the 1980s and it was not unusual for Iwamoto to knock on
the door long before breakfast time, having been up all night working out new
fingerings and techniques to deal with the new pieces. With Japanese
dedication to detail and respect for the task in hand Iwamoto helped Denyer to
extend the range of the shakuhachi.

A series of delicately conceived pieces resulted: *On On — It Must Be So*,
then *Wheat*, and *Quite White*, the first two having percussion parts. The first
piece used bass drum and castanets, but Denyer wanted to look further for
appropriate percussion. What he calls the 'mass-produced quality' of these
instruments clashed with the 'naturalness' of the shakuhachi sound. In *Wheat*
he used stones, metal, sandpaper, glass, wood.

It is difficult to avoid the reference to Japanese sounds when listening to
these pieces. It is also true that they are genuinely composed pieces which
would not have been written in Japan. The culturally specific sound of the
shakuhachi, however, does highlight a basic point. If you write for an
instrument you also take on its entire history as a cultural force which is
embedded in its very construction. (Denyer claims that some instruments have
the capacity to transcend their roots. I feel that this is largely up to the
composer.) We may not hear this so powerfully in a new piece for the Western
violin or trumpet because the culture is too familiar.

The standard methods of training instrumentalists take on these culturally specific assumptions without question. Therefore to realize music which genuinely goes beyond the load of tradition it becomes imperative, as Denyer says, to "redesign the players". This is a more difficult task than composition.

Although not a perfect solution, one of Denyer's major contributions to music-making has been his scoring for non-standard instruments. He regards this as one way of trying to break the iron grip of Western art music. He is not the first to have done so. The music of the American Harry Partch springs to mind, none of which can be played on anything other than the ensembles of instruments the composer specifically designed and built. John Cage, from his early percussion and prepared piano pieces to his use of radios as musical instruments, took a similar route. We might say that the European development of electronic music followed a similar and uniquely contemporary line, but Denyer and others have not found this to be the human solution they prefer.

An instructive story is that of trombonist Jim Fulkerson's suggestion that Denyer write a duo for them to play. Denyer confesses that much as he admired Fulkerson as a person and a musician he thought the idea of a duet for piano and trombone was unworkable.

Denyer began by going back to basics. His own account, written in a programme note, outlines the dilemma and the way through. "The difficulty was that I could not find a way into the trombone and I have absolutely no thoughts at all for the piano... Then the obvious struck me — if Jim lost his trombone he would be no less of a musician and I certainly didn't feel tied to keyboards. With the instruments off our backs I felt as if released from a heavy burden and the piece was written relatively quickly." The work that resulted was for two male voices and percussion.

As I looked at the score of *A Monkey's Paw* I commented that it was unlikely that Denyer could expect many performances. His response was that this was the story of his compositional life. He has still not heard some of his own music. "Yes. It worries me considerably", he says and then roars with laughter. "Would you like to see the sea drum?"

He went upstairs and returned with a huge hexagonal 'drum' made to his own design by instrument maker David Sawyer. The drum heads, made of thick paper, were three inches apart. Inside was a quantity of lead shot. There were handles on either side. Two players hold the drum between them. By tipping it this way and that the lead pellets roll around to produce a sound uncannily like the sea on a pebble beach.

I realized that making sound is a peculiarly magic activity. Within seconds I had been taught by cooperation and participation how to make long waves and short waves, even little trickles, with the sea drum. An object that is designed to make sounds links with whoever plays it.

This enquiry into the fundamentals of making sounds does not belong to Frank Denyer alone but the physicality he brings to his search is typical of the man and unique. It was prepared by his questions about avant-gardism, revealed in his ethnomusicology studies and field trips to East Africa and India, and is now transmitted via his own music.

The revelations of local folk music are paralleled in internationalism. We are not only equal in our own regions. If giving voice or even just listening to 'the people' has any substance it must also apply to East Africa, India, Japan. Denyer took this possibility into his creativity. One reason why *A Monkey's Paw* threw the new music buffs at Darmstadt is that it is imbued with a profound challenge to European *and* American ethnocentrism. That is why it is important.

Although aware of the drive to question context, function and content, Denyer's experiences in India and Africa seem to have allowed him to continue composition without being dominated by current intellectual debates. The almost tragicomic dilemma of postmodernism, for example, is that it is self-consciously aware of all limitations. It even sees its own opposition as, of necessity, a product of what it opposes.

One reason I admire Denyer's work is that in a constructive way it addresses other issues, but not in ignorance. I had been close to issues labelled Marxism, community arts, democracy, and by implication sexual and racial politics, postcolonialism, structuralism. All this in itself is an ethnic tradition outlining the concerns and mythologies of an intelligentsia which, although cosmopolitan to a degree, is decidedly Western. Denyer's fieldwork showed him that music can be played according to radically different values. Of course, he remains a European, but by opening his ears to the globe he has been able to address less ethnocentric concerns. It may be a fragile gesture but it is surely worth the effort.

The sense of liberation I find in Denyer's music comes partly from his musicianly way of investigating anything that seems like a possibility given his familiarity with Western and non-Western musics. He has an astonishingly direct way of presenting his findings. One is tempted to ask how he does it. The answer is the monkey's paw.

Unfinished Symphony

Voluntary : Musical Democracy /
Sonic Harvest

PROGRAMME NOTE

'Musical Democracy' refers to a principle embedded in the art, act, processes and products of music itself. It is not primarily concerned with how music fits into a democratic society, what it should do, if anything, in relation to political ideas, nor how or if it should be supported by a society that considers itself democratic.

For centuries composers have quoted, parodied or arranged musical ideas that suggest regional dances, street music, the everyday milieu. But it was only in the Romantic era that one sector of the population dubbed the 'folk' was self-consciously sought out and given a label. This exactly parallels the rise of democratic ideals.

In the twentieth century, consciously or not, composers and animators have habitually performed a peculiar balancing act in search of musical democracy, not without occasionally falling off their own tightrope.

Amongst even the most innovative musicians there is not one who has not felt the need for absorption (if only temporary) in musical traditions of supposed age and conservatism. La Monte Young, one of the boldest experimenters, studied Indian singing with Pandit Pran Nath. John Cage has based a large part of his output on one of the oldest books of traditional wisdom, the I Ching. Cornelius Cardew felt the need to renounce avant-gardism in favour of conventional tonality, popular and folk tunes. The furthest out Afro-Americans (Coltrane, Coleman, Archie Shepp, Sun Ra, Cecil Taylor, Anthony Braxton) invoke the blues. And so the list goes on. There are no exceptions. It is a psychological necessity. And, it seems, the further out you get the more comprehensive your conscious need to compare what you do to something 'pre-formed'.

Yet, to be stuck in the mud eventually loses its charm. I found that my self-imposed sixteen-year silence had become deafening. In a sense I had seen all I needed to see. Nothing I ever wrote would now be free of that now that I was free of it.

- 1 -
Voluntary : Musical Democracy

Walking across Bodmin Moor one evening, listening to the skylarks and the sheep, I became convinced that John Cage's *4'33''* is the ultimate musical gesture, and therefore the greatest piece of music in history. The new complexities warbled out by one small bird put the entire post-war European avant-garde to shame and still managed to have a comprehensible melodic framework. The bleats of sheep added punctuation points. A faint slow-moving breeze was the backdrop.

Would I say the same thing in the middle of a city rush hour? The truthful answer is that I would — sometimes. But then, there would also be occasions when the skylark wouldn't bother me either. So it all depends on my condition of life and whether I'm listening. Traffic noises *are* interesting. I insist on this even when they're irritating.

So the real problem occurs, as Cage would agree, when music is intentional rather than ambient. At this point prejudices — we can hardly call them anything else — come into action.

There was a time when I considered Cage to be the wisest person in musical history, and if music *were* purely a matter of sound, or even 'organized sound' as Varèse said, I doubt if anyone could argue otherwise. But I sense more.

For some time I too asserted that music is simply organized sound, but was unable to access a feeling that this is insufficient. Then I realized that in order to register sounds as music some activity has to take place: either listening, playing or responding in some other way. The 'organized sound' formulation then becomes a typical trick of Western dualism. It refers to the object (music) as if it were distinguishable from the subject (the activity of listening, playing etc.).

Just as sounds are not independent of listeners and players, so the business of listening cannot be detached from the whole person. Once looked upon as a unity of subject and object, music becomes transformative. Put simply, a person who isn't listening is not experiencing music on anything other than a subliminal level. In order to experience sounds as music you have to hear them as music. Attentive listening exercises a human faculty. As any form of exercise strengthens muscles, my powers of audition are refined by continued listening. Therefore I am transformed, even if only a little bit.

So I'd propose that music is transformation through hearing and playing sounds. This description does not isolate the sounds 'out there' as if they could be independent of what we do.

Unlike the skylarks or rush-hour traffic (which are music if you're listening) music often happens when more than one person intends to make it. They either announce that they're going to play it or record it or they spontaneously let it happen. This will be a transformative experience whether we like it or not. Some artists have argued that art doesn't transform but I don't believe this. Paint is transformed into image, silence into music, even if, as Cage discovered, we merely put a frame round it. It might be profoundly transformative. It might simply pass a few minutes pleasantly. It might affirm or question what we already know. Whatever, if we were better off without it it is reasonable to assume that after millennia we'd have found a way of abolishing it.

If music is viewed as a process of transformation requiring activity, then it is obvious that this activity must happen in a context of some kind — a concert hall, country pub, college seminar, on Sunday mornings, on the radio, at a street parade, wedding, funeral. In order to bring music about, living beings normally have to devise ways of making it via certain sounding devices, in certain social relations, through specialists (or not), by reading it from notation, via aural tradition, improvising, co-ordinated by a leader (or not), and so on. My description of music is abstract until we introduce specifics. Then, the happenings we call music occur in genres.

A distinguishing feature of performance genres, from telling a dirty joke to Wagner's *Ring* cycle, is that they are marked off from the rest of life's processes by rituals and agreements. They also carry expectations with them. In the 1960s it was often argued that the gap between art and life was narrowing. This cannot be so unless we view them as separate in the first instance. However, the ritual distinction between the two is another convenience which appears to be perennial.

So music occurs in contexts. These include the individual and his or her personal psychology, local and wider culture, the moment in history, economics, religion or world view, and so on. Music doesn't express or create other matters. It *is* them. Paradoxically it is also only itself. The paradox comes by thinking about it.

As I picked my way through the thickets of theory throughout the 1970s and '80s I found nothing in Western thought which totally expressed this view of interdependence in a comprehensible way. It is *there* in semiotics, structuralism, postmodernism, but to a significant degree I experienced a dislocation of 'out there' and 'in here' in all I read. More importantly, a feeling of paralysis inhabits the Western approach as if what is 'out there' should be reformed so that what is 'in here' can reach some kind of harmony. This dualism leaves us little to do, for the problems of contemporary society and music's part in it are too vast and inhibiting. In attempting to decode the myth contained in an image, text or assumption, I am overwhelmed by the sheer complexity of the matter.

In the Japanese Buddhist concept of *esho funi* I found I was able not only to deconstruct but also to reconstruct. As reconstruction must now surpass the craze for its opposite I offer a brief explanation.

Esho is a contraction of *eho* and *shoho*. *Shoho* refers to what the West would call the subject (me on Bodmin Moor). *Eho* is the object (the skylarks and the sheep). They are run together into one word to show that they are inseparable. Life and its environment are therefore 'two but not two': *funi*. They appear different but are united in their essence.

Esho funi goes further. If the way music is regarded by society, or its relationship to society, is problematic this is nevertheless a case of *unity*, the one inseparable from the other. The implication is clear: if musicians hope to change society through their work, then they must make similar adjustments in themselves. Yasuji Kirimura writes: "...the formation of one's environment must coincide with the emergence of one's life in this world; a person cannot simply appear without an environment, simply floating in space... An environment is a reflection of the inner life of the individual living within it; it takes on characteristics which accord with the life-condition of the person in question". In other words musicians affect their environment by changing themselves. They do not have answers. Rather, they ask questions that characterize the world they live in, which includes themselves.

The last piece of music I wrote before my sixteen-year pause was presented at a composers' seminar. I had been unable to find classically trained musicians who would take it seriously, so two musicians plus myself on piano played alongside a group of visual artists. The musical details of the piece have now passed into a haze but I left the visual artists free to interpret their material in any way they wanted. At one point I remember looking up from the piano to see three people in fluorescent green overalls wearing different masks — one was a wartime gas mask.

It was a peculiar and decisive sensation. I was stunned by the power of the imagery these people had dreamed up, the more so because my hand in it was slight. But a stronger emotion was one of utter futility. Who the hell cared about those green people in their masks or, for that matter, the sounds I was coaxing out of a grand piano? It wasn't a question of being in a minority. I have always accepted that as a precondition of the way an artist lives. It was more a feeling that there was a lack of connection with anything, any person.

It struck me at the time that in our efforts to break down the barriers between art and life all we had really learnt about was the irrelevance of art. For who is really bothered about the struggle with tradition other than those who are leading actors in it?

After this experience I found it impossible to proceed as a composer. I destroyed all my work and resolved to write nothing new until I felt clearer. I was not to know that this process would take over a decade and a half.

Somewhere between The Ambling Band and A Monkey's Paw I started composing music again. It wasn't that I had found the answers to all my questions, at least not in any way I could formulate. But, having pinned my hopes in various places and on various people, I eventually got bored looking. It just took an inordinately long period of personal enquiry to discover the simple truth: the answers lie in the questions themselves.

Democracy, musical or other, is not located in a system, a set of values or anything else. It is a myth. En route to this self-evident fact I have encountered various doctrines. One of the most powerful, because it is tied up with the most basic insecurity — money — is community arts. In community arts funding circles a desire to follow one's own path was taboo. Art, one has heard it said, is now part of the social services.

The artist, by giving people things to do (and notably it is the sitting targets that get the brunt of it — kids, the elderly, the unemployed, disabled people) defuses real social engagement into occupational therapy. It diverts rather than subverts. Its creative potential is minimized because, despite its response to the historical moment, it proceeds according to unsolved contradictions of process and product, trained and untrained, the guidelines laid down by art tradition. Community arts is vitally attached to funding systems which insist on this conservatism. There is no allowance for art's right to be useless.

Music has trodden these paths in some of its guises. Cage could say in 1967 "I may be wrong, but I think art's work is done". This had a ring of truth. There would still be reverence for the concert works of the past but as far as new composition was concerned there were only two choices that I could see: either continue to go beyond or deliberately ignore the genuine challenges of the new.

"Art's work is done" does not imply that there is no more need for aesthetic experience, or even for the kind of events that some of us might label 'art'. It is a critique of the role of the artist, and the art work, in modern society. And, as there is no essential difference, it is a critique of society too.

My greatest problem with folklore and community arts, with which I was concerned during my interregnum, was their lack of creativity for the artist. It was impossible to find an uncompromised way of implementing creative ideas within their frameworks. The experience was important, nevertheless, because the limitations taught me the value of connectedness. It forced me to question the doctrines — community participation at any price (helping with the Queen's Jubilee celebrations?), the deskilling of the artist for the sake of levelling, abandonment of vision.

Now it is obvious. These currents were necessary phases in the questioning and abandonment of structures, practices, implicit ideologies that are no longer necessary. The myth of democracy, as it progresses, forces these issues upon us because they are the same issues that individuals face in their efforts to identify where they can be useful. Choices are not necessary, only actions. Those actions can use, or refer to, any and every possibility we have discovered.

Via folklore I was consciously seeking a non-commercial, more 'natural' condition of music-making. In the village singers, but not in the folk revival, I thought I had found this, and having done so realized that it had to stay just too raw in order the fulfil these conditions. I noted clear lines of demarcation beyond which individual creativity would not be appropriate. The new music I had engaged in had been liberating in its attitudes but it had not offered a sufficient sense of connectedness. Both had affirmed a new vision of living, one by looking back, the other by looking forward.

Their failing (and perhaps I should be more honest and say *my* failing) had been a blindness to the opposition between ideology and reality. Therefore I continually felt as though possibilities were being suggested rather than actualized. Some of these included greater participation, decentralization and the jettisoning of the music academy educational framework. These are what excited me in improvisation groups and country pubs alike.

Success could only be measured musically. If music *could* be produced according to these ideals it affirmed the ideals. If not, the whole pack of cards flopped with the music. If there were reservations these were consistent with the ideals — fundamentally one had reservations about them too.

And there were reservations — for me most of the time. The folk scene rarely inspected the forces that created and shaped it, or those that it opposed.

There were times when it was impossible even to mention popular culture without feeling as though one was swearing in church. All schools of thought are based on taboos. Therefore, like avant-gardism which had similar weaknesses, it was easy to ignore or recuperate.

Cornelius Cardew became aware of such contradictions and turned his attention to political analysis. It feels almost grudging to point out the weaknesses of a man whose practice was always to modify and evolve but it must be said that Cardew treated the proletariat as an object. This is a tenuous solution because the proletariat (if one accepts the myth) is a *capitalist* class no less than the bourgeoisie. He was well aware of this, and his tragedy is that circumstances did not allow him the time to develop in directions which may well have been fruitful.

Yet I know how disarmingly easy it is to fall into this trap of objectifying — in my case improvisation, methods of notation, folklore, conditions of music-making, and a number of highly talented and articulate individuals. I assumed that, within these chosen objects, an approach to music-making could be found. It was obviously not so because the results were not fulfilling. Hence my years of disquiet.

It almost sounds too clichéd to present as a conclusion, but the signs point to neither 'out there' nor 'in here'. Neither devotion to exterior influences nor introspection can provide anything more than provisional courses of action. Only when what is 'in here' finds a degree of harmony with what is 'out there' does dualism, alienation and disquiet cease. May every person discover this in their own way.

It is easy to assume that the 'folk' are an objective fact outside oneself, less easy to accept that each individual creates the 'folk' according to the meanings they seek. 'Out there' a few people know a few old songs. 'In here' is a need. So we create the relationship, the 'folk', the myth. It is a form of idolatry, for our needs inhabit our myths precisely because they are needs. Our worship, or reverence, is *ergo* directed to our own needs.

The musical mainstreams do nothing to discourage this myth-making. Success for a performer or composer still begins with mastering approved techniques, knuckling under to the unpleasant business of marketing one's accomplishments, winning prizes and competitions. Many of the musical possibilities I have discussed in this book suggest serious need for change. Yet ultimately it is no good merely to apportion blame. Change comes about more quickly through positive action than negative criticism.

Musical democracy rests on one essential premise: everyone is (has the potential to be) musical. The ethnomusicologist John Blacking, whose book *How Musical Is Man?* is required reading for the musical democrat, asks whether music might be a species trait. I have encountered sufficient evidence in my fieldwork to agree, albeit tentatively.

In the 1980s I collected playground lore from schoolchildren. I employed a very simple technique. With the permission of the Head Teacher I stood or sat in the playground at break time. Within seconds a few children would inevitably ask me who I was and what I was doing. My reply was something along the lines of: "I'm interested in songs. Do you know any?" This was an acceptable, logical answer to most children. After perhaps a bit of giggling I would be offered playground parodies, pop songs, rude rhymes. In no time at all a crowd would gather. On some occasions it seems that I had the whole school pressing towards my tape recorder.

Some directive questioning on my part would lead on to skipping rhymes, action songs, rhymes and songs for clapping, bouncing balls, accompanying games. I rarely encountered a child who couldn't 'sing'.

I noticed certain divisions. Far more girls than boys offered material. Boys' efforts tended to emphasize male pursuits such as football. These tendencies I took largely as a response to the sex roles in adult society.

There was another division that was less easy to account for. It was undoubtedly true that some children emerged as leaders. They knew more rhymes, games and songs than the rest. And, despite peer group pressure, some were less interested. Such divisions could exist within one family, between two sisters for example.

On one occasion I was touring in the Lake District visiting primary schools with music workshops. During each session the children would be asked which songs they knew. They usually offered standard clapping games such as *When Suzy Was a Baby.*

When Suzy was a baby
A baby Suzy was
And she went: Ga ga gagaga
When Suzy was a schoolgirl
A schoolgirl Suzy was
And she went: Miss, Miss I can't do this
I got my knickers in a twist

And so on through Suzy's life until she dies, becomes a skeleton, a ghost, and finally nothing. I always warmed to the 'nothing' verse.

When Suzy was a nothing
A nothing Suzy was
And she went...

At one tiny rural school the repertoire was overwhelming. Once started they went from one song to another, covering some with actions, dances, games, parodies. I had never heard so many songs from one group of children.

As it happened I did not have my tape recorder with me at the time. So a year later, when I was compiling a double album of field recordings for Folkways Records, I fixed to return to the school. From Devon to Cumbria is a very long journey. It takes a day, a lot of petrol, and accommodation at the end of it. I boggle now at the level of commitment which took me on such a chase.

When I started recording the children I was frankly disappointed. What had happened to that vast repertoire? Why were the songs performed with no more enthusiasm than I could have found at any local school in Devon? What had happened in twelve months?

The Headmistress explained. The girl who had led these activities had left in the meantime. She hadn't even been a particularly popular child, many children making faces at the mention of her name. But she was one of those people who led the tradition and probably extended it.

This was a learning experience for me. It contained a big enough truth to be formative. What it told me was that although everyone had the ability to participate or respond in some way I had seen living proof that if this was to be enhanced and developed then this depended on the enthusiasm of particular individuals.

The most damaging possibility which musical democracy leads the unwary towards is the view, prevalent in socialist and egalitarian philosophies, that, in Stockhausen's words, "Progress entails the majority of this planet's inhabitants attaining the same abilities". He sees this as restricting whether it happens in socialist countries or in "so-called free countries, since the commercialization of music and educationalists' excessive ambitions of explaining everything demonstrates the same symptoms".

His warning is appropriate. His nightmare of the Yamaha system ruling the world, reducing everything to banality and mediocrity, is the exact opposite of the ambitions of democracy. Yet, of course, the technology exists to do just that. I had come dangerously close to this possibility by following the logic of folklore to what I saw as its conclusion. In doing so I had found myself in situations, as a community artist, whereby I felt obliged to shelve my own uniqueness in favour of, for example, accompanying a local Country and Western singer with stars in her eyes.

Although there is a time and place for enabling or assisting others I found it insufficient as an aesthetic unless I could pretend I had no further vision. I feared this possibility in the community arts movement, and participated in it in the folk revival.

I do not attack anyone else's practice. I merely offer comment lest a practice itself become a religion. If the practice itself is a genuine exploration of matters that can only be approached via music, poetry, theatre or dance (and incidentally code concepts of society, politics, relationships) then it is valuable. In such cases the practice comes, like the plethora of songs in that one school playground, from individuals unashamed of their own uniqueness. They are leaders not because they are better than anyone else but because they have acknowledged that in a certain small area of life they are proactive.

Stockhausen answers the question "Why shouldn't the instrumentalist just intuit on his own? Why does he need a composer?" by reference to universal laws. "Why does a spiritual group need a guru? Why has an atom a nucleus? Why in the whole universe is there nothing that doesn't have a centre? Why aren't there only moons? Why isn't every planet a sun? The composer has to fulfil the role of gathering together those people who are good interpreters, but by nature are not original sources. Why are there fountains in the world and why doesn't the water come from everywhere?"

It took many years of experimentation to realize that an arts practice which *denies* the artists the right to be themselves is profoundly reactionary and anti-democratic, although superficially it may not look that way. For if democracy is about anything worthwhile it has to involve itself in uniqueness. This is not something we apply to everyone but ourselves. It starts with ourselves.

I began to see the challenges of musical democracy as a red herring. There is considerable difference between typically Occidental and Oriental patterns of living. In the West we have the tendency to think then act, to get the theory right before we dare to practise. The Eastern impulse has more emphasis on taking action and evaluating later. Neither are complete approaches. To grasp the nettle of action and thought, thought and action as indivisible — to be or not to be — that *is* the question.

The musicality which John Blacking suggests is a 'species trait' of mankind — this is the raw material a composer may work with. There *are* vital questions of why modern society limits this trait, how its methods of musical education discriminate between people at an early age, what is the relation to commercialism, and so on. But the musician, composer or animator confronts these questions by creating music. That is why his name is Mozart and not Socrates.

- 2 -
Sonic Harvest

Lovers of the book of Ecclesiastes may have recognized in my narrative a barely concealed search for the grand solution. Having eventually realized that the more we look the more we see ourselves looking, the advice that "he that increaseth knowledge increaseth sorrow" seems near the mark. It would appear that "eat, drink and be merry (and, if you like, make music)" is the most radical solution on offer. The necessary caution is to remember that if we are artists at all it is likely that our future work will contradict the cherished positions we now take.

But there is more to it than that. It would be horrifying if the grand solution was available for, according to delicious paradox, every single approach, action or idea is entirely what we are seeking. As long as we are not attached to it being so. Or may I suggest that action itself, in this case musical action, is the very key — not theory.

The world of sound has much to teach us in this respect. Sounds have no purpose, no manners, nothing to say. If it is possible to press them into musical service with this in mind we are likely to create huge good fortune for ourselves. This may sound like a restatement of Cage's core philosophy but, as he would no doubt agree, it is the assumption that he or anyone else has got it right which makes it wrong. In fact, as soon as we give up the idea of anyone being right or wrong we're on the right track. Or the wrong one. Does it matter?

What does matter (to me because I happen to be interested in it) is the pattern of musical democracy which emerges when we take an overview of all the paths, contradictory though some may appear, which have led us to the present. Musical democracy does not appear in any particular guise. It enters musical practice in many ways. Historically it happens simultaneously with the rise of democratic and egalitarian ideas in other walks of life. It is based on the growth of the idea of equality as a desirable condition of life. Although equality itself needs to be demythologized, the growth of egalitarian ideas has been inexorable even including those periods when liberal democracies have been governed by parties which appeared to favour privilege.

Why do I constantly refer to democracy as a myth rather an ideal? Because I see it as the central reference point for political, artistic and other aspiration. In times when people believed the sun (or any other natural phenomenon) should be worshipped it was assumed that it pervaded life. Therefore it was central to life. God fulfilled the same role in later societies. All was ultimately referable to Him — life, death, the social and moral order. Democracy is the new myth. Like God it can't be proved to exist, and there is no example of it working perfectly.

In all areas of life the new myth took time to grow because it involved the overthrow of previous belief systems. From our perspective it is hard to imagine that a social system based on hierarchy was, at one time, taken as normal or natural. Feudalism, the Divine Right of Kings, a highly structured church, exclusive social groupings, and so on into the industrial era with its secularized systems of domination and control — all these were normal patterns.

E.P. Thompson's classic history *The Making of the English Working Classes* begins by quoting the first of the 'leading rules' of the London Corresponding Society, dated March 1792. The rule reads: "That our members be unlimited". The qualification for joining had nothing to do with income, estate, status or influence. It was that a person was convinced in principle that "every adult person, in possession of their reason, and not incapacitated by crimes, should have a vote for a Member of Parliament". The leaders were subsequently arrested on charges of High Treason. That is how unusual the concept of equality was in the late eighteenth century.

Just as on the social and political scene battles were fought to establish the new myth, musically, over the same period, we find it encoded in some interesting forms. In 1823 a small book of what we might now call 'folk carols' from the West of Cornwall was published. The collector of the songs was one Davis Gilbert, an inventor. The title page proudly boasts that the songs are given exactly as taken down from the mouths of the people. There is little remarkable in this until we consider that it was an almost revolutionary statement for its time. To regard the peasantry of West Cornwall, untrained, untutored, by some standards even unmusical, as worthy of such attention implied a shifting of attitude. Davis Gilbert's collection is often cited as the first authentic English folk music collection to be published in such a way, and although not perhaps strictly true, it is symbolic. It could be said to be a forerunner of the folk song movement.

It is interesting to reflect that the folk song pioneers themselves came from a peculiar position of conservative radicalism. They too saw the old order breaking down, and basically regretted it. Their appreciation of 'the people' was hardly neutral, and not without its patronizing side. Yet, simultaneously, they afford the people the honour of a degree of the limelight, leading, eventually, to a folk song revival which, I suspect, many of the early collectors would have disowned.

As the old social hierarchies were breaking down this was reflected in art music, the composers being in a similarly contradictory position to that of the folklorists. Wagner's ambiguous tonalities and chromaticisms stretched the classical tonal and functional harmonic systems almost as far as they could go without disappearing. Debussy wrote music which almost abolished the old systems — any chord could follow any other, limited only by the composer's taste and sense of form. Atonality followed in which all notes, in theory, had equal weight.

Like the appearance of 'the people' in other schools of art music, atonality was also a revolutionary concept. Only a wink of an eye earlier (in historical time) all music had been based on strictly determined relationships between intervals of the scale. Most obviously, every piece had a tonic note, the key and final tone which served as 'home'. Upon each note of the scale chords were built, all of which had varying degrees of 'pull' towards each other and the tonic. It was a very well worked out system related to deep structures in society and religion.

To find oneself impelled to atonality, as Schoenberg and others did, must have had a psychological impact of huge proportions. Like the conservative radicals of the folk song movement, the atonalists brought onto the musical stage a concept of equality which was potentially more revolutionary than any beliefs they personally held. For all the religiosity of Webern his actual musical universe was atheistic.

This freedom was a liberation, but it was also a problem. Should it be organized according to a system now that there was no apparent reason for one sound to follow another? Serialism was one of the most powerful solutions, but it is somewhat analogous to state communism in which equality is systematized and imposed from above. In historical time its invention coincides with the Russian Revolution, a fact which I do not regard as entirely coincidental.

It was typical of Europeans subsequently to create a strong avant-garde which followed and refined the lead of Schoenberg and Webern. This led to that highly complex, internally democratic music which, it may be recalled, I found difficult to play or correctly hear.

As far as music in Europe was concerned it could be said that High and Low culture were still slugging it out, even as the bourgeois stage was redefining itself. Bartók and the folk devotees invited democracy into the concert hall via echoes of peasants and workers with mud on their boots. The serialists invited it in via tightly worked out, refined systems. It is not surprising that the greatest challenge to both came from the United States.

America, with only a few hundred years of historical tradition, produced what Europeans liked to think of as musical eccentrics. Scott Joplin had raised ragtime to an art form, although he hardly won the struggle to get it out of the brothels and wasn't accorded any widespread acclaim until the 1960s. Charles Ives copiously quoted ragtime, jazz, patriotic hymns and rallying calls, folk melodies and the like in sonatas, symphonies and a number of impressionistic works. He self-consciously aligned himself with American philosophers of democracy, albeit of a slightly mystical turn of mind — Emerson, Thoreau and the like. Henry Cowell explored pure sound and percussion music. (Percussion music? In Europe? No harmony? No melody?) Harry Partch invented his own scales, systems and musical instruments. Indeed, he tried to reinvent music. Only an American would feel free to take on such a task.

John Cage was quite clear about America's advantage in being far from European tradition. He emerges as a seminal figure because, in a sense, he went *beyond* democracy, largely, I feel, due to his involvement in Oriental philosophy — the *I Ching*, Zen Buddhism. In the 1950s his compositions by chance methods superficially contained a similar message to that of the European serialists of the time. Every note, every sound, was equal, none having any more functional value than the others. It might be said that Cage too invented systems every bit as rigid as the serialists, and perhaps this is fair comment. There are more than subtle differences in the results and the paths they pointed to. Whereas the Europeans discriminated against any group of notes that might suggest tonality, with Cage if such a sound happened by chance it was afforded equal weight to all the other sounds surrounding it.

In Cage's aesthetic every sound is not only equal in a democratic sense: it is a Buddha. This takes the matter beyond the myth-making of politics and into the realms of the Self, enlightenment, alteration of Mind, and ultimately life itself.

America, of course, also produced jazz. Ragtime broke in the 1890s, and from there to electro-acoustic-jazz-funk-free-rock and Uncle Tom Cobbleigh and all is a remarkably compact history. Again, there is precious little coincidence here. The conditions for democracy had been created, especially in America. It was a task which got to the heart of prejudices to extend this to Blacks and people of differing ethnic origins.

From the point of view of democracy jazz and blues indirectly led to one of the most problematic musical phenomena of the era: the rise of modern pop music. Although now a long way from its origins, it remains so that modern pop begins with rock and roll, a kind of commercialized blues and boogie. The popular masses, the marketing target, are now a factor in the creation of music. There is also the suspicion that they are thus open to manipulation.

Folklore, serialism, indeterminacy, improvisation, jazz, pop — these were the available options in the 1960s when I first became consciously interested in making music. Subsequent developments have included two which have occupied me enough to deserve mention: community arts and postmodernism.

Community Arts took root as a movement in the late 1960s and became a buzzword in Britain throughout the 1970s. Although I was often funded from community arts sources (Arts Council, Southwest Arts) I found it problematic. My personal reservations have been hinted at elsewhere in this book. Stated bluntly they amount to this: there appeared to be little room in community arts ideology for artists to genuinely inhabit their own integrity. All was sacrificed on an altar of accessibility and participation by members of communities. Many community arts events espoused idioms of real conservatism and banality. The romantic notion that "anyone can produce art" was dressed up in ideologically convincing statements and positions, but there was something seriously wrong with the tendency to deskill down. Context, function and participation were weighted with an importance that was previously accorded to accomplishment, content, personal vision, devotion. As a debunking exercise it had much to offer, but it overbalanced.

It could be that I simply found myself in the wrong bag, but I doubt it. For the artist with more commitment to ideology than art community arts was a stimulating banner. It served the function of reopening an old debate about populism versus elitism, which gets to the heart of democracy in the arts. I learnt much from it.

As part of my song collecting activities I was once led to a local produce show in Kingston, a tiny village in South Devon. Competing for prizes were all manner of curiosities. The one I remember best was the class for three potatoes. There were a number of entries. The contestants had lovingly grown their spuds, cleaned them, and arranged them on a plate or small basket. The displays were aesthetically very pleasing and actually said much about the values and world view of those who created them. I remember musing: if someone had stuck three spuds in the Tate Gallery it would be called art, but this was just a vegetable show. A cheap point, true. But I already regarded three spuds as art. That much I had learnt from folklore and community arts, but it probably merely confirmed suspicions I had had many years earlier.

It has become clear that the cases of artists such as O Riada, Cardew and MacColl were examples of a desire to fully relate to the implications of the democracy myth. Put better: they understood their era in depth, yet they didn't resolve its contradictions. Instead they took refuge in ideologies — the Irish tradition, Marxism-Leninism, the folk.

One of the major problems of music-making in those traditions which historically follow on from the Baroque, Classical, Romantic European line is the insistence on notation as a means of fixing an individual's musical ideas. Musical sound is assumed to be analogous to a form of knowledge that we can 'get right'. Thus, in good scientific fashion, it can be presented in a semi-precise system of signs.

These written conventions are a social agreement. Those initiated into the language 'know' what the signs imply in terms of sound. Music, however, is not merely a matter of equating sounds with signs. It is also vitally concerned with which sounds, which ways of playing. Very few of these can be written down. The signs, for a composer, may be a way of fixing what has been imagined. For the performer/interpreter they are also a means of excluding all possibilities not supposed to be in the composer's mind. There is nothing wrong with this established agreement provided it makes no claim to be the whole story.

It is still difficult for many Western classically trained musicians to create in the realms of what has not yet been imagined (improvisation) because it cannot be signed in any known form. Yet this is exactly what characterizes most non-Western traditions and many folk, popular and jazz traditions in the West. Our classical tradition and the new music which follows from it, in terms of global music history and current practice, is erratic. It is slow to catch up with the idea that a 'composition', the written or orally communicated item, may consist of an outline and no more.

FISH MUSIC FOR MUTED STRINGS

FISH MUSIC

For muted string players and fish.

The score is prepared as follows:

A large fish tank or aquarium stocked with fish is placed so
that both performers and audience can see it. (If the piece is
played in a public aquarium - eg. in a zoo) seats should be
arranged so that all can see.

Five strips of black masking tape are placed parallel at
equal spaces apart. These are large musical staves which can
be read in whatever clef is appropriate to each instrument.

Performance:

String players (muted) each choose one fish. As the fish
passes across the stave in either direction, up or down, play
the notes it passes using glissandi. If the fish recedes away
from the front of the tank take this as a diminuendo. If the
fish come to the front of the tank take this as a crescendo.
If the fish makes sudden movements echo these on your
instrument. If the fish remains static hold the note it has
landed on.

Apart from notes you pass through during glissandi all other
notes are naturals (no sharp and flats).

NB: Leger lines may be imagined or drawn more faintly.

The piece lasts any length of time.

The drawing above is an illustration of the principle.

Sam Richards 1968 and 1980

Before I left London I had experimented with forms of notation which were concerned with writing down what had *not* been imagined by me. The object was to stimulate the imagination and responses of the performer. The composition I remain most proud of from this period (which I have recently produced a new score of) is entitled *Fish Music*, although it actually calls for very precise notation reading from a group of string players. It plays with the idea that music could be created on musical staves, yet nothing in detail had been previously imagined by me, the composer. How could this be done?

Fish Music for muted strings simply consists of creating a large musical stave on the glass of a fish tank or aquarium. Each player chooses one fish and follows it, meticulously playing the notes the fish passes through as it swims backwards and forwards. If the fish stays still, as fish often do, the player pauses. Any gesture the fish makes (a sudden swish of the tail, fast swimming, diving etc.) are directly echoed by the players.

A degree of improvisation is called for here, but not much. In other pieces where the object was to stimulate the imagination and responses of the performer the details were less precise. Because such pieces implied no general agreement as to which sounds were suitable I was happy, in theory, to accept anything as long as it was sincerely offered.

But theory and practice rarely matched. And there was no way of demanding sincerity. Many performances left me unsatisfied. Folk music, again only in theory, seemed to offer the possibility of non-notated performance via long established practice or tradition. In order to turn this theory into reality one had to ignore much of the folk revival and seek out the increasingly rare village singers and musicians.

What folklore taught me most of all was how a social agreement to make music need not use bourgeois tradition as its basis. Nor was it in the least motivated by the cash nexus. Under these circumtances (and admittedly with a radical Romantic eye on the whole thing) I began to see music and singing as a celebration of who we are coupled with a strong sense of time and place. Exactly how, or if, this could be turned into creative composition without falling into a kind of fey new ageism was the problem I faced until I heard those Irish language psalm settings of Sean and Peadar O Riada.

Sean O Riada's example helped to reveal a few windmills that I had habitually tilted at. The old ways of composition, the accepted and generally taught relationship with the concert tradition certainly needed demystifying. However, if you depose the king you don't necessarily have to go on to assassinate him. He may still be a valuable man with years of insight and practice behind him. This is exactly so with musical resources.

Having abandoned conventional notation, tonality and repetition as contradictory to either serial or indeterminate logic, many were surprised to hear the notated, tonal, repetitive music which has flourished since the 1960s. This music has acquired the label 'minimalist', although postmodern is a better designation. (There could be few composers more minimalist than Webern or Feldman, neither of whom belonged to the new 'school'. Paragraph 7 of Cardew's *The Great Learning* is composed from even more minimal resources. And, as usual, Cage had made the ultimate minimalist statement in his silent piece, *4'33''*, in the early 1950s.)

The music of the Americans Terry Riley, Steve Reich, Philip Glass, John Adams, Meredith Monk, to name only the best known, does not necessarily contradict modernism, although I have heard it argued that it represents a failure to come to grips with modernism's challenges. The rise of the postmodern generation, of which Cardew was a British precursor, signalled an interregnum for idealism. Was the myth of democracy dead or just resting?

For my own purposes as a composer I felt (and still feel) compelled to go beyond the myth and guess at what lies behind it. A long period of probing and disquiet had convinced me that ideology was not only a limited basis for art; if taken literally it stifled creative activity. Yet, of course, we are caught in some ideology or other — unavoidably. It is this dilemma which makes postmodernism fascinating.

The sounds of Glass, Reich, Adams and, to a lesser extent, Meredith Monk often suggest a flat surface. They hint at a subtext which does not actually exist. The element of parody suggests that *something* is being parodied, but when we get closer we encounter nothing other than what we thought we heard. The subconscious is of no account. The whole thing is hard-edged. We are being drawn closer to facing who and what we are by the very fact that the composer gives us no clue.

Postmodern music, of course, broke modernist taboos. Yet its strong identity as a 'school' or sect makes me wary of regarding it as anything more than a revelation of further options. In the same way, although I am perhaps more devoted to experimental notation than ever before, it is useful to realize that, as occasion demands, a traditional system can be used or adapted at will. Likewise a whole gamut of ways of making music, traditions, experimental approaches and techniques — including none at all if the composer so wishes — are now available as resources. If all resources can be regarded as equally viable without hierarchy then even classical harmony and counterpoint can be reinstated as one possibility, no better or worse than any other.

Beyond the myth of democracy lies, I believe, a fact, a truth. Democracy strives to make us equal, which, I have suggested, we are patently not if we only take into account those things a materialist would consider — wealth, status, physique, ability and so on. But the truth is that no matter how different we are, how we may espouse opposing ideas, manifest talents, gravitate to differing styles and points of view, these are essentially a matter of what we, individually and collectively, inherit. We choose who we are in the face of this inheritance. That choice is not always conscious, but choice it is. This leads to another truth: we are not obliged to make these choices. We are capable of discovering what and who, in the essence of life, we really are.

Equality, therefore, at root, is not a matter of politics and economics, although it has to be negotiated for. Equality is really about what is left of ourselves when such temporary involvements are dissolved. What, we might ask, is left? Ultimately only life itself, a changing, incomprehensible force most of which we never perceive. The fact that we all live it is what makes us equal. This fact has no value in the sense that a price, an ideology, a world view can be pinned on to it. Yet, as Kant observed, "Whatever...is above all value and therefore admits of no equivalent has dignity." There is no equivalent to life.

It is this realization which, I sense, democracy and its musical experiments are intuitively about. If you listen to the music of peasants with attentiveness you respect the dignity of their life. If you listen to jazz, classical music and its twentieth-century developments, improvisation — whatever — you respect the dignity of the people who make it and the sounds they make. For the dignity of life inheres in sounds too. This is what Cage means when he refers to each sound as a Buddha, complete in itself, ultimately enlightening.

But what happens when we compose as opposed to listening? Appealing though the possibility sounds, you can't just sit there and ask people to respect the dignity of your life. You have to make sounds, Cage's silent piece notwithstanding. You make choices as to which sounds, how they will be stimulated, organized.

My way forward has been very simple, too simple perhaps for those who insist on theory. It is simply to review all the types of music I have been drawn to, and also to acknowledge those types more marginal to my own taste. The twentieth century provides a long list.

I began to see the twentieth century as both the harvest of seeds planted in the previous century and as the seeds of whatever would grow in the twenty-first. The seeds are sounds and styles of various kinds in a bewildering but beautiful profusion. If I took them as my palette my canvas could be as small or as wide as I wished. I was beginning to argue that self-conscious allegiance to style was the very thing that hampered its achievement. Looking through musical democracy to its spiritual base offers us everything. We no longer need accept or reject anything on principle. Our fund of resources is limited only by the amount of time and energy we have in a lifetime. It is a wonderful position to be in.

Rather than being over-concerned with how we write or compose, we may begin with the fact that we *are* composing, or wish to. The framework we draw up, or are offered (when asked to write for particular purposes), is a convenience which we will invent according to who we are. This can be anything, musical or not.

One of my recent compositions, *Travels*, places groups of musicians in different locations — a town square, a landscape, an industrial estate, a waterfall on Dartmoor, a church, a concert hall — and takes the audience round in a coach. When they reach each location music is already playing. They are encouraged to leave before it finishes. This is a framework in itself. Superimposed on this are two other factors: the ten stages of a shaman's psychic journey and a desire to use as many local musicians and ensembles as possible.

When I began to compose this piece I had to get the coach route right first, choose the locations and make sure they were all possible. To do this I needed to drive around for many days estimating whether a coach could get down some of the narrow Devon lanes, whether locations would be useable, what restrictions there would be, and so on. During this I realized, of course, that I was composing. It had never occurred to me that this kind of activity could be regarded as musical composition, but in fact all the same considerations were as relevant as when composing at the keyboard: would this location go with that, what would be the effect of a long journey from one location to another, how did the texture of each place marry or clash with the next? It was very enjoyable being a composer behind the wheel or on foot.

In 1989 I was invited to contribute musical ideas to a new festival, the Lynton and Lynmouth Festival of the Arts and Countryside. It was to take place in May 1990. Although known to the organizers as a folklorist I was determined from the outset to plan a concert which, taking the countryside as its theme, showed a range of musical responses, a small but convincing selection of available options.

There are certain givens in a landscape: the lie of the land, the paths of streams and rivers, the soils, the rock. Although it is possible to change some of them by quarrying, diverting streams, putting a new road through a hillside, these alterations are relatively small. We cannot redesign the contours of the land to make a mountainous area out of a plain.

What does change more frequently and profoundly than is sometimes admitted are the details we paint onto the landscape. If we want to farm an area, use it for forestry, tourism, build a city, a motorway we impose on the base a superstructure. This not only alters the visual appearance, it also speaks volumes about how we feel, value and relate to the land. Therefore the landscape changes in detail but not in essence. (Continued unsympathetic usage may in time damage its essence, true.)

By extension I applied this idea to music and song. The way we create these apparently innocent activities signals a similar set of relationships, not only to landscapes but to life itself. Far from being static, our ideas are changing constantly. I called the concert 'Music in a Changing Landscape', aware that in one sense I was the landscape.

As well as the occasional item for The Ambling Band, and *Fool's Holiday*, I had been composing music again for some years. It had all been either recorded in a studio where I experimented with different textures and methods, or written for dancers. None had been written purely as music for itself. With 'Music in a Changing Landscape' I decided to change that. I composed two pieces, *Ireland's Glory* and *Exmoor Landscape*, specially for that event.

There were also contributions from folk singers, jazz musicians and improvisers. The concert managed to explore all the musical themes and relationships which had demanded attention ever since that experience in Sean O Riada's house in County Cork two years earlier.

The folk items sounded only superficially like local traditions, with the exception of my friend Vic Legg. One side of Vic's family were Gypsies, although Vic insists on their preferred designation of 'travelling hawkers'. He got many songs from his mother and two aunts, Betsy and Charlotte, in Cornwall. You can hear this connection in the way he sings.

His singing partner Lar Cann, also from Cornwall, is a painter and art teacher. He plays guitar delicately and tastefully, and sings with a rather more directly revivalist approach. The two of them gave roots and continuity to the concert.

I knew I was playing a game — deliberately using the mythology of folk to suggest qualities of permanence and history. The dubious accuracy of this myth had long ceased to bother me. In any case, the contemporary conclusion was to be vastly different from the self-conscious use of 'folk disciplines' I had followed, sometimes reluctantly, as a revival singer and songwriter. The idea of 'bringing the tradition up to date' had ceased to be interesting, even allowing for its ideology. On a musical level those folk-like parameters of stanza form, popular poetry and simple melody could be stated as convincingly as need be by songs which were fashioned with that conviction. If the song was convincing it was at least partly because the people who helped make it were convinced. They had responded to their cultural era, helped create it, and now, as recontextualized as Mozart on CD, their work deserved to be heard and evaluated entirely for its ability to speak to us now. Vic and Lar approach traditional songs in this spirit and make a superb job of it.

Two improvised items responded equally to the environment but did so via an exploratory method which owed little to past traditions. We called ourselves The White Horse Ensemble — four players who did little together after this event — Mark Joseph on tenor sax, Helen White, vocal, Tom Cook on conga drums, and myself on keyboards.

Our response to the countryside had been formed by direct contact. We had chosen two locations on Dartmoor — Merrivale Quarry and Wistman's Wood. To prepare our music we drove and walked to these places and improvised on site.

We did this for about forty minutes in each place. The quarry gave a lot of scope for playing with distance, images of falling, resonance and echo, the sound of machinery. I looked at the gouged-out rock face and noticed intricate scarring patterns that had been made by machinery, the years, the weather. This was as suggestive of ways of playing sounds as many graphic scores I had seen or written in the past. I played it.

We recorded our improvisations and listened to them in the car and later at home. There were long passages which had the uneasy feeling of doodling but I had committed an act of faith and was prepared to see it through. My friends were not experienced musicians, they could not read music fluently, and I felt some degree of responsibility to act as guide. (I now see this as arrogance. What evidence was there that I was more qualified to guide than the others just because I could read music and had more years of experience behind me? Had we been playing the classics this would have been justified. But we weren't. We were experimenting with something new to all of us. We were equals in this sense.)

Our rehearsals at home attempted to keep some of the feeling and imagery of the quarry and the wood but we had to let go of what we had played there. After a few sessions each piece began to shape up. Nothing was written down except a few chords I had stumbled on and wanted to remember. Was this typical of the only trained musician in the group?

The two improvisations we did in the concert were as well co-ordinated as many a written piece but they retained the freshness of improvisation. They stated a response which was in some ways opposite to the contributions of the folk revivalists.

Between these poles were the two compositions I had written. One of them,

Ireland's Glory, may well have been a homage to the country where I first
located the creative stirring which led me onwards. It is based on a studio mix
of the late Joe Heaney, one of Ireland's greatest ballad singers. He is first
heard singing a Gaelic language song. Soon another recording of the same
performance is introduced, thus creating a round. This happens a third and
fourth time, producing a complex, unpredictable tonal texture. Over a period of
around ten minutes reverb was gradually increased in the mix, eventually
producing a sound like voices in a distant cathedral, all swirling into one
another.

A choir, using an English translation of an old Irish text, is given precise
instructions on how to sing sustained textures, swelling and fading at signs
from a conductor. Their notes are chosen from any heard on the tape. A series
of organ chords acts as a drone throughout.

Two soloists — Mark Joseph on flute and Helen White singing — were
invited to improvise a dialogue over this texture, using a passage from Joyce's
Ulysses as text. The dialogue was strict, with only slight overlapping being
allowed. It had been rehearsed many times.

As *Ireland's Glory* wound down I knew that at last whatever questions I
had been asking for twenty years or more were receiving attention — not in
words, concepts, 'answers' (there aren't any), but in musical activity. Whatever
issues, political or otherwise, had fogged the view, there was now a solid sense
of certainty that they were finally embedded in the sounds we were making
rather than in a theory which suggested which sounds to make. This sense of
freedom had been hard earned.

The second piece, *Exmoor Landscape* (illustrated opposite), was problematic. How could I possibly create a piece of music which, despite being abstract,
was in some way related to the landscape itself? Phoney quotations from local
songs — and I knew plenty — struck me as a desperate measure. The whole
idea was to move on from that mythology, to build a new one more consistent
with my own experience of life.

One afternoon I looked at an Ordnance Survey map of Exmoor. I found
Dick French's farm near Brendon. Despite years of driving round the place the
map told me that I knew little about the lie of the land. The positioning of
many features — hills, crossroads, villages — came as a surprise.

I took a black pen and a ruler. I drew a fine straight line from Dick's farm
across some high hills and down to the first road, somewhere near
Challacombe. Looking at this line I had the enlightening sensation that this was
my composition. I enlarged the map a few times on a photocopier so that I
could see more clearly the detail on either side of the line.

The symbolism of that line only gradually dawned on me. What I had done
was to start the line where I thought I had found my mud some years earlier.
Dick's farm had been a second home for some years. It was here that I could
forget the pretensions of being a folklorist, a folk revivalist, and merely
observe, accept and participate in a tradition. It was also here that some
powerful personal memories lived, hilarious, painful, shocking, educative. And
it was here that I had often admitted to myself, but no one else, that the reason
I enjoyed myself so much around this part of the country was that it was so

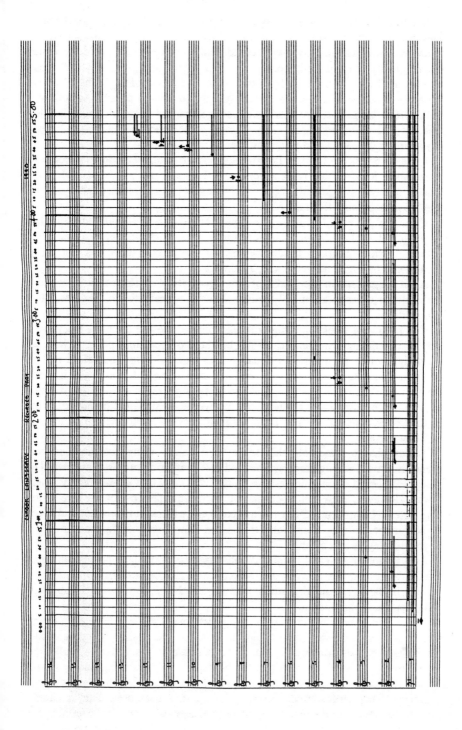

different and so far away from my own experience of life, the culture I knew. This had its difficult side. By allowing myself to identify so strongly with a tradition which was not my own I could, and sometimes did, avoid the issues that originally brought me there.

The line I drew went *away* from this point, over some of the highest hills on the moor. It knew where it had started, and it was always possible to follow it back to the farm. Yet it pointed away, suggesting the route of a solo journey that I would now embark on. This was no coincidence. I could have chosen anywhere on that map as my starting point.

I had to begin the journey literally solo. I had actually to do it to begin to sense what it was like. With a compass, the map and a few sandwiches I started out one Sunday afternoon, following my line across territory I had previously seen only from the road.

Climbing the hills I began to imagine a huge musical sound getting higher in pitch but without losing its foundations. The landscape is like that. The bottom doesn't disappear. It accumulates mass as it ascends. When you get to the top you feel lighter, weightless, awake.

As it happened, in the midst of this speculation, it started to rain and I realized that I wasn't as fit as I thought. I beat a retreat back to the farm. But I had started.

The following week, working with the contour lines on the map, I devised a way of translating space into time and height and depth into pitch. I chose an ascending series of notes and equated each one with its equivalent rise in contour. The first note, a low C, would be heard at the outset and would sound throughout. At a point exactly calculated by taking a millimeter as five seconds in time, the occurrence of the next contour would be signalled by the next note in the series. And so on. The twenty-minute piece went to the top of the hill and down again.

I was able to assemble this score in a studio using sustained sounds, precisely timed, adding some synthesized swells in an improvised manner. The piece was scored out in minute-long units, just so I would know roughly where I was. However, these units became the basic time periods for the live score. The notes which occurred in each minute were written out in boxes and given to performers to use in any way they liked. The first performance used two keyboard players and a flute.

Using another series of numbers I was also able to include percussion parts. Each player had the same score, which consisted of squares with numbers written in them. If your first square had the number 3, for example, you made three sounds in that minute.

There were many features in the landscape that I did not have time to use but I was aware that they could have made the basis of composition, improvisation, performance. It would be possible to feature trees, buildings, road crossings, water — anything encountered — by creating single simple scores and positioning these in the musical texture at the appropriate timed moments. These ideas need not be restricted to a composer. They could be offered to others in workshops, to young people, local musicians, communities. A performing group could be assembled to play regularly together, improvising, working from different kinds of scores.

Plymouth was the location for the second performance of *Exmoor Landscape*, although at the Plymouth Barbican Theatre I was able to work with a larger ensemble — three saxophones, three keyboards, more percussionists. I saw some time later that the line I had drawn from Dick's farm did, if extended down to South Devon, pass right through Plymouth. Now that *is* a coincidence.

In a local pub there is a functions room where different bands play: jazz, folk, soft rock and popular music. Sometimes there's a good crowd, sometimes not, depending on the weather, time of year, rival attractions, the popularity of the featured band. I was offered an evening and accepted, then realized I had absolutely no idea what I was going to play.

The context was fascinating. What would happen if experimental approaches normally reserved for specialist venues were offered in a place used to traditional and familiar idioms? The only conclusion I came to before composing was that the music would need to be immediate. This determined a certain amount. I had three months to fill in the rest.

Working with four or five musicians in mind I started to compose *Influence*. Each page of music was a composition in itself with its own approach to notation, its own demands on players and listeners. The composition as a whole was based on a classic Buddhist text, *The Lotus Sutra*, which has twenty-eight chapters, one per page of music. (Illustrated overleaf)

I recorded each chapter as I worked on it, not attempting to understand it as I read it aloud. Later in the day I played back the recording, simultaneously drawing shapes on large sheets of paper. Sometimes these shapes became musical, sometimes not. If the particular notation used for the page I was working on was to be staff notation I wrote down a few musical ideas as they occurred. Otherwise I kept the drawings for a while and studied them, then often threw them away. They served their purpose by focusing my imagination.

Gradually the page would be built up. Many of them were like board games. Others were purely pictorial. Many had sounds specified. A series of chords emerged as important, allowing for some unintentional continuity from page to page. A great deal of improvisation was called for but it was always structured in some way by the material given. Over three performances to date it has been noticed how similar each interpretation sounds.

There were two rehearsals with three keyboard players, a saxophone, and a poet who read some of his work alongside certain pages. In the performance we only got through about half the pages. I realized, as I had suspected, that the complete piece needed five or six hours to itself. The pub got two and a half hours.

There were around thirty people in the pub for the first performance. Few left, and many arrived at the start and stayed right through. Some of the music was tranquil, some was very noisy. There were moments of melody, moments of chaos. I heard that the bar staff considered me to be mad, but I took this as a compliment as they are friendly people. I had found out what I needed; now I wanted to play the music elsewhere.

In a subsequent performance at the Exeter Arts Centre I invited non-specialist performers, including beginners, to a workshop for two days. By

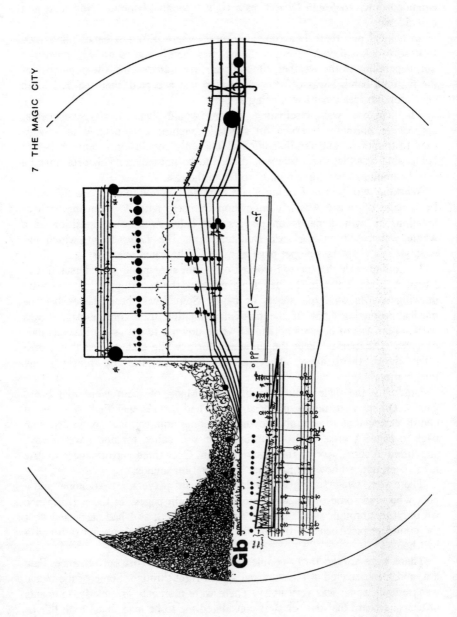

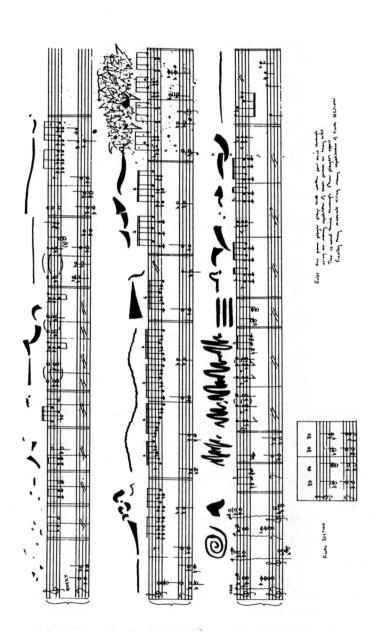

demanding much from them I was able to create a performance in which they played together with those who had worked on the piece before.

I am in favour of a music of utter stupidity. The dilemmas outlined in this book, my own and those of others, are largely the inevitable outcome of too much sense. O Riada's depression over his musical direction was very sensible. MacColl's rigorous switch from theatre to folk revivalism was supremely sensible. Such sensible actions have been influential but it seems to be the stupid things that challenge us most.

Cage's ridiculous decision to devote his life to composing music by chance, Cardew's outrageous conversion to tonality and simplicity, Denyer's preposterous orchestra of invented instruments for *A Monkey's Paw* — these gestures would never have been committed by people whose vision was limited by common sense.

With the village singers I noticed an important difference between them and the folk revivalists, myself included. They were spontaneous. Dick French, Jim Sanders, Pop Hingston and the rest carried their repertoires in their heads. With good instinct they usually pulled out appropriate songs as if from nowhere. I took a list of my songs everywhere, usually tucked away in my concertina box. When I was called on to sing I had already checked my list and knew what I was going to offer next. This totally sensible expedient allowed the security of rational response and I was always conscious of its implications. It suggested that I was not entirely at home in the traditional singing milieu. I needed a system, a piece of logic, something to think with, something to rely on.

When Dick French gets that glint in his eye and decides to take the pub apart he might sing half a dozen songs on the trot, each one compelling, well 'programmed', calculated to get the best out of the situation. But that's the point. It isn't calculated. It is canny, but calculated — no. To get up in front of a crowd of people with no idea of what you're going to do is, by most artistic yardsticks, stupid. Because I am by nature a thinker this degree of stupidity is hard-won.

The stupidity I refer to is the willingness to take a leap in the dark, a state of mind which grasps at nothing and therefore tends to receive everything. The improvisations of AMM are a superb example. The trick is to not be clever. The way to be calm is sometimes to rage. Those who refuse to rage are never calm. The point is to stop trying to be the way you think you want to be and get on with just being. Exactly like sounds.

I took a leap in the dark when I left the London music scene and refused to write another note of music until I had sorted out some fundamentals. I am proud of this creative silence because it was so stupid. I hit problems when I tried to rationalize the gesture, to work out what I had done and what I was now doing.

In the same way a common-sense approach to composition demands plans, directions, predictions, relationships which are outlined beforehand. This obsession derives from economic factors. The idea of spending our time on projects whose outcome (if there is one) is uncertain contradicts a pervasive belief that time is money and that money is a measure of value. For individuals this may be an important dilemma, causing attachment to that which can be seen. Socially it is a disaster and it held sway in that desperately materialistic period of the 1980s in Britain and elsewhere.

From the standpoint of music-making and the arts there are serious consequences in the materialist world view. Public or private funding is normally based on what is sensible. Application forms demand precise plans, beneficiaries, marketing strategies based on work not yet accomplished, detailed budgets and so on. It is not that such things are wrong in themselves. But when they become objects of worship we might as well forget about art.

The sensible approach, as opposed to the stupid one, leads into one of the biggest fallacies of musical and artistic democracy generally — that it is about majorities. Local arts associations and various other funding organizations, particularly if they are public bodies, often seem to work with a barely concealed conscience clause lurking in the shadows. The 'bums on seats', appealing-to-the-whole-region mentality is really a case of Thatcherspeak and we are better off without it. We have seen how the folk revival was a minority interest, even in its heyday. But without minorities there would be no jazz in Britain, no experimental music and, indeed, no European tradition of concert music.

Thinking in terms of majorities is the status quo. Our political democracies are imperfect and this is often due to their lack of imagination, risk-taking, stupidity. Why take on the least democratic elements of the myth? Music and the arts are a perfect standpoint from which to question the materialist world view for the very simple reason that in strict linguistic terms they are redundant.

In the past couple of years I have been asked to serve on ad hoc advisory groups for local arts provision — one for folk and one for new music (these opposites will follow me for ever). Sincere, rational people, all keen to do our very best for music, the people, the region, we sat round tables, shuffling papers, airing opinions, appearing sensible. On each occasion, after some hours of application to logic, I wanted to suggest that we tear up all the papers, shelve most of the ideas and consult the *I Ching*. But this, of course, would have been too stupid.

Musical democracy, and I guess by implication *all* democracy, begins with this pledge to abandon one-sided rationality, to include what appears to be non-logical (note: not *illogical* — there is a difference). Or, we might say, it includes oneself in 'the people'. If you can't get it right for yourself, you won't get it right for anyone. To find my spot I took a leap into folklore.

It took me many years to realize one remarkably simple fact. The challenge is not to arrive at a theoretical position about others' music but to discover the most appropriate ways to make your own music. This implies the most appropriate ways to live your life. In this you are only doing what others have already done. The music others make is not offered in a spirit of analysis. It is offered in a spirit of music.

This is exactly what I mean by being stupid. The narrow focus of sensible, rational one-dimensional thought *avoids* the very reason music exists — it acts in a way that words and concepts cannot grasp. Let us forget all those musical academics whose inability to run their lives is often reflected in their obsessional desire for theory. I invite all musicians who are in the least interested in a fair society to begin by making music.

My current work, based as it is on landscapes, has already introduced me to one life issue which undoubtedly needs reforming. Like most composers I have believed for years that the way to write music is to sit soberly at home, perhaps with a keyboard close by, working out and writing down musical ideas and eventually arriving at something called a composition. Now I ask: is there any reason why this should be so? Do I really wish to spend long periods of my life sitting in a room scribbling, trying to imagine sounds and ways of playing? No. Should anyone wish to find me while I am composing I may be out for a walk, taking a drive to the sea, having a drink in a local pub, talking with my friends. *This* is when composition happens. When I return home with my notebooks, a few sketches, objects I have picked up on the way, information, addresses — well, then, I have to sit down and get the ideas together. But this should be done as quickly as possible so as not to interfere with my health.

I no longer believe in an 'ideal' situation. Any situation is ideal for making music.

Bibliography

Bailey, Derek. *Improvisation: Its Nature and Practice in Music.* Moorland Publishing, 1980.

Baring-Gould, Sabine. *Early Reminiscences (1834-64),* 1923.

Baring-Gould, Sabine. *Further Reminiscences (1864-94),* 1925.

Blacking, John. *How Musical Is Man?* Faber, 1976.

Braden, Su. *Artists and People.* Routledge & Kegan Paul, 1978.

Cage, John. *Silence: Lectures and Writings.* Wesleyan University Press, Conn., 1961.

Cage, John. *A Year From Monday. New Lectures and Writings.* Wesleyan University Press, Conn., 1967.

Cage, John. *Notations.* Something Else Press, N.Y., 1969.

Cardew, Cornelius. *Scratch Music.* Latimer New Dimensions, 1972.

Cardew, Cornelius. *Stockhausen Serves Imperialism.* Latimer New Dimensions, 1974.

Cardew, Cornelius (ed.). *The Treatise Handbook.* The Gallery Upstairs Press, Buffalo, N.Y., 1967.

Cott, Jonathan (ed.). *Stockhausen: Conversations with the Composer.* Robson Books, 1974.

Denyer, Frank. *The Shakuhachi and the Contemporary Music Instrumentarium: A Personal View.* The Contemporary Music Review.

Fromm, Erich. *The Sane Society.* Routledge, 1956.

Griffiths, Paul. *Modern Music: The Avant Garde Since 1945.* Dent, 1981.

Harris, Bernard & Freyer, Grattan (eds.). *Integrating Tradition: The Achievement of Sean O Riada.* Irish Humanities Centre & Keohanes, 1981.

Kennedy, Peter (ed.). *Folksongs of Britain and Ireland.* Oak Publications, 1975.

Kirimura, Yasuji. *Fundamentals of Buddhism.* Nichiren Shoshu International Centre, Tokyo, 1977.

Kostelanetz, Richard. *Conversing with Cage.* Omnibus Press, 1989.

Lévi-Strauss, Claude. *The Raw and the Cooked: Introduction to a Science of Mythology.* Jonathan Cape, 1970.

Lloyd, A.L. *Come All Ye Bold Miners.* (Revised and enlarged edition). Lawrence & Wishart, 1978.

Lloyd, A.L. *Folk Song in England.* Lawrence & Wishart, 1967.

Lomax, Alan. *Folk Song Style and Culture.* Transaction Books, New Jersey, 1968.

MacColl, Ewan & Seeger, Peggy. *The Singing Island.* Mills Music, 1960.

Prévost, Eddie. *Improvisation.* (Article in a booklet published for the Cornelius Cardew Memorial Concert, Queen Elizabeth Hall, 1982)

Sharp, Cecil. *English Folk Song, Some Conclusions.* (ed. Maud Karpeles) Methuen & Co., 1954.

Stockhausen, Karlheinz. *Towards a Cosmic Music.* Element Books, 1989.

Tilbury, John. *The Music.* (Article on the music of Cornelius Cardew in the booklet published for the Cornelius Cardew Memorial Concert, Queen Elizabeth Hall, 1982)

Watson, Ian. *Song and Democratic Culture in Britain.* Croom Helm, 1983.

Williams, Alfred. *Folk-songs of the Upper Thames.* Duckworth & Co., London, 1923.

Discography

The music discussed in this book falls neatly into two categories: that which you can get anywhere, and that which is harder or impossible to come by. I cannot do anything about the impossible. And the likes of Bartók and Webern can look after themselves. So all I can really do is to list a few recordings that fall into the 'hard to come by' category.

AMM, *Ammmusic*. Elektra Records, 1967. EUK 256.

AMM, *The Crypt*. Matchless Recordings, Shetlock's Cottages, Matching Tye, near Harlow, Essex, CM17 ORR, 1968. MR5

AMM, *Generative Themes*. Matchless Recordings, 1982. MR6.

AMM, *The Inexhaustible Document*. Matchless Recordings, 1987. MR13.

Cardew, Cornelius, *The Great Learning: Paragraphs 2 and 7*. Played by The Scratch Orchestra. Deutsche Grammophon, 1971. 2561 107.

Cardew, Cornelius, *Thälmann Variations* . Cornelius Cardew, piano. Matchless Recordings, 1975. MR10.

Cornelius Cardew Memorial Concert (First Movement for String Quartet, Octet '61, Treatise, Paragraph 1 of The Great Learning, The Turtledove, The Workers' Song, Thälmann Variations, Croppy Boy, Watkinson's Thirteens, Smash the Social Contract!, There Is Only One Lie, There is Only One Truth, We Sing for the Future) Impetus Records, 1985. IMP 28204

Denyer Frank, *A Monkey's Paw* with *Stalks, After the Rain, A Fragile Thread, Winged Play*. Continuum, 1991. CCD 1026.

Denyer, Frank, *Wheat, The Music of Frank Denyer (On On—It Must Be So, I Await the Sea's Red Hibiscus, Wheat, Quick Quick the Tamberan is Coming, Quite White, Voices)* Orchid Records, 1 Town Farm, Harberton, Totnes, Devon, 1984. OR3.

Hall, Reg; Plunkett, Mervyn with Bulwer, Walter; Cooper, Billy; Bulwer, Daisy, and Wortley, Russell, *English Country Music*. Topic Records, 1976. 12T296.

Isca Fayre (Unaccompanied harmony singing from The Exeter Traditional Folk Song Club), *Then Around Me Young and Old...* Candle Records, 1976. CAN761.

Kennedy, Peter (Series editor), *The Folk Songs of Britain* – ten volumes. Topic Records. 12T157, 12T158, 12T159, 12T160, 12T161, 12T194, 12T195, 12T196, 12T197, 12T198.

MacColl, Ewan & Seeger, Peggy. For a catalogue of a representative selection of albums of traditional and new songs contact Blackthorne Records Ltd, 35 Stanley Avenue, Beckenham, Kent BR3 2PU.

O Riada, Sean, *Ceol An Aifrinn.* (O Riada's first Mass). 1971. CB3.

O Riada, Sean and O Riada, Peadar, *Go mBeannaitear Duit* (Psalms in the Irish Language). (The Cuil Aodha Choir directed by Peader O Riada). Gael-linn Records, Eire, 1987. CEF 125.

O Riada, Sean, *Mise Eire.* (RTE Symphony Orchestra). Gael-linn Records, Eire. CEF 080.

O Riada, Sean, *O Riada's Farewell.* Claddagh Records, Eire. CC12.

O Riada, Sean with Ceoltoiri Cualann, *O Riada Sa Gaiety.* Gael-linn Records, Eire, 1970. CEF 027

O Riada, Sean, *Vertical Man (Hercules Dux Ferrariae for Strings. Ten Poems Set to Music).* Claddagh Records, 1969. CSM1.

Richards, Sam (Musical Director), *Just One More Song. Music and Folklore from Devon.* The Daylight Company, Honiton, Devon, 1987. LD5030.

Watersons, The, *Frost and Fire, A Calendar of Ceremonial Folk Songs.* Topic Records, 1965. 12T136.

Yamaguchi, Goro (shakuhachi player), *A Bell Ringing in the Empty Sky.* Nonesuch Explorer Series, 1969. H72025.

The following are field recordings of Westcountry and other traditions compiled by the author and colleagues.

Devon Tradition: An Anthology from Traditional Singers. Topic Records, 1979. 12TS349.

An English Folk Music Anthology. Nursery songs, Children singing, Songs associated with rituals, Country singers, Travellers, Urban singers, Recent songs of unknown authorship. Folkways New York, 1981. Ethnic Folkways Records FE38553.

Index

PROKOFIEV

by David Gutman

Born and raised in the Russia of the Tsars, Sergey Prokofiev established himself as an *enfant terrible* of the musical world in the years up to 1918. After the revolution he lived abroad, first in the United States, later in Paris. Then came the thirties and, little by little, reconciliation with the new Soviet Russia. He spent the last 17 years of his life in the USSR, stimulated as well as stifled by the cultural policies dictated by Stalin.

Prokofiev contributed to the standard symphonic repertoire more new music than any other composer of our time: music for the stage, music for films, symphonies, concertos, oratorios and sonatas. The composer as humourist is familiar enough from *Peter and the Wolf, Lieutenant Kijé* and the *Classical Symphony*. But the masterpieces which attest to a deeper side of his genius — the wartime sonatas, the Sixth symphony, the epic *War and Peace* — remain comparatively neglected.

David Gutman argues that Prokofiev's music is closely bound up with the social upheavals of its time, and it is this which has presented intractable problems for critics and public alike. All too often, the life and works have been viewed from the standpoint of ideological warfare with little obligation to achieve a real understanding. This new and balanced assessment, the first British study to appear for many years, draws on the reminiscences of Prokofiev's friends and colleagues as well as making use of his extensive letters and diaries.

David Gutman studied history at St John's College, Cambridge, specialising in Soviet politics and culture. A contributor to *Brio* and *Books and Bookmen*, he has written on subjects as various as Sir Michael Tippett, Olivier Messiaen, Galina Vishnevskaya and John Lennon.

45 photographs, numerous illustrations and examples, catalogue of works, bibliography, select discography

ISBN 0 946619 32 8   £12.95 net in UK

Amber Lane Press, Church Street, Charlbury, Oxford OX7 3PR